# WE REFUSED TO DIE

## *My Time as a Prisoner of War in Bataan and Japan 1942–1945*

✪

Gene S. Jacobsen

THE UNIVERSITY OF UTAH PRESS
*Salt Lake City*

First paperback printing 2010

The Defiance House Man colophon is a registered trademark of the University of Utah Press. It is based upon a four-foot-tall, Ancient Puebloan pictograph (late PIII) near Glen Canyon, Utah.

19 18 17 16 15 2 3 4 5 6

LIBRARY OF CONGRESS CATALOGING-IN-PUBLICATION DATA
Jacobsen, Gene Samuel, 1921–2007
We refused to die : my time as a prisoner of war in Bataan and Japan, 1942–1945 / Gene S. Jacobsen.
p. cm.
ISBN 978-1-60781-125-1 (alk. paper)
1. Jacobsen, Gene Samuel, 1921– 2. World War, 1939–1945—Prisoners of war, Japanese. 3. World War, 1939–1945—Campaigns—Philippines. 4. World War, 1939–1945—Personal narratives, American. 5. Prisoners of war—United States—Biography. 6. Prisoners of war—Philippines—Biography. 7. Prisoners of war—Japan—Biography. 8. United States. Army. Air Corps. Pursuit Squadron, 20th. I. Title.
D805.J3J23 2004
940.54'7252'092—dc22

2004008110

# WE REFUSED TO DIE

THIS BOOK is lovingly dedicated to the officers and men of the 20th Pursuit Squadron, United States Army Air Corps, who survived the battles for the Peninsula of Bataan in the Philippine Islands during World War II and who, through their indomitable courage and by the grace of God, endured the starvation, disease, slave labor, and the vicious brutality of the Japanese military for three and one-half years as prisoners of war. These were the men for whom life and freedom were so precious that during the long months of captivity they refused to die.

# CONTENTS

# PROLOGUE

THE 20TH PURSUIT SQUADRON came into being at Moffett Field, California, on February 1, 1940. It was part of the 35th Pursuit Group, GHQ Air Force, Moffett Field, California. The squadron comprised enlisted men from Randolph Field, Texas, Barksdale Field, Louisiana, and Moffett Field, California. Seven P-36 airplanes were assigned to the squadron on the day it was formed.

The 20th was transferred from Moffett Field, California, to Hamilton Field, California, on September 10, 1940. During October 1940 the squadron lost, through transfer, 75 percent of its original personnel.

On October 23, 1940, the squadron received orders to prepare to move, and at 4:00 p.m. that day, with fifty experienced enlisted men and one hundred seven inexperienced recruits, it left Hamilton Field and arrived at San Pedro, Port of Los Angeles, at eight o'clock the following morning. At eight o'clock that evening their ship, the *SS Washington,* put out to sea.

On the morning of November 5, 1940, at 6:30 a.m., the ship arrived at Honolulu, Hawaii. From there it sailed to Shanghai, China, to evacuate American citizens. Families of Americans stationed in China boarded the ship. On November 19 it set sail for Manila, Philippine Islands, where it docked on November 23, 1940.

To the squadron were assigned P-26s and, later, P-35s. Additional officers and enlisted men joined the squadron throughout the following year in an effort to bring the organization up to full strength.

After six months at Nichols Field, Manila, the squadron was reassigned to Clark Field, where it received twenty-five P-40s. It was at Clark Field when Japanese planes bombed and strafed it on Monday, December 8, 1941, the same day Pearl Harbor was attacked by other units of the Japanese military.

The squadron continued to operate from Clark Field until Christmas

Eve 1941, at which time it received orders to relocate near Mariveles Field, then under construction, on the Peninsula of Bataan. After building revetments for replacement airplanes for a number of days, the men served as infantry troops until all Allied forces on Bataan were ordered to surrender.

On Bataan the officers and men suffered severely from the lack of food and medicine and the proper military equipment with which to wage an effective defense of the Bataan Peninsula.

The surrender took place on April 9, 1942, and four days later the infamous Bataan Death March began. During the next few months thousands of Americans died from starvation, dysentery, malaria, and brutal treatment at the hands of the Japanese military.

Men from the 20th Pursuit Squadron served for three and one-half years as prisoners of war in various work camps throughout the Philippines and in Japan and Manchuria.

The data gathered to date reveal that of the 207 officers and men who made up the squadron at the beginning of the war, 142 or roughly 70 percent were killed or died in prison camps. Sixty-five returned to the United States, and sixteeen were still living as of September 2003. All of us are eighty years of age or older.

# 1

# ATTACK ON PEARL HARBOR

"OUT OF YOUR SACKS, you bunch of gin hounds! Pay the penalty for all of your boozing! C'mon, hit the dirt. Roll call in five minutes."

Ten minutes later, 7:00 a.m. sharp, all had dragged themselves to the parade ground just west of the shacks and, after considerable stumbling and confusion, managed to get themselves into their assigned squads.

"Stand at ease," said the first sergeant.

The previous daylong celebration at the NCO Club in honor of a departing master sergeant had left its mark on more than a few. Others required far less of an excuse for a hangover in that tropical vineyard where gin could be purchased for thirty-five cents a bottle. Everyone knew, because it was well advertised, that San Miguel A-1-1-A Gin had taken the prize for being the best all-around gin entered at the San Francisco World's Fair. Besides that, the long-time army regulars in the Philippines counseled the newcomers, "Leave the booze strictly alone. If you feel that you must drink, drink gin. In the heat of the tropics it will do less harm to your body than anything else you can drink except water. It's even better than most water in the Islands because, while it may contain parasites, it makes them so happy they don't make you sick."

We stood for an unusually long few minutes, and by the time the first sergeant screeched, "Tension!" the bright red sun had already begun its lazy ascent over Mount Arayat. In the Philippines it always seemed to be smiling at us. We had the impression that it was really advising us not to get overly eager or enthusiastic while we were in the tropics because the tempo of life is properly slow. Just no sense in burning up excessive energy in the heat.

Once the squadron was at full attention, the first sergeant, not greatly appreciated by all because he had a tendency to be a bully and seemed to feel that it was necessary for him to have all of the answers all of the time, dispensed with the routine procedure of morning assembly. Instead, he announced that the squadron commander, who was present along with the officer of the day, had information that he wanted to share with us.

Although the CO wasn't much older than most of us and a lot younger than a number of the squadron veterans, he was "The Old Man" to all of us. That wasn't a derogatory title at all, merely one that confirmed he was the squadron commander, our commanding officer, and as such was in complete charge. He hadn't been our CO when the squadron left Hamilton Field, California, but a few months after our arrival in the Philippines he had been awarded his first command when the major was transferred and given group leadership responsibilities.

"Men, my message is not a happy one," the CO stated quietly. "I will make what I have to say brief because we all have a great deal to do. This morning, Sunday in Honolulu, the Imperial Japanese forces made a sneak, cowardly, and disastrous attack on Pearl Harbor and other military establishments in Hawaii, including the airfields. At this time we are not fully informed concerning the extent of the destruction. We have learned, however, that serious damage was inflicted on both military equipment and personnel. It appears many Navy vessels were docked or anchored in Pearl Harbor, including battleships, and most, if not all, were destroyed. How the Japanese were able to approach the Hawaiian Islands undetected appears to be a mystery. They did just that, however, and, consequently, our effectiveness in this outlying post is likely to be seriously challenged.

"As you are aware, the pursuit squadrons in the Philippine Islands are at full or near-full strength. Recently there hasn't been much talk concerning the location of these squadrons, but we do know that they are organized and able.

"Orders just received direct us to keep at least one of the squadrons in the air at all times in an effort to learn of the enemy's movements and to prevent the Japanese from destroying militarily strategic locations, facilities, and equipment and from making a successful invasion of the Philippines.

"I don't have any more information to share with you at this time. You fully understand the seriousness of the situation, I am sure. All leaves are canceled and all men are to be at their stations constantly. As further information is received, it will be relayed to you as quickly as it is appropriate for us to do so.

"I strongly urge all of you to remain on constant alert. Keep yourselves in good physical condition. Eat your meals regularly and keep your morale high. It is a crisis such as this that we have been preparing for. Our planes are in good condition, and we have capable pilots and support personnel. I have little doubt this squadron will account well for itself whatever happens."

Apparently having nothing further to say and not wishing to attempt responses to questions for which he had no answers, the CO turned and promptly left the area. He, a dedicated career officer, was far more serious than I had ever known him to be before, and while his office door was always open to squadron members, officers or enlisted men, he was basically a serious person—all military.

Momentarily we were too stunned to move or to talk. We just stood and looked at each other. However, the initial shock passed quickly.

"Who would have thought that those Japs would have had the nerve to pull a dirty trick like that?"

"How in the devil did they ever get clear to Hawaii without ever being spotted? Our forces there must have all been on vacation!"

"One thing for sure, they'll pay!"

"We'll blow those little yellow fellers right off the face of the earth!"

"I'm for the U.S. bombin' Tokyo off the map right now! They're just too dumb to know who they are foolin' around with!"

"Tention!"

"Listen to you," bellowed the first sergeant. "You make me sick to my stomach. It's because of smart alecs like you that we're in this mess! Look at yourselves! I doubt that some of you could fight your way out of a paper bag this morning. The time for all of the stupid talk is over!

"Now, get yourselves over to the mess hall for breakfast! It may be the last meal you'll ever get! And then get to work! The first guy I see goofin' off today gets fed to the Japs by me personally!

"Dismissed!"

## 2

# ENEMY OVER CLARK FIELD

AT AGE NINETEEN I, Gene S. Jacobsen, was the squadron supply sergeant. I hadn't really aspired to be supply sergeant. My career objective had been to become a technically competent airplane mechanic, not a pencil pusher. However, I was pleased with the assignment and the promotion after only a few months as supply clerk and was grateful to the CO for giving me the greater responsibility. As I became fully involved in the leadership activities of the office and able to perceive the importance of it to the effective functioning of the squadron, I found myself to be enthusiastic and came to thoroughly enjoy the assignment. Especially satisfying to me was the opportunity to be of service to a group of great fellows, both officers and enlisted men.

I headed for the supply shack eager to be alone, away from everyone, to collect my thoughts. One thing for sure, I had no appetite either for breakfast or for the kind of dialogue that would be taking place in the mess shack.

Clark Field was large, but it really wasn't much of an air base. Situated down mountain from Fort Stotsenberg, the Philippine Scout Artillery and Cavalry Post, it bragged a wide dirt runway bordered by three not-too-large hangars. Across the road from the three hangars were two more of the same size and vintage and a temporary building that housed the squadron mess. Not much farther up the road toward Fort Stotsenberg was the operations shack.

For five months the enlisted men of our squadron had been living in one of the hangars adjacent to the airstrip, sleeping on folding cots. In one corner of the hangar, fenced off by extra footlockers and one large table used for poker on paydays, had been my supply room. Only a week before we had moved into the small, newly constructed, mat-walled buildings that were to serve as temporary quarters until more permanent ones could be constructed.

One of the tiny grass shacks on the outer fringe served as the squadron supply office. It wasn't much more convenient than the corner of the hangar, but there was privacy and far more security. I had a bunk in the shack, which made me, along with the first sergeant, someone rather privileged. However, that also meant that I could be on call twenty-four hours each day.

Once inside the shack I stood as though dazed, unable to organize my thoughts or to plan any course of action. I felt numb all over. The feeling wasn't one of fright (that came later), but it was almost as if I were in a stupor. I just couldn't bring myself to believe that the Japanese would have or could have made an attack on my country. I felt both disgust and anger. The feelings of anger were directed toward both the Japanese and the Americans who had permitted the invasion of Hawaii. We had talked some of the possibility of a war with Japan, but it had been just talk. No one with whom I associated really seriously thought that the Japanese would ever venture that far from home. And it had never occurred to me that any part of the United States could ever be vulnerable to an attack from any aggressor.

Finally, I forced myself to survey the contents of the supply building, wondering what I could do or should do that might be helpful. The supply shack was my area of responsibility, so I knew that this was where I would help make preparations to resist the enemy.

"How would my efforts here be helpful today, though?" I asked myself. A feeling of almost contempt for myself swept over me as I considered the possibilities. Here I was, a member of a fighter squadron with no contribution to make for repulsing the enemy.

The sight before me was almost disgusting. There were the poker table and the footlockers that served as the room-wide counter across which supplies were dispensed. Stacked in one corner as a nesting place for bedbugs were a few extra mattresses for single cots. The better ones had been issued. Extra mattress covers, sheets, and blankets were piled along the back and one side of the building.

"The Japs would be really frightened to see all of this stuff," I muttered.

The pistol rack was empty—the 45s having been issued to the officers and the senior noncoms some days earlier. There were four racks of 12-gauge sawed-off shotguns to be issued to the squadron riot squads in case of parachute troops or local disorders. I had the dubious honor of being squad leader of one of the four groups charged with "keeping the peace" in the area surrounding the U.S. air base. Each squad also had one Lewis .30-caliber machine gun and several drums of shells. All machine guns could be depended upon to jam following a few bursts of gunfire.

Sadly I concluded that there wasn't much in the squadron supply shack that would hinder, help, or in any way impress the Japanese if they did overrun the Philippines.

Turning the radio on, I switched from station to station to learn the status of the attack on the Hawaiian Islands and the anticipated attack upon the Philippines. All excitedly reported the events at Pearl Harbor and the area surrounding the naval base. I soon had heard enough of the sickening disaster so turned the radio off.

As the morning dragged on, each minute seemed like forever. No one came to the supply shack to conduct business. Consequently, I directed my attention to counting the number of pairs of socks and shoes, coveralls, underwear, shirts, trousers, etc., I had stored in the place. I had been meaning to do that for some time.

I really wasn't supposed to have any extra clothing on hand. The regulations were clear. When clothing was worn out, I was to collect it from the men and, after I had accumulated a reasonable amount, I could request that an officer from the Quartermaster Corps at Fort Stotsenburg come down to survey it. He would eventually arrive in the company of a Filipino worker who carried a brush and a bucket of red paint. After the survey, I could then take the paint-spattered clothing and properly authorized requisition to the quartermaster warehouse, where I could exchange the discarded items for new stuff.

Following each visit of the officer and his man, I would carefully sort through the items of wear and remove any that the paint slosher had missed. These I would set aside to be surveyed again at a later date. Or, if I could easily tear out the part of the item that had been dabbed with paint, I would do that and save that item for a future survey. Those at the warehouse never checked the surrendered items against the requisition, so there would be little risk involved.

After a few months of this, I had been able to build up a sizable reserve of extra clothing items for distribution to the men who needed more changes than the official allocation permitted. In addition, I was usually able to persuade the quartermaster workers to permit me to keep all of the clothing and sheets to be used as rags by those who serviced the planes on the hangar line. I really was rapidly developing into a pretty savvy supply sergeant.

At roughly 9:30 a.m. I locked the supply building and wandered over to the operations shack to check on the action there and to see if I could be of any help. There I learned that the squadron's P-40s had just been ordered into the air. Crew chiefs and the radio and armament men were standing by their planes and the pilots were getting final briefing.

I watched the planes as they roared, one by one, down the dirt runway and became airborne.

"This really is a great squadron," I said to one of the crew chiefs nearby. "I hope that each pilot makes a good account of himself and returns with honor if the flights intercept the Japs."

"They are a super bunch of guys," he responded. "What I hope is that all of them make it back safely."

As the maintenance crews returned to the operations shack from the airstrip, there wasn't much of the usual chatter. Everyone was grim and unusually thoughtful. I could easily sense their feelings of frustration and concern and of growing uneasiness. I wasn't exactly sure concerning the nature of my own feelings. However, I could feel the tension increasing within me. Could it be fear that I was experiencing? I really didn't think that I was afraid.

With the departure of our planes, the airstrip seemed almost deserted. At the far edge across the field from us were the B-17s, newly arrived from the States and tied down safely some distance from the hangars. Now that we were at war with the Japanese I couldn't understand why those babies weren't right then attacking the Japanese air bases on Formosa. That Japanese-held island to the north of the Philippines was within striking range for the B-17s. Earlier in the morning they had left Clark Air Base only to return within a relatively short period of time.

In an attempt at self-solace as I wandered around a bit, I reminded myself that we were not entirely unprepared for war. Earlier, several trenches had been dug, one near the operations shack and others around the hangars and the mess shack. It wasn't intended that these trenches would accommodate the men and officers who made up the squadron because at any one time, most would be at various duty stations. I recalled that, while the trenches were being dug, a variety of comments had been made relative to the intelligence level of those inspired to initiate such a stupid assignment. Now, I could see men eyeing the trench by the operations shack with what appeared to be considerable respect.

Minutes of the morning dragged into hours. As the time passed, my anxiety level increased, as did that of others. At least, I was sure that they shared my feelings although I discussed that subject with no one.

Shortly after eleven o'clock that morning our planes returned to Clark Field and were soon lined up on the strip across from the operations shack for refueling and a quick maintenance check. The pilots reported no unusual movement either in the air or on the ground or at sea. The usual joviality of the atmosphere after return from flight was completely absent. Instead, there seemed to be feelings of quiet reverence. The pilots and members of the maintenance crews appeared apprehensive knowing, I am sure, that in the very near future the training war games in which they had participated would now become the real thing.

Planes from the squadron at Iba, the gunnery range on the west coast, and those from another squadron at Nichols Field, Manila, had replaced ours in the air. We didn't learn until some time later that while our pilots had not sighted the enemy, our planes had been detected by the Japanese bomber pilots whose mission was to bomb bases in the Philippines. Their planes, already over the Islands, had been turned back out to sea.

I returned to my supply shack. Then, with my mess kit in hand, my training gas mask dangling from around my neck, and my World War I steel helmet on my head, I started for lunch across the large open field that separated the mess hut from the supply shack. The distance was approximately two hundred yards.

I had gone nearly a third of the way when my attention was attracted by the noise of approaching planes. Because our planes were visible on the ground, I promptly assumed that those I was hearing belonged to the other two squadrons that had replaced ours when our planes landed. I stopped and scanned the sky. It wasn't until the planes were reasonably close to Clark Field that I was able to spot the large flight approaching from the northeast.

"What a beautiful sight," I breathed to myself. Then I realized that the planes were much too large and too slow to be fighter planes.

"Hey, good old Uncle Sam has come through with support!" I shouted to no one, "and just when we needed the planes so badly!"

The bombers began a slow left bank over Fort Stotsenberg and were over the bachelor officers' quarters at the edge of Clark Field before I spotted the Rising Sun grinning down from the underside of each wing.

"Jap bombers!" I screamed as the bombs began their blood-curdling descent.

With bombs whistling as they fell toward earth, I dived instinctively to the ground where, on my belly and protected only by my WWI steel helmet, I watched the completely one-sided show.

Having had no more forewarning than I, our pilots, crewmen, and radiomen were caught by the first explosives to hit the ground. The planes had just barely begun taking off when the bombs from the Japanese bombers began to explode shrapnel among them. Those not crippled immediately roared down the runway in a heroic effort, only to be blown to bits before they could get off the ground. Just three of the twenty-five managed to get into the air. The rest were rubble, scattered all over the dirt airstrip.

I learned later that the three P-40 pilots who escaped the Japanese bombs made initial contact with Japanese escort fighters and, learning immediately that the P-40 was no match for the much lighter and far more maneuverable Japanese Zero, abandoned Clark Field temporarily in hopes of being able to locate and bomb the Japanese aircraft carrier from which the fighter planes were launched. Prior to returning to home base, they were able to make a most responsible accounting of themselves.

Those of the men servicing the planes who were not already killed or seriously wounded sprinted for the safety of the trench by the operations shack. "Run! Run faster!" I shouted.

In spite of their heroic efforts some didn't get to the trench in time. I watched four literally cut in two by the bomb shrapnel. A fifth, Sgt. Bill Hainer from Wisconsin, was running well and then seemed to move as if in slow motion before falling forward on his face with a gaping hole in his back. Others were more fortunate and were able to plunge headfirst into the newly dug trench.

The destruction was unbelievable. The bombers, as they made a swing over the field, completely destroyed the hangars and most of the planes, including the B-17s that had recently landed and were being refueled and loaded with ammunition, and scored a direct hit on our mess hall. The black smoke from the briskly burning gasoline and oil-fed fires quickly and effectively obscured the field from further view.

As soon as the bombers had passed over, I leaped to my feet, sprinted back into the squadron supply shack, and grabbed a sawed-off shotgun in anticipation of Japanese parachute troops.

Charging outside, I ran directly into S/Sgt. Carl Nyberg, who was also after a shotgun. Before we could turn back to the supply room, we were forced to the ground by Japanese fighter planes swarming over the area. We later learned these were Zeros that had flown fighter protection for the Japanese bombers and had remained over the field on clean-up detail as the bombers flew toward Formosa.

The nearest place that offered any protection for Nyberg and me was a huge pile of sand that construction workers had unloaded that morning directly in front of the supply shack. We promptly dived to one side of it and from its protection watched the whole tragic show.

The Japanese Zero fighters at first concentrated on what was left of the P-40s and the B-17 bombers. Passing back and forth, back and forth, almost completely unmolested, they shredded our planes. Next, they made their close-to-the-ground strafing runs over the burning hangars and operations shack, further encouraging the briskly burning fires started by the bombers.

Not once during the entire raid did I hear fire from the American artillery that was supposed to be surrounding the air base. It could have been that antiaircraft guns were blasting away continuously and that I was just too occupied with my own problems to be aware of their efforts to adequately defend what was left after the bombers had rained down their destruction. (These National Guard outfits had also arrived only recently from the States.)

Each Japanese fighter plane, in addition to machine guns, carried a 20-mm cannon in the nose, and between the bursts of machine gun fire could be heard the whomp, whomp, whomp of the cannon as the phosphorus-laden shells were fired into stationary targets. Because of the smoke screen effectively generated by the crackling fires, much of the airplane activity was obscured from our view. As the planes made their strafing runs back and forth across the hangars, however, they crossed the housing areas, giving us ample opportunity to observe firsthand the grinning faces of the Japanese pilots. They had much about which to be elated.

Suddenly out of the smoke roared the plane of the commander of one of the American P-40 squadrons. It was clearly distinguishable by the three stripes running from the top of the plane to its belly. Two Japanese planes closely pursued him, guns firing.

Seeking the safety of the smoke, the CO promptly reappeared, this time on the tail of the Japanese planes, which seemed to be sticking together for protection. Tracers from the P-40 wing and nose .50-caliber guns made it possible for us to score the effectiveness of the attack. We watched one

Zero go down over the field and we learned later that the other crashed in the jungle not far from the field. Despite our own predicament, we cheered the kill scored by our CO!

For lack of a better target, and because of what appeared to be the complete lack of interference from our ground forces, the Japanese pilots then concentrated on the living quarters and personnel. Their leisurely passes back and forth must have been sheer pleasure for them.

All of the Japanese fighters were equipped with belly tanks and these, when emptied, were dropped around us. We at first thought they were 500-pound bombs, and when they didn't explode on contact we assumed that they were of the delayed-action variety. I didn't have the technical savvy to realize that they were merely disposable gasoline tanks to be dropped once the gasoline in them had been used.

Thanks to our team effort, Sergeant Nyberg and I were able to survive the attack unscathed. We remained with the pile of sand throughout the entire siege. As the planes strafed back and forth across the personnel area, we would run around and around the sandpile. We must have made at least a thousand trips around that protective heap of sand. If planes had come at us from different directions at the same time, we would have been in real trouble, because shells from the planes were kicking up sand all around us. All during the attack flashbacks of my youth passed before my eyes. I recalled vividly numerous childhood experiences of years long past. These troubled me somewhat because I remembered having read that people near death often have such experiences, and I wondered if this was to be my time to go.

How long the Japanese fighters remained I don't know for sure. It seemed to be for eternity.

When they finally did depart, I lay on the sand for a long time panting, completely exhausted. Still clutched in my fist was that useless sawed-off 12-gauge shotgun, the barrel and breach fully packed with sand. In complete disgust I pushed it away.

Hardly had the Japanese left when our CO landed his plane amid the holes and debris scattered everywhere. There was no question of his being a hero of the day!

Another hero of the day was Cpl. Harold Poole from the armament crew who, seeing a Lewis .30-caliber machine gun that was unmanned, jumped into the trench where it was mounted only to find that the ancient thing, living up to its tradition, had jammed. Ignoring the one-sided battle that was raging around him, he calmly stripped the gun and reassembled it, and he then shot down one of the Zero fighters attacking his area. He reported that the plane dived directly at him with guns blazing. He returned the fire as it approached, directing the shells into the radial engine. It passed over without hitting him and crashed just off the field. He later was awarded a silver star for heroism. Shooting down a plane with a .30-caliber Lewis machine gun was an almost impossible feat.

A quick check revealed that seven pilots and fifteen enlisted men had been killed on the runway and many were injured, though several of those wounded were not in serious condition. Our planes and equipment were nearly a complete loss.

Word came by radio that the gunnery base on the west coast had been bombed with nearly all of the squadron's planes destroyed and many men killed. The bombers had caught the men in the mess hall and had scored a direct hit. We learned also that the Nichols Field Air Base was not attacked seriously during the first day.

At late afternoon it was a stunned, tired, and sick-at-heart group of officers and men who, under the direction of the CO, moved by foot off Clark Field to bivouac by a river several miles away. Each could take only a blanket. Because I was the keeper of the CO's bedroll, I had the privilege of carrying the monstrosity. It didn't weigh more than fifty pounds, but it was bulky and terribly awkward. While the assignment didn't seem to me to be in keeping with my high rank and position in the outfit, I figured that if the CO could fight Japanese in the air when outnumbered at least fifty to one, I probably could carry his bedroll without serious harm to my ego. Truthfully, I had tremendous respect and admiration for the man. To be of service to him, at that time especially, was a privilege.

By the time we had ploughed our way through approximately two miles of fairly rough country and reached the river, I was starved. I wished then with all my heart that I had taken the CO seriously when he told us that morning to eat our meals.

There was no food. So, as soon as our exodus came to a halt, we rolled up in our blankets for rest and sleep. We were all hoping for some word of explanation of just what had happened, but none was forthcoming. Our CO's problems and concerns were undoubtedly far greater than ours. He was a fantastic combat pilot and a great human being. Even as tired as we all were, I suspect all of us would have been glad to do about anything asked of us by him.

In spite of the upsetting activities of the day, I had not yet experienced great fear. That was to come later, I learned sadly. Consequently, I went to sleep almost immediately after stretching out on the ground with my blanket over me. Others enjoyed the same experience. It seemed clear no one really wanted to hash over the events of the day. With the two exceptions noted, there was little over which any of us felt great pride.

I couldn't have been asleep for more than a few minutes when I was shaken awake by my former supply officer, Lieutenant Ploy. He was a flight leader and a fine gentleman. I liked him a great deal and enjoyed our relationship in the squadron supply business. He wasn't at all pushy and seemed pleased with my administration of the squadron supply. From time to time he asked me to type reports dealing with a variety of squadron activities for him. I gladly obliged because I truly appreciated him as a colleague and was eager to help him progress as an officer.

"The CO has directed me to return to Clark Field to receive fighter planes from Nichols Field. It appears that we are to maintain Clark Field and continue to use it as a base for our planes. Do you think that you can find your way back to the base? I would be grateful if you would go with me."

I knew that I could get us back to the base.

"Why shouldn't I know every foot of that trail?" I thought. "I had a good look at it as I carried that bulky bedroll."

"Lieutenant, I can get us back there, and I don't mind at all going with you," I responded.

Having slept in my clothing, I didn't have to dress, so without further conversation we moved off into the darkness.

For at least twenty minutes as we walked slowly toward the field, he was silent. Then he asked, "How do you feel about what is happening?"

I told him that I didn't much relish the thought of the United States being at war with any country but, "If we have to defend the Philippines against an enemy, it can just as well be against the Japanese."

"As far as I am concerned," I continued, "if war had to come, this is as good a time as any for me. I am on my own and really don't have any family responsibilities or anyone except my parents to think about me. They have six other kids, five boys and a girl, to worry about."

"I wish now that I were in your situation, but that is not the case with me," he said. "I am terribly afraid, not especially for myself, although I am now convinced that the enemy will be no pushover. My fear is for my family. I have a wonderful, loving wife and two beautiful daughters in the States. I love them so much and just have to make it through this war to return to them. I've just got to!" he said in desperation.

I hadn't even known that the guy was married. He had never said so. But then, he had never talked much about anything outside of squadron business. I supposed he shared personal feelings with officer colleagues. He talked now, though, and I listened. By the time we had arrived at the base I knew all about his wife and kids and felt sorry for all of them.

"Guess his wife must be plenty worried, also," I thought to myself.

When we returned to the base, everything was strictly business and I could see his self-confidence return as he saw the replacement P-40s. He got a special gleam in his eyes like "Now, you hot shots. Let's just see who is going to be in charge of the show from here on out."

# 3

# JAPANESE INVASION OF THE PHILIPPINES

IT WAS NEARLY THREE O'CLOCK in the morning when the lieutenant and I arrived back at the river completely exhausted, hungrier than I had ever remembered being, and eager to roll up in our blankets on the ground again. The only contribution I had made during the night was providing direction and company to the lieutenant as we made our way through the unfamiliar landscape between the river and Clark Field.

Protected by the cover of night, bulldozers from the base had filled in the immense craters left by the Japanese bombs and had pushed the debris of the day off the field. The Nichols Field pursuit squadron had delivered its P-40s for our pilots at Clark Field and, for some reason, hadn't seemed too upset over having to give up their fighting machines. Because the hangars had been completely destroyed, the only potentially safe spot to place the planes out of the sight of the enemy was a heavily wooded area located at the edge of the landing strip, halfway down its length. Revetments had not been built, so that was a task awaiting our squadron members or others assigned to the job.

By the time I awakened much later in the morning, the sun was already high in the sky. Some of the men had gone back to the airfield, and the rest, those of us not needed immediately to work on the airplanes, had orders to wait by the river until vehicles could be secured to carry us all back to the base.

As can be imagined, the talk of the morning focused on the predicament in which we found ourselves. There was much speculation concerning the length of time it would take the United States to get over to the Islands with men and equipment and wipe the Japanese off the face of the earth. There was no question but what our immediate situation was perceived as serious, but not to the extent that any of us feared the Japanese would overrun the Philippines. Right then we were more concerned about when we would get something to eat and the opportunity to learn in more detail what had happened to Clark Field the previous day.

It was nearly noon when the trucks finally made their way across the rough terrain to the place where we were waiting. By that time we were eager to get back into action, to more thoroughly survey the air base, and to look after our own possessions.

While in the heavily laden trucks going back to the air base we had our second experience with the Japanese air force. This time two Japanese planes appeared out of nowhere. By the time they had been spotted flying barely above the trees, they were diving on the trucks with their guns firing. They made only a single pass at the vehicles and the men and missed both. Everyone dived out of the moving trucks into the safety of the undergrowth in the anticipation of another long siege. Other than to get a bit dirtier, no one seemed to be much worse off from the short-lived attack, and the exercise left us all in much better spirits. It was almost as if we were playing a game and were looking for the opportunity to outsmart the opponent and then taunt him. There were many threats and jeers as we continued our way back to the base.

The trip was short. Upon arrival we found the air base to be almost completely deserted. The living quarters were empty, and the entire post had the air of a ghost town. No one had bothered the contents of the buildings even though the doors were left unlocked. It appeared that the people living in the vicinity thought the most unsafe place would be the air base and, for that reason, stayed completely away.

I hadn't been back at the field long until my supply-sergeant instincts began to direct me, and I decided it might be wise to see what I could do in the way of getting together equipment the men might need at a later time. To date we had received no information concerning our future activities or where we were to be located, but we hoped we wouldn't be expected to reoccupy our recently vacated living quarters. We had ample evidence they offered little protection from the Japanese.

After some thought I stacked together all of the extra blankets and other equipment that I felt might be usable. The first sergeant finally advised each person to strip down his bed, at least to take blankets, and also to get together a small supply of clothing and toilet articles. The balance of our possessions, valuable or valueless, were to be left behind if we abandoned the base. We were to be ready to travel fast if necessary.

After getting together readily movable items, I wandered over to the new post exchange to see what could be found of value there. Like those of most of the other buildings on the base, the doors of the place had been left unlocked, so I walked right in. What a fantastic sight greeted me!

On the tables of the eating area were glasses of Coke half finished, remains of ice cream sundaes partly eaten, sandwiches unfinished, and other evidence of people having abandoned the place in a hurry. When the Japanese struck, safety had been much more important than food or drink. How things were to change!

During the next hour or so I made numerous trips back and forth to the PX, where I filled barracks bags with cartons of cigarettes, candy bars, and any other items I thought would be usable. I was able to collect a good bit before the word got around. It wasn't long, though, before the place was completely stripped of anything that held any attraction for the men. Of course this amounted to looting, but the attitude was, "Let's get the stuff before those from off the base move in!"

During the balance of the afternoon, those of us not working on the planes just sat around contemplating our future. Apparently the Japanese were concentrating their activities elsewhere, because we were left completely alone.

Along toward evening the CO instructed us to move from the air base into the hilly canyon just above Fort Stotsenburg. The squadron had only a ton-and-a-half truck and two small pickup vehicles. These were to be used to move kitchen equipment and supplies and other materials that would be needed in the bivouac area.

When counsel was sought, I was advised by the CO not to take anything from the supply room. From then on, each person was to be responsible for his own belongings, including his bedding. As much as I was reluctant to leave the supplies, I was relieved not to have them to worry about. I did lock the supply shack and put the loot from the PX on one of the small trucks to be dispensed at a later date. Then I began the hike through Fort Stotsenburg to the hills.

Our new living area in the canyon above the fort was not too far from the base, so we walked the distance with little effort. We were advised to dig in and from there send men to the airfield as needed to maintain the airplanes that had been assigned to our squadron and that would be used primarily for reconnaissance flights. Our pilots were to take advantage of opportunities that presented themselves and defend themselves when attacked, but because the planes were so necessary for use in observing the movements of the enemy, they were not to be placed in any greater jeopardy than necessary.

It was nearly dark when we arrived in the canyon. About all we had time to do was to pick out what we each perceived to be a safe spot where we could spend the night. No food had been served since noon of the previous day, but back at the base we had found plenty to satisfy ourselves. It was a good thing we had, because no evening meal was prepared.

Rolled up in my blanket, I reviewed the events of the past two days. Only two days old, the war seemed to have been going on forever. How long those two days had been! My morale wasn't too good right then, but, thankfully, I was physically exhausted and sleep quickly took over.

The following morning we promptly went to work digging in. It was an enthusiastic group of men who wanted to give first priority to their own individual foxholes but instead received directions to donate immediate attention to preparing trenches in the group area—places where the cooks would be preparing and serving food and where the business of the squadron would be conducted.

We chose to dig our foxholes and trenches in the most heavily wooded area. After we had time to assure ourselves we couldn't be detected by the enemy, one of our pilots flew over the area to determine if any signs of our camp were visible from the air. After we had taken the necessary additional precautions as advised by that pilot, we felt reasonably sure we would not be high-priority targets.

The first two days in our work area were spent digging holes for ourselves and for the pilots and airplane maintenance men, who were required to spend most of their time down on the line with the planes. The ground was hard and rocky, but there weren't too many complaints about the digging. In fact, most of us approached the task with considerable enthusiasm. By evening of the second day we had holes and trenches all over the place. The work and bivouac areas looked almost like a prairie-dog town.

As long as we were busy, we didn't have time to consider seriously the situation in which we found ourselves. But once the holes were dug, there wasn't a great deal of work to do in the canyon and only a limited number of men were needed at the airfield. The labor work force rotated so that everyone had the opportunity to do his share, and it wasn't long before the planes were well concealed in revetments in the underbrush.

About the fifth day, with increased bombing by the Japanese, no reliable information from the United States, and practically no information from locals, the bravado we had demonstrated so vocally began to be replaced by fear. Shortly, the gravity of the situation was to hit most of us with full force. Where once we openly vocalized our bravery, now we were frightened. No longer was there talk of what we were going to do to the Japanese and what Uncle Sam was going to do. The evidence was mounting in favor of the Japanese. There was little question but what they were the ones who were calling the shots, at least in that part of the world. We were told by those who monitored the news that General Douglas MacArthur had been placed in charge of all of the war efforts in the Islands. The question was "Given his record thus far, what great leadership can be expected from him?"

As far as we were concerned, General MacArthur had to date been a complete failure as a leader. The reputation he had established thus far among those who knew him was that he was an arrogant, pompous phony who had established himself as a sovereign in a foreign country. The Manila Hotel had been his castle. From there he had reigned, available to only a chosen few.

During the daylight hours we had to fight ourselves to keep from remaining in or near our deep foxholes all of the time. Each day we dug the holes a bit deeper and dug additional holes, just in case. Unless we were assigned to work at the field or in the camp area, we remained close to cover and protection. There was little talking and no longer any kidding with each other about those ridiculous Japanese. When darkness fell, we knew the chances of survival were much better, at least until daylight.

Fortunately, for most of us that awful feeling of fright lasted only a few days, and then we were back in full charge of ourselves. There were, however, three of our men who were never able to regain personal control. Initially, we continued to try to help them, because we understood their problem well. Most of us asked ourselves repeatedly if the same thing could and might happen to us. Later, our patience exhausted, these three cowards became the scourge of the outfit. No amount of threatening, bullying, or name-calling ever brought them out of their world of fear. There were times when I was in complete agreement with those who firmly maintained they should be shot.

One of the three men was a sergeant who had kept pretty much to himself during the thirteen months we had been in the Philippines. He seemed not to have or to want any close friends. He was a good-looking, well-built fellow who apparently knew well the technical aspects of his work assignment. Now, in the canyon, he made no display of his feelings but went quietly off by himself, where he remained under cover at all times. In the beginning we made attempts to try to bring him back to the world of reality. Finally, we gave him up as a lost cause. There were times when he came out of hiding but only when he was at the point of starvation.

The second in hiding was a tall, thin private from one of the southern states. He and a buddy had joined the Army Air Corps together. In fact, they had grown up together. However, in spite of the constant pleading and the threats of his once-close friend, he was never able to shed the terrible fear that possessed him to the extent that he could make any productive contribution to the war effort. During the time we were involved in the conflict, he was completely useless.

The third permanent coward was a private first class, a big fellow who was a cook. All during the time our outfit had been together he had tried desperately to dominate the activities of the squadron mess. He was so disagreeable that few cared for him, including the officers. He was not overly bright, and during the pre-war period spent most of his off-work hours drinking alone.

Because of his size he was able to badger and bully, and even though many of the men outranked him, he was fairly well in control of the serving areas of the squadron mess. He didn't have many friends, so everyone received the same treatment. One thing that could be said about him was that his behavior was consistently intolerable. He had always seemed to get a great deal of satisfaction from being just as miserable as he possibly could be.

Once this person was identified as a coward, open season was declared on him and many experienced considerable satisfaction and pleasure over his constant misery. There were those who went out of their way to make life as unbearable for him as possible, and it was difficult for me not to want to join in the crowd. More than anything else, I have hated a bully. A mere shout of "Here they come!" was all that was required to send him underground, where he would remain for hours.

While most of us weren't overly enthusiastic over going to work at the airstrip, that was almost better than having nothing to do in the canyon. At least, there we had the opportunity to assist with the maintenance of the airplanes and the areas where they were tied down after each flight.

From the air, according to our pilots, the trees where our planes were kept stood out like a circus attraction. No one could understand why the

Japanese didn't level all of the underbrush. They must have known that the planes could not have been placed in bombed-out and burned-out hangars, and they did know our planes were flying off Clark Field.

Many times during each day the Japanese planes bombed the airstrip, the hangars, and the area where we once lived, but not once, at least to my knowledge, did they ever directly strike the bushy area along the side of the field. After each of their bombing missions, men would hop on bulldozers that had been placed around the field and fill in the bomb craters. In a matter of minutes the landing strip would be usable again.

On one of those December days, several of us were working in the vicinity of three planes well concealed in the brush. The P-40s were warming up in preparation for flight. Those of us who were not airplane mechanics had the responsibility of working as helpers to the mechanics. It was our duty to maintain the foxholes and trenches and to be constantly on the lookout for enemy planes. We had no mechanical warning system.

On this particular morning Corky Holmes, one of the young mechanics, came across the airstrip in a cut-down pickup truck. Corky and I had been good friends, and we were especially close after the outbreak of the war. He was from Ogden, Utah, and when he enlisted and was sent to Hamilton Field, California, he left a sweetheart in Ogden whom he planned to marry when his hitch in the Air Corps had been completed. Those long-range plans were demolished one day at Nichols Field when he received a "Dear John" letter from his girl. He was truly devastated over that news but continued to be a heck of a good soldier and a delightful friend.

Standing at the edge of the brush, I waved to him as he approached.

Not far from where I stood he stopped the truck and got out. He took from the seat of the truck a box of cigars he had scrounged from somewhere. He opened the box and placed it on the truck's hood. Then, he dipped both hands into the box and came out with a double handful of cigars. Coming toward the trees, he began shouting, "Cigars? Cigars! Does anyone want a cigar?"

Laughing at his antics, I turned around to see if he had any takers. No one was in sight.

Instinctively I turned toward the small tower that had been constructed. Sure enough, the red flag was whipping excitedly in the breeze as if its very movements alone would be sufficient to alert us of approaching enemy planes.

Almost simultaneously I heard the shrill, chilling whistle of the bombs from the Japanese planes overhead as they made their treacherous descent toward Clark Field.

The noise from our own airplane engines had drowned out the roar of the high-altitude approach of the Japanese bombers.

Spinning around, I made a dash for one of the trenches we had dug. Corky, who was smaller and faster than I, got into the brush ahead of me. He didn't, however, see the heavy vine that I had ducked under. Catching him under the chin or across the face, it halted him abruptly. Amidst exploding bombs, flying shrapnel, and dust, I dived into a trench.

When the bombers had passed over and everything was again reasonably safe, I got out of the trench with others and made my way back a few yards to where I had last seen Corky. I fully expected to find him cut into bits by the shrapnel. He wasn't there. I felt myself becoming ill.

"Hey! Hey! Hey! Hey, you guys!"

I ran over to where the call came from, and there lying full length along the bottom of a trench on his back was Corky. His clothing and face were covered with dust, but he had a big smile on his kisser. In his two hands he still held the cigars.

He looked up out of the trench, and in the most pitiful, pleading voice asked, "Don't any of you guys want a cigar?"

# 4

# THE ORANGE PLAN

AS THE DAYS PASSED, each daylight hour was filled with uncertainty and frustration. Only constant activity kept us sane.

Long before Christmas the Japanese had made successful invasions of the Philippine Islands from the north and were moving up from the south, where they had met little opposition in their landing at Camarine Norte. Because of Corregidor and Forts Frank and Drummond, they were not able to gain access to Manila Bay for their transports and warships. They were, however, going to be able to take the capital city of Manila because of the land drives from both the north and the south.

The cavalry and field artillery of the Philippine Scouts fought bravely at Lingayen Gulf, but their horse outfits were no match for the mechanized units that were landed by the Japanese forces under the protection of a superior air force and their navy. Many stories of the bravery of these horse-mounted Filipino soldiers trickled back to us at Clark Field, and it was not at all difficult for us to imagine the great odds that confronted our Filipino allies.

When we learned a few days before Christmas that Clark Field was to be abandoned, I reactivated myself as supply sergeant and informed the CO that much of the men's clothing was still in the laundry at the port area of Manila. By this time our clothing had become dirty, and in spite of efforts at scrubbing, all troops badly needed the fresh changes.

With some persuasive help from my supply officer, Lieutenant Roberts, a newly added non-flying officer, the CO authorized me to take the ton-and-a-half truck to Manila. The distance wasn't far, only about eighty kilometers. With a colleague to assist with the driving and the loading, we made the trip with little difficulty. We encountered no harassment from the enemy and were able to claim our belongings from the quartermaster laundry with ease. We even had time to stop briefly at the YMCA for a bath and a final ice cream sundae.

Manila was expecting to be invaded momentarily. The residents were frightened and had already reconciled themselves to the likelihood of the occupation of the area by the Japanese. They, too, found it difficult to believe the Japanese could defeat the American forces even for a short period of time. Like us, they had perceived the American forces to be invincible. Little did any of us know then what was in store for us.

While in Manila we learned that General MacArthur and President Quezon were to move their headquarters to Corregidor. That bit of information didn't affect us one way or the other; we had never perceived either to be a great asset to the war effort. Rather, MacArthur had recently served effectively only as an impediment. We just couldn't get over the tragedy of losing our B-17s to the Japanese on the first day of the war. It wouldn't have been so bad to have lost them in combat, but to have them destroyed while sitting on the ground was a terrible fiasco.

Later, when questioned by superiors concerning the failure to send the bombers to bomb Japan, General MacArthur maintained that he had never been contacted by anyone concerning the use of the planes against the Japanese Air Force assembled on Formosa. He went on to say that had a request been made to him he would have not authorized the flight because fighter protection was not available. It was interesting to learn from bomber crews that fighter protection for the B-17s was not needed. They could fly high enough to stay out of the range of the Japanese fighters.

Following the end of the war, our former commanding officer, General Moore, attended a conference of American and Japanese Air Force officers held in Japan. At one session he was seated next to a high-ranking Japanese officer who spoke English fluently. During his conversation with that officer he inquired concerning his assignment on the first day of the war. The Japanese officer informed him that, as a young officer pilot, he commanded a squadron of planes based on Formosa.

He said to General Moore, "On the morning of the outbreak of the war, a large number of Japanese planes were based on Formosa in readiness for the air strike on the Philippines. When we arose early that morning, a heavy fog engulfed the entire area, including the air base. The fog was so thick we could hardly see our hands in front of us.

"Fog was not common in that area and we were both dismayed and extremely concerned about our situation. We were well aware of the B-17s on Clark Field and anticipated they would attack our planes sitting on the ground. With your Norden bombsights we knew the fog could be penetrated effectively. Had those planes made a strike during that morning, it is possible the outcome of the Philippine campaign would have been much different. The fog finally lifted at about eleven o'clock in the morning and successful strikes against the planes in the Philippines were made."

On our return trip to Clark Field with the truckload of clean laundry, we encountered American and Filipino forces moving pieces of heavy artillery toward the Peninsula of Bataan. From them we learned that Manila was, in fact, to be declared an open city. Our forces, under what was to be known as "The Orange Plan," were to move to the Peninsula of Bataan and, with the help of the troops on Corregidor, hold Bataan and Corregidor until reinforcements from the States arrived. From those two locations we would then launch an offensive and drive the Japanese completely out of the Islands.

Back at Clark Field, after considerable negotiations with a motor-pool officer at Fort Stotsenburg, the CO managed to secure a five-ton truck for squadron use. After that it wasn't too difficult to convince the supply fellows at the fort that they should be generous with our squadron. After all, their men had left days earlier.

"Isn't it better that clothing be issued to us than confiscated by the Japs?" I asked. With that, they told me to help myself to whatever the men could use.

Assisted by several fellows from the squadron, I loaded the huge truck with socks, shoes, khakis, coveralls, underwear, blankets, pup tents, and several large tents.

Leaving the supply depot, we proceeded to the evacuated post exchange at the fort, where we found the unlocked building still well stocked. There we secured toothpaste, soap, towels, shaving equipment, and quantities of other usable toilet articles. This high load we then covered with a huge canvas. By this time the truck was dangerously top-heavy.

The Allies wisely did declare Manila an open city, and it was evident to us by the time we abandoned Clark Field what was going to happen to the strategically important areas of the Philippines: they were soon to be occupied by Japanese forces.

On December 23, our CO officially informed us concerning the Orange Plan. He wasn't definite concerning the exact time of our move to Bataan, but he informed us that we should be ready to leave on a moment's notice. Planes still in flying condition were to be flown to Bataan Field on the Peninsula of Bataan. All usable parts were to be stripped off the planes earlier grounded. With approximately two hundred men eager for work, the time required to dismantle the inoperative planes was minimal.

Along about dusk on Christmas Eve, we obeyed orders to assemble our convoy on a road leading from Fort Stotsenburg to Clark Field. Never again would be seen such a conglomeration of men and machines. The convoy was made up of almost every type of vehicle imaginable. GI trucks were almost unobtainable, so the forces had to rely on civilian vehicles to move the organization.

One group of men had commandeered a large LaSalle convertible. The owner of the vehicle, even though a loyal patriot, hadn't been thoroughly convinced he should give up the automobile. He followed the takers to the convoy, and it required the intervention of the CO before the matter could be settled. As it turned out, the occupants of the sedan were permitted to keep it. The owner was given a receipt authorizing payment for the car when American forces were again in control of the area.

After much confusion and delay and considerable concern that the Japanese might drop bombs on us, the convoy began moving slowly down the road toward the city of San Fernando.

It was with mixed feelings we departed. Thus far, our contribution to the war effort hadn't been anything to brag about. Most of us were quietly suffering the humiliation of the defeat already experienced, although few talked about this openly. Our hopes now were that, once on Bataan, we would be reequipped with planes and given the opportunity to function as a full-fledged fighter squadron. While several of our now-experienced combat pilots had serious reservations about our ability to compete effectively in the air against superior Japanese planes, most continued to be capable and eager. And the ground support crews were competent. Needed and hoped for was a reasonable chance to redeem ourselves.

I drove the big supply truck with a dozen or more men on the top. The vehicle, already loaded high with clothing and equipment, was made more top-heavy by the men who tried desperately to cling to the load. Those fellows, during the long black night, more than earned their ride by guiding me in the dark, helping me to keep the truck on the road right side up.

It was a despondent group of men who passed through Angeles, a town usually bright with light from all the places catering to servicemen from Clark Field and Fort Stotsenburg. The city had been the scene of many enjoyable activities. Right then I thought of Chicken Charlie's, a place where weekly we used to get a whole deep-fried chicken, French fries, and home-made bread for a peso. Quite often we would go there early in the day. Later in the evening when all other festivities ended we would return for a second feast.

Rumor had it that one of the best friends of the Clark Field men, a furniture-store operator, turned out be a Japanese spy. Before the outbreak of the war I never heard anyone speaking of the possibility of spies nor felt concerned about the matter. In fact, no one that I knew of seemed to take very seriously the possibility of war with the Japanese. Who was interested in war when everyone was having such a good time?

By midnight we had reached San Fernando, a city through which we had driven dozens of times on our way to Manila. Thus far, we had covered no more than thirty miles, but then it was almost impossible for the convoy to maintain any speed while driving without lights. As the vehicles halted in the city square, the bells in the Catholic church began to chime. We received word that there would be a short stop here for rest.

Sitting slouched in the seat of the truck, I felt my morale right then drop to zero. I was tired, despondent, and terribly homesick as I began to recall other Christmases. Two years before I had been with my girl, and even last Christmas in the Philippines I was having a great time. In fact, until the bombing of Pearl Harbor all of my army experiences had been nothing short of terrific.

"Those lousy Japs!"

5

# RAW RECRUITS

AS I SAT RESTING MY HEAD on the steering wheel of the truck, completely exhausted but unable to sleep, I couldn't help but ponder the events that had led to my present situation. Enlistment in the Army had not been a long-range goal for me. Instead, it stemmed more from the lack of anything better.

Not long after graduation from high school I entered the hospital for a long-delayed hernia operation and spent the balance of the summer recuperating from that event. I had no interest in college and didn't have any money anyway, so about the middle of September I had gone to Shelley, Idaho, with a couple of other fellows. The need for spud pickers was great, and we hadn't experienced any difficulty in securing employment for a couple of months.

During the following six months I managed a duck-pin bowling alley in Montpelier, Idaho. By the first of April of 1940 I had about enough of the bowling-alley business and began to yearn for a job that didn't keep me inside all the time. Our part of the country was beautiful, especially during the spring, summer, and fall, and I was eager to be out in the sunshine.

About the middle of April my potato-picking buddies and I had secured jobs on one of the sheep and cattle ranches owned by the Cokeville Land and Livestock Company of Cokeville, Wyoming. Our place of work was the Sublette Ranch located about five miles from Cokeville, up the Smith's Fork River. The pay was forty-five dollars per month, but for that amount of money we had to work seven days a week. All in all, we were fairly satisfied with the arrangement.

On Saturday evenings we would go to town to a dance. That was about the only recreation we had, but after long working days we were generally eager to hit the sack shortly after the evening meal was served.

At one of the Saturday-night dances I met a fellow whose father owned several herds of sheep. During my brief discussion with him, I indicated I would like to get a job with a sheep herd. He told me he didn't know whether or not his dad was hiring any new men but he would tell him about my interest anyway.

It was about the middle of May when his dad, a French Basque by the name of Pete, visited the Sublette ranch and asked for me. He told me that after the lambing period had ended he would have three summer herds, each consisting of about three thousand head of ewes and lambs. One of the three would be herded by a fellow who had been working for him for ten years. He had come to the United States from France as a very young man and had remained with Pete continuously, saving nearly all of his money to enable him to return to France and purchase a farm for himself.

At the outbreak of the war between France and Germany the herder, who also had the name of Pete, was ordered to return to France to help in the defense of his country. He notified French authorities he was not ready to return because he still had not been able to accumulate adequate funds to purchase the property he so badly wanted. The response to him was to the effect that if he did not return, the money he had on deposit at home would be confiscated by the government.

After serious deliberation, he decided he would never return to France but would apply for citizenship in the United States instead. That meant he would have to learn to speak and write the English language. That was where I fitted into the picture.

The conversation with the owner was enjoyable, and at the end of the discussion he offered me the job. It paid sixty dollars per month along with board and room. I accepted and told him I would be ready to go as soon as I finished the day's work and collected my gear. He came back to the ranch for me the following morning.

I threw my gear into the bed of the truck already occupied by a couple of sheep dogs that had found sleeping space between several western and pack saddles and other odds and ends. The dogs, I was to learn, were necessary for effective sheep ranching.

We drove to Cokeville, where we loaded the rest of the truck with food supplies and rock salt, the order for which had been placed earlier. By 10:00 a.m. we were on our way to the lambing herd, which was on the range in the mountains between Geneva, Idaho, and Star Valley, Wyoming. What a beautiful day and how I enjoyed spending it with my boss, who turned out to be a most delightful fellow!

The ewes were just beginning to lamb, and all of them were together in one large herd. When about a third of them finished lambing, they and their lambs would be separated from the main group and would begin grazing in a separate area. The same thing would happen when half of those left had lambed, leaving the final third to finish the lambing season. It was hoped that all would be lambed out by June 15, giving the last group at least two weeks to toughen up prior to the long trek to the summer range.

At the cook shack I met the fellow who cooked for the six men who worked with the sheep. He was a Mexican who spoke English well and who turned out to be an interesting person.

Pete then told me my first assignment would be as an assistant to the Mexican cook. My hunch was he arrived at the decision after I told him how much my mother had taught me about cooking and how I truly enjoyed cooking. I didn't mind the assignment a bit.

The days on the lambing ground passed rapidly. From the cook I learned a great deal about sheep-camp cooking and about life in general. He immediately set about teaching me to make sourdough bread, an important part of the sheepherder's diet. As soon as I passed the test to his satisfaction, bread-making became my major responsibility. In addition to making bread, I helped prepare food for the three large meals served each day. I had never imagined individuals could eat as much as the Basques did. They worked hard and ate well.

Late in the afternoon of June 27, the boss sent word we should start moving our herds toward the trail to the summer range the following day. I was thoroughly elated! We were far enough away from the trail that it would take us a full day to reach it. All herds moving from our part of the country toward the summer range would use the same trail to assure that no more pasture land was spoiled than was necessary. Once they had reached the national forest, they would split off and go to their different summer grazing areas.

My responsibility on the trail was to prepare an early breakfast and then help get the herd moving. Once the sheep were on their way, I would strike camp, pack the camp gear, load it on the horses, and move out in the direction the herd would be going. Before long I would pass the herd, and by the time it had caught up to me at noon, I was expected to have food ready, including freshly baked bread. The sheep would rest in the shade during the heat of the day, and by the time they were on the trail once again, I would be way ahead, setting up camp for the night. My responsibility included selecting an area appropriate for assuring feed and safety for the sheep.

On the Fourth of July our three herds went through the counting in corral. Pete Espil, the herder for whom I was to tend camp, promptly took charge of our herd. Our allotment was the one at the head of the Salt River. What a beautiful part of the world it was!

That summer was one of the greatest I had ever spent. The mountains were rugged and beautiful, the streams were filled with trout, and we had good saddle and pack horses and three dogs far wiser with the sheep than was I. And Pete Espil was something else! What a super guy he was! He was an eager student and learned rapidly. In no way was it a one-way affair, either. I learned much from him daily, not French, Spanish, or the Basque language—all of which he spoke fluently—but about sheep, horses, bear, and how to cook using a Dutch oven. That guy really loved food, and the better informed I became about cooking, the more I came to enjoy it.

Each Friday we killed a large lamb, always an unbranded stray, never one of our own. When I questioned Pete concerning the honesty of that practice, he responded, "I don't know it isn't one of ours we didn't brand. Even if it isn't, other herders are killing and eating our strays."

Our days were filled with interesting activities and study. If I had free time when he didn't, I would go fishing. Pete was always supportive of that activity because he loved a dinner of fish more than anything else, and there were big ones in the river just waiting to be taken.

Snows come early to the high mountains of Wyoming, so by the tenth of September we were trailing back to the lower foothills. On the 19th of the month, my birthday, we were poised with our herd on the mountain ridge just above Cokeville, ready to drive our eighty-pound lambs to the stockyards. Three days later I picked up my check for the summer's work, and feeling I deserved a vacation, I headed for town. I felt good about what had been accomplished during the summer. Pete had learned to speak English very well and was progressing rapidly with his writing. We parted as good friends.

After a weekend of festivities with my friend from the Sublette Ranch, he and I decided to stop at the post-office building in Pocatello, Idaho, to inquire concerning life in the U.S. Navy. It so happened that we arrived at the recruiter's office at noon, when he was out to lunch. His friend, the Army recruiter, was in his office directly across the hall and invited us to wait with him until the Navy man returned. Thinking back now, it occurs to me that right then may have been the time when we made a serious strategical error.

While we were cooling our heels, the Army sergeant was eager to tell us about the Army, and we were interested in hearing him tell about life in the various branches. He informed us that there were openings in all areas of the service for men who had graduated from high school. The most romantic opportunity right then, he pointed out to us forcefully and convincingly, was membership in the Army Air Corps.

"This," he said, "is a relatively new organization, and it is desperately in need of men. Promotions will come fast!"

"I don't know," I said. "If I ever went into the Army, I think I would want to join the cavalry. I know horses and like to work around them."

"What are you talkin' about, man? You mean you would want to spend your life playing nursemaid to a horse? Horses are on the way out. The cavalry is becoming mechanized. The Air Corps is the place for high-school graduates. You could probably be sent to a technical school right away to learn to be an airplane mechanic. And those guys are really in demand in the Air Corps and with civilian airlines."

"If I didn't join the cavalry, how about the medical corps?" I asked. "I think I would like to work around a hospital."

"What! You mean to tell me that you want to be a bedpan boy? I wouldn't carry those stinkin' bedpans around for anyone! In the Air Corps you might even get a chance to fly a plane. They still have flyin' sergeants, you know.

"Listen, fellas, like I said, the Air Corps is a new organization. Promotions are gonna come fast. You've got high-school diplomas. You'll move right up in the organization. You're just the kind of guys they're lookin' for. If I could, I'd transfer into the Air Corps myself right now!"

By the time the Navy recruiter returned from lunch, we had our fists full of papers to take home for completion and for the signatures of our parents. We were both under the age of twenty-one, and the Air Corps needed written approval.

It wasn't difficult for me to convince my mother the Air Corps was the place for me. She knew I was terribly restless and was eager for me to get new experiences. And she was convinced I would do great things for and in that organization.

My dad didn't give in quite so easily, though. He had never been very impressed, so he informed me, with the caliber of men he had seen wearing Army uniforms, and he reminded me the pay of soldiers was low and would undoubtedly continue to be so. I countered with the information the Air Corps was something new, and the opportunities there were unlimited. He finally gave in and signed my release, but with considerable reluctance.

I recalled how jubilant I had been in Salt Lake City, Utah, when I was sworn into the Air Corps and was told I would be assigned to the 18th Pursuit Squadron at Hamilton Field, California. I had never been to California. In fact, I had never been much farther away from home than Salt Lake City. I did know everything I had ever heard about California had been good and exciting.

Dean, my ranch work partner who had inquired about the service with me in Pocatello, lost his enthusiasm after we returned home, and when I went for induction, he still hadn't made up his mind to join. By the time he decided in favor of signing up, I was already in basic training. He arrived at Hamilton Field about ten days later and was assigned to the headquarters squadron of the group in which my squadron had membership.

Basic training was something else! Upon arrival at Hamilton Field, I, along with a great many from all over the United States, was assigned to the second floor of one of the many temporary two-story buildings that had been recently constructed. There I received GI clothing that didn't fit, a footlocker, and other odds and ends. I also kept my civilian clothing, which we were authorized to wear on and off base when we were not on duty. The staff sergeant in charge of the men on our floor was really a nice guy. From him we learned much concerning what we should and should not do if we wanted to stay out of trouble in the Army.

I didn't mind the marching part of recruit drill, but the drill master, a sergeant from the infantry, was really an obnoxious jerk. On the morning we first fell out for drill, he stood in front of us, hands on his hips, and quickly demonstrated to us what a dummy he really was.

"I'm your drill sergeant, and I'm your boss while you are on the drill field! What I say goes! I'm gonna work the rear ends off you smart alecs! I know your kind too well! You think because you're in the fly corps that you're better'n anybody else! I'm here to show you insignificant imbeciles what a real infantry soldier looks like!

"By the time I finish with you, you'll hate my guts! I don't want any nonsense from any of you while you're in training under me. After that's over, if you think you've got the guts, you can come around to my building, and you can have a crack at me. I can beat the whole bunch of you all at once!"

He was so ridiculous it was hard to keep from laughing, and as I carefully looked around our group it seemed to me there were among us those who just might be more than a match for the big-shot sergeant.

Three weeks passed rapidly without serious incident, and I learned about the U.S. Army Air Corps and about the men who served in the organization. I really had been a green kid fresh off the farm. Personal privacy, which had been so important to me while growing up—forget it. In the Army everyone and everything was on display on command. I believe the worst part of the introduction for me were the "short arm" inspections that were conducted regularly for the purpose of identifying those who had contracted venereal disease. Not only was I embarrassed, but this seemed to me to be the ultimate in the invasion of personal privacy. Later, I learned why these regular inspections by medical personnel were so necessary.

In the beginning everyone in uniform rated a salute from me. Later, I began to be somewhat more discriminate and saluted only those who had stripes or bars or brass on their collars. I undoubtedly gave considerable pleasure to a number of privates first class.

Army rules and regulations were never very difficult for me to accept, as long as they were implemented fairly. In our home we had learned discipline. My mother was not a harsh disciplinarian, but she was a most proper lady and had taught us to use the right language and to have respect for authority. The authority figure in our home was my father, and although he was not a severe man, we had learned early to abide by his counsel and decisions. He didn't punish often, but punishment when administered could be quite severe. Our family was large, income was limited, and Dad had to work hard to provide a good home for all of us. He didn't have much time for nonsense. Never have I known a man who was more fair or honest in his dealings with others.

My first evening in the squadron mess initiated me regarding dining-hall etiquette. At each table sat ten or so men with a sergeant at the head. We were served family style with squadron privates taking their turn on KP. The instructions were that we were to hold up a plate for refilling when it was nearly empty. KPs would then come and get the plate or bowl from us.

During the course of the dinner, the bread plate came by me. I took a piece of bread and set the plate in the middle of the table.

"Hold up the plate, stupid!" directed the master sergeant at the head of the table.

"But there are several pieces of bread on it," I responded, holding up the plate for him to see.

"Listen, wise guy, I said hold it up and don't give me any of that back talk!"

I held the plate up, and a KP came and took it away to be refilled.

Several evenings later in the same mess hall I was in line to scrape my plate. Two garbage cans had been provided—one for scraps and one for paper. As I proceeded to scrape my plate, a paper cup fell into the wrong can.

"Dummy, don't you know enough to put a cup in the can for paper and not in the can for scraps? Can't you read? How dumb can you be?"

"I didn't intend to put the cup into the can," I said. "It fell in, and I was going to reach in and pick the thing up and put it right in this little can which is for cups and other things."

"Don't get smart with me. All we got around this place lately is a bunch of you smart alecs!"

Back at the barracks I talked with the staff sergeant who supervised us there. I told him of my two experiences with the master sergeant and wondered what recourse I might have if this type of harassment continued.

"Well, he is a noncommissioned officer, and there is really not much you can do; that is, unless you get him in a situation where you can call his bluff in front of a group of men. Then, he will either have to settle with you man-to-man, or he will be shown up for what he apparently is. If you challenge him, make sure the cause is legitimate."

The third time the master sergeant cut loose at me was when we were alone in the day room. I had written a letter to a friend and had placed it in the outgoing mail receptacle. Without turning around, I reached into the open box and took out the letter to make sure that I had written my return address on the envelope. Then he grabbed the letter out of my hand.

"What in the hell do you think you are doing, going through the United States mail? Don't you know that's a criminal offense? You could be put in the brig for a stupid trick like that!"

I tried to show him I was only looking at my own letter, but he wouldn't listen.

"You are lucky I don't turn you over to the military police right now. Don't you ever let me catch you doing anything like that again!"

That settled the matter for me. I made up my mind to have my turn at the turkey.

My opportunity came sooner than anticipated.

The very next day we were dismissed at noon from recruit drill, not far from our barracks. Because the mail was delivered during the morning, all of us raced for the day room in hopes of a letter. Like most other buildings on the base, the one housing the day room was a temporary construction and not too stable. A group of us reached the door at the same time, but I burst into the room ahead of everyone else. The building really shook from the force of our enthusiastic approach.

In one corner of the room at a card table four NCOs were seated, playing cards. One of the four was my friend, the master sergeant.

Jumping up from his chair, he shouted, "You dumb bastards! Where do you think you get off charging in here like that? All of you get your asses out of this building and right now!"

"Hey, back off! Wait a minute, sergeant," I said. "We have just as much right to be in this day room as you or anyone else does. Now, I don't know about the rest of these guys, but you've been on my back ever since I got here, and I've about had a gut full of you. Why don't you just pull off your shirt with those stripes you think give you the right to be the bully you are and step outside with me to settle our differences like gentlemen?"

His mouth fell open, and he stared at me dumbfounded. I am sure he couldn't believe what he had heard.

After several moments, which seemed like hours, he turned and went back to the table without another word. To make matters worse, all of the new guys with me cheered.

The sergeant never bothered me again.

During our fourth week at Hamilton we learned that one of the squadrons on the base was the 20th Pursuit Squadron. It was trying to entice new recruits from other outfits to transfer in to bring it up to full strength prior to its being shipped out to the Philippine Islands. We were told the entire squadron, with the exception of a few "old timers," was to be made up of men newly recruited into the Army Air Corps.

The rumor was that our present squadron, the 18th, would leave in a few months for Alaska, but it was only a rumor. Since I had lived in "cold" country all my life and greatly enjoyed the out-of-doors, Alaska had considerable attraction for me, although I had to admit that I didn't know much about the U.S. possession in the far north.

After drill one evening Dean, my friend from home, was waiting to inform me he had been transferred to the new squadron and encouraged me to request a transfer so we could be together. He assured me volunteers would be accepted eagerly. So, I formally volunteered for the change.

The following day a runner came out to the drill field with a note for the drill sergeant. He read the note slowly and then, looking directly at me, commanded, "Jacobsen, you poor dumb bastard, the Philippine Islands for you!"

# 6

# GOODBYE, GOOD LUCK, AND GOD BLESS YOU

MY NEW OUTFIT, the 20th Pursuit Squadron, did not originate at Hamilton Field, California. The squadron had been transferred from Moffett Field, California, not too much earlier, but only a few experienced men had been retained in it. Consequently, there was the need for many recently recruited young men to build it up to full operating strength.

The squadron was commanded by a major by the name of Grover. The balance of the officers corps consisted of two first lieutenants and eight second lieutenants. My initial contact with those who were already members of the squadron was good, and I looked forward to enjoyable experiences both with them and with those who just a few weeks earlier had been civilians representing almost all parts of our country.

The next two weeks were busy ones for the men in the 20th. We had to take typhoid, cholera, yellow fever, and tetanus shots, and all of us underwent a thorough physical examination. Field packs were issued and packed, and office and hangar-line equipment was crated and labeled. While much of what went on seemed to be a waste of time, no one complained much because of the anticipation of new and exciting adventures.

Two days before we were scheduled to leave Hamilton Field, my hometown buddy, Dean, was notified that his shot record had been lost. There wasn't time for him to repeat the shots so he was transferred out of our squadron and reassigned to the headquarters squadron of our original group. I was disappointed as was he, but not even that information dampened my spirits. I had met new fellows and had made new friends and was rarin' to go, and the sooner the better.

The day for a trial run finally arrived. With field packs slung, we assembled on the hangar line on that air base alongside of San Francisco Bay. Several important-looking officers gave us a careful once-over and concluded that we appeared to be properly organized for the move. That was followed by roll call by one of the first lieutenants. In the short time that I had been with the squadron, he had been able to become a pain in the neck to most of the new men.

As he walked down the line of men calling names, each responded with "Here, Sir!" except a shave-tail private who responded merely with "Here."

With his face close to the respondent's he demanded, "Soldier, don't you know enough to say sir to an officer?"

"Yeah," the private responded.

"Get your butt out of line and down to the squadron mess on KP!" the lieutenant shouted to the private.

The fellow just smiled and sauntered off toward the kitchen.

Most of us were pleased and appreciative when that officer was transferred out of the squadron shortly after our arrival in the Philippines.

Finally, with Fox Movietone cameramen there to record our departure, the squadron once again assembled on the hangar line, where the commanding officer of Hamilton Field addressed us. I didn't pay close attention to most of his speech but his concluding remarks captured my attention completely.

"Men, you are going to the Philippine Islands, some of you never to return. Goodbye, good luck, and God bless you!"

That closing remark created more than a little stir, with one man exclaiming, "What in the hell is this guy saying, 'some of you never to return'? If that is the case, by damn I'm goin' to change my mind about goin'."

It wasn't until some months later that we finally came to understand what the speaker back at Hamilton Field had in mind.

In single file we marched to waiting trucks. The police, with sirens screeching full blast, escorted us to the city of San Francisco, where we boarded a train for San Pedro. That night I learned the hard way how not to play blackjack. I was also confronted with the challenge of learning how to manage completely without spending money while we sailed from San Pedro to Manila via Shanghai.

Our vessel, the SS *Washington,* was huge and beautiful. She had been chartered by the U.S. government to sail to China to pick up American refugees from the war between China and Japan. Our squadron had luckily been assigned to this ship for the trip to the Philippines.

Joining us for the first leg of the trip between San Pedro and Honolulu were a large number of infantry troops assigned to serve in Hawaii. For the first few days the ship was a bit crowded, but no one seemed to mind at all. Once the ship docked in Honolulu the infantry troops promptly disembarked, leaving the entire ship to the crew and our squadron.

The ship was scheduled to be at dock in Honolulu for three days, which gave us ample time to become marginally acquainted with the city. Two bits of information that I picked up there were quite disturbing to me. The first was that a man could get sick if he drank too much cold pineapple juice when he was overheated. The second was that a man had to get into line if he wanted to visit a prostitute. I didn't, but as we walked down one street we observed a long line of men stretching from a door on the second floor, down the steps, out the walk, and down the sidewalk.

"What the heck is that lineup all about?" I asked.

"You are looking at a bunch of really dumb soldiers waiting for their turn with a whore," was the disgusted response. No doubt about it, I was getting some learning that wasn't available in our schools at home or on the street either.

As we enjoyed the sights of Honolulu, I had to keep pinching myself to be convinced that I was really in Hawaii. I just wished that I could be sharing some of the exotic beauty with the folks back home who could rarely find the time to spend a few hours on a fishing stream, let alone find the time and the resources to take an extended cruise to the Hawaiian Islands.

There were enough beautiful staterooms on Decks A and B to accommodate the men of our squadron. Two of us were assigned to each stateroom, with all of the comforts and courtesies extended to first-class paying passengers. In fact, the service was much too good for a bunch of dogfaces. We seemed, however, to be able to adjust ourselves to this improved level of living.

The trip from Honolulu seemed short because of the good times we were enjoying. The ship's first-class dining fare, the swimming pool, the gym, the movies, and all of the other luxurious attractions kept us well occupied and extremely contented. Somewhere in the South China Sea the ship confronted a typhoon that was vigorous enough to keep the promenade deck awash for a couple of days, but, as rough as the seas were, few of us missed any meals.

While sailing up the Yangtze River into the Wangpoo, we got our first look at the devastation caused by war. The buildings lining the river showed scars from heavy shelling, many being completely demolished.

We heard from the news that thousands of Chinese had been left homeless and without ample food, clothing, or medicine. Japanese gunboats escorted our ship and were close enough to permit us to get a fairly good look at some of those who had been so ruthless with the Chinese people and destructive to their lands. By the time we exited the area we had seen enough destruction to cause us to have less than happy thoughts about the Japanese military.

Off Shanghai our vessel anchored in the middle of the river. Some of the new American passengers, mostly women and children, were promptly brought to the ship in lighters.

Swarming around our ship were dozens of small boats filled with Chinese men, women, and children. Those people begged for food constantly and crowded and struggled to get near the garbage chute. It was a sad, pitiful sight and caused me to give serious thought to my life thus far and to the many privileges I had enjoyed as an American. Most of the families in our little town enjoyed only a modest living, but compared to these poor Chinese, we were richly blessed.

All the while we were anchored off Shanghai, Japanese planes were continually flying overhead, and their gunboats patrolled the river constantly.

After two days of taking on passengers, we slowly made our way down the Wangpoo and into the Yangtze River under Japanese gunboat escort.

With all of the beautiful ladies now aboard ship, the level and quality of festivity increased considerably. In addition to being without funds, I wasn't experienced enough or sophisticated enough to understand how one attracted the companionship of female strangers. Those who were, however, enjoyed the added attraction of having party dates and a dancing partner. Some of those were the ones, also, who learned that a single bed could readily accommodate two under certain circumstances.

Even without a girl of my own, I wasn't at all unhappy. I greatly enjoyed the ship's new atmosphere and was not eager for the journey to end.

Between China and the Philippines we encountered rough seas once again, but this landlubber experienced no difficulties. I had earned my sea legs long ago standing in the bed of an iron-tired wagon being pulled down a bumpy road by a team of spirited horses. A number of my colleagues didn't fare quite so well, however. I felt sorry for them because the food continued to be nothing less than fantastic.

Not only were the meals super, but we were welcome any time of the day or night in the galley, where we could serve ourselves from huge stacks of sandwiches and from an attractive assortment of drinks. What a life that was!

On Thanksgiving Day, my father's birthday, after twenty-three days aboard the "floating palace" turned "floating fun house," we finally reached Manila Bay. As the ship glided slowly and smoothly into the bay, we lined the decks and began scanning the shoreline of Manila, the city that was to be our home for the next two years. The greenish-blue water was without a ripple.

Forts Frank and Drummond were pointed out to us, as was the Mariveles Port on the Peninsula of Bataan. Next, we approached Corregidor, an island fortress that meant nothing more to us at that time than did any of the other beautiful scenery. Little did we realize how important these islands and the Peninsula of Bataan were to become.

As we docked, a Philippine Army band was on hand to welcome us, and there was hustle and bustle everywhere. With our stuffed green barracks bags over our shoulders, we staggered down the gangplanks and into waiting trucks. It was great to be on land again permanently.

As we rode from the docks to our base, Nichols Field south of Manila, I commented that Manila wasn't at all what I had expected. I had anticipated tropical jungles with thatched-roof homes. Instead, we drove through a modern, beautiful, well-kept city.

Dewey Boulevard, with the palm-tree-lined beach on one side and the gracious Spanish homes on the other, was nothing short of magnificent. "What a great place this is going to be!" I announced to myself.

From the road, Nichols Field, our new home, could not be seen. Situated in the barrio of Baclaren just south of Manila, it was surrounded by homes and huge, old trees. It reminded one of a gracious southern plantation as shown in movies more than it did an air base.

We found our squadron barracks to be located on the second story of a large, well-screened building just to the left of the base entrance. The first story housed the day room, which was a large airy space filled with pool and card tables. There were also easy chairs and stacks of magazines. The atmosphere was warm and attractive and subsequent visits there were all pleasant experiences for me. Never having been in a pool hall in my life, I didn't know the first thing about the game, and after watching a few of the many pool experts, I concluded that there was no way that I was going to impress anyone as a player. Cards held no attraction for me either after my earlier experience on the train, so for me the card tables were also off limits.

On the first floor were also the barbershop, the kitchen and mess hall, the shower and latrine rooms, and the squadron office and supply room. Most of the second-story space was filled with double-decker metal bunks with mattresses, pillows, and mosquito netting. There were also spaces for a foot and wall locker for each squadron member. One end of the sleeping area was walled off into several small rooms reserved for the senior NCOs, including the first sergeant.

Among the enlisted men, those with the most seniority had the first choice of bunks, so that assured me an upper bed. Sleeping below me was a buck sergeant who later got busted from sergeant to private. He was also moved out of that bunk, which suited me fine. I still didn't rate a lower berth, however.

Each of us signed for one of the iron bunk beds, a mattress, pillow, mosquito net, four sheets, and a blanket. The bedbugs were included with the bed, mattress, and mosquito net—we didn't have to sign for those.

For health reasons we were quarantined to the base for two weeks. Most of us didn't mind because there were plenty of interesting attractions to keep us occupied. The local Filipino and Chinese merchants were authorized to come on base, and it wasn't long before most of us were in hock for at least a new pair of handmade shoes and various pieces of clothing.

During the first week we unpacked squadron equipment so we could begin to function as an active squadron. Eight P-26s were assigned to our outfit, and the pilots began daily flights in the stubby contraptions.

Almost every new man in the squadron wanted to be an airplane mechanic. This presented a serious problem for the first sergeant and the commanding officer because cooks, clerks, and supply men were also needed. Each morning 150 or so men went down to the hangar line, where many of us would spend most of our time sweeping and dusting. As we returned from the hangar line each morning at eleven o'clock for lunch, the first sergeant would give the old pep talk about the benefits to be derived from assignments as cooks or clerks. I was determined to stay in there pitching until those who were going to be airplane mechanics were selected.

Finally, after having learned all that I needed to know concerning the sweeping and dusting of airplane hangars, I succumbed to pressures applied by the first sergeant.

"I have been going over your personal file carefully," he said to me, "and I found you are able to type and you have also had a year of record-keeping experience in a bank in your hometown. If you will accept an assignment as clerk in the squadron supply, I will recommend a promotion to the rank of private first class for you with a fourth-class-specialist rating. You won't be able to receive the salary increase that goes with the rank and rating until you have completed the first three months of your enlistment. After that time your monthly salary will increase from $21.00 to $36.00 per month."

I was persuaded and promptly went to work as a supply clerk. The supply sergeant, Ralph J. Kearney, was a handsome, super fellow, and I enjoyed him from the very first introduction. A young fellow from Oregon by the name of Norman D. Thompson was the other supply-room clerk, and he too was a very special person. He had been in the squadron for several months and was reasonably well informed concerning the overall operation.

Our work day at Nichols Field began with roll call at 6:30 a.m. Breakfast began at 7:00, and we were to be at work by 8:00. Everyone knocked off for a short break at 9:30 and at 11:00 for a shower before lunch. That was the end of the normal work day for most of us, although we were on call twenty-four hours of each day. There was no air conditioning in any of the work stations, and the afternoon heat and humidity made productive activity almost impossible.

Because of the intense heat, most of us chose to sleep for several hours until evening breezes from the ocean brought relief. For most, getting acclimated was no small undertaking. Initially, I longed to be back in Wyoming's cool nights and delightful days. What I really wanted was to be in the Philippines with Wyoming's climate. Idaho's climate would have been satisfactory also.

In the early evening we could play basketball, visit the well-stocked library, go swimming on the base or in the bay, which was only about a block from the base, or even golf. The planes flew from the golf course during the morning hours, but the golfers had priority during the afternoon and evening hours except for special practice flights and emergencies.

Each man in the squadron was assessed a fee of five dollars per month to pay the salaries of the Filipinos who worked at KP and served as barracks boys. Pay for the laundry also came out of the five-dollar allocation.

Thus, none of us had to serve on KP or had to make our beds, clean the living quarters, or send out or receive our laundry. Extremely tough life! There was no restriction on the amount of laundry that could be sent out weekly. With practically no domestic responsibilities and not a great deal more squadron work, everyone had more than enough free time to pursue his individual interests.

At Nichols Field were two other administrative and supply squadrons. Those were older outfits whose men kept pretty well to themselves. Not far from our barracks was the post exchange, the theater, the library, and the gymnasium. A tailor and a shoe shop, operated by the Chinese, were also conveniently situated.

For two dollars the tailors would form-fit a pair of GI trousers and a shirt. It got so no one but a cheapskate would be seen in regular issue. For five dollars the Chinese shoemakers would make any pair of shoes ordered. All they needed was a picture of the style desired and foot measurements. By the end of the two-week quarantine period we were sharp-looking fellows, and the Chinese had cornered most of our ready cash and also some of what we were to receive in the future. They kindly did not charge interest on the unpaid balance.

For another two dollars a month we could get a daily shave at the barbershop and a weekly haircut and two shampoos each month. We were expected to feed ourselves and scrub our own backs in the shower, but most of the demands were reasonable.

We learned that the richest fellow in the squadron was the one who was in charge of the day room, because he managed and took a cut from all of the gambling. Anyone with money could easily find a way to lose it or loan it in the day room. The going interest rate there was 20 percent per month. A ten-dollar bill loaned would yield two dollars per month interest, or twenty-four dollars per year. Unfortunately, there were far more borrowers than lenders, and there were some who just paid the interest owed each month and never did get ahead enough to pay any of the original loan back. The twenty-percent men did heavy business, especially along toward the end of the month. The day room in our squadron must have been the forerunner of present-day Las Vegas gambling casinos.

When one deducted money paid to Filipino workers, the laundry, and the barber, he still had fourteen dollars left each month and that was about all he needed if he was reasonably careful with his finances. It was possible to do a considerable amount of business with the Chinese specialists and still remain free from debt. Once my salary was increased to thirty-six dollars each month, I arranged for a fifteen-dollar-per-month allotment to be sent to my dad for deposit in the bank at home. As I received promotions and my salary grew, I increased the size of the monthly allotment.

By the end of the time we were restricted to base, we were eager to get to the city of Manila. Drinkers had been able to get plenty of the hard stuff to drink, and beer was available in the PX. In the barrio of Baclaren a quart of gin cost about thirty-five cents, and a quart of imported Canadian Club rye whiskey cost only two dollars.

In preparation for the time when we would be turned loose on the local populace, we were fully oriented concerning the evils of drinking and of sex with local prostitutes. Base doctors warned that most prostitutes in whorehouses and street girls, all of whom were available in great numbers, were infected with one or more types of venereal disease. Films vividly and dramatically presented the penalties in store for those who didn't refrain from personal contact or who didn't take necessary precautions before and after affairs with the Filipino girls. Everyone was required to carry at least one prophylactic on his person when he left the air base. When stopped by the military police, he could be returned to the base if he couldn't produce the required protective device.

Much to our surprise, the medical doctors suggested to those men who felt they needed the companionship of a woman that they select one whom they liked and bring her on the base for a thorough and no-cost medical examination. If she was found to be free from disease, she and the GI could live together in a common-law arrangement. The doctors let us know they were not promoting the practice of common-law marriage, but they had found soldiers were safer, were more content with their lives, and performed better as soldiers under such arrangements rather than with short-time-only contacts.

I don't know of any of our gang entering into this type of living arrangement, but I later talked with a fellow from a different outfit on base who had a common-law wife. He found that she could get along reasonably well on an allotment of roughly fifteen American dollars per month. That amount would take care of the girl's rent costs, her food, and her clothing.

On the afternoon of the day we were released from quarantine, five of us paid a con-artist taxi driver six pesos for a two-peso ride into the center of Manila, where we went to a movie. After the movie we had a sandwich. It was then that the talk got around to women. It seemed every Filipino wanted to be helpful in recommending Filipino companionship for us, and our waiter at the sandwich shop had a taxi standing by to take us to the Golden Gate Bar when we finished eating. We learned later a taxi driver would be paid for bringing customers to a bar, and he in turn would take care of the person who provided him with customers.

The Golden Gate Bar was a large, unattractive, and unoccupied building at five in the afternoon. Each of us ordered a drink of our choosing, and each had his drink personally delivered and served by his own private girl. These girls were small; most were reasonably attractive, and all were scantily clothed.

The girl who chose me was fairly aggressive, and I promptly became nervous but not so much so as was Dick Watts, who told me that he wanted to leave right then. I agreed we shouldn't be in the place but was reluctant to leave for fear we might miss out on something interesting. And some parts of these ladies were interesting.

It wasn't until one of our group and his lady friend began playing keep-away with a prophylactic that I agreed with Dick we should leave. He was actually shaking with fear, and I was plenty nervous. It was clear we knew we shouldn't be in that place. Both of us grew up in a culture where such behavior was totally unacceptable. We concluded the shaking was a message to us that we were in the wrong place and had better make a hasty exit.

The months from November 1940 until July 1941 were fantastic! Each day was glorious! We tried to budget our money carefully so activities for the month could be financed properly without going into debt. Clothing and good food were free to us, and goodies in the PX were most inexpensive. We read a great deal and played basketball and swam, when we had the energy. At times I even served as a sparring partner for two squadron boxers who were training to be world champions. One could have been great except that he trained on booze. The only thing the other had going for him was that he was bigger than anyone else around. Both were far better fighters than I. The heavyweight did win the heavyweight title of the armed forces, far-eastern division, because a Navy heavyweight knocked him out after the bell had sounded following an early round.

We learned that commissary cigarettes, which cost us a dollar a carton, could be sold off base for a huge profit. The problem was that we were permitted to purchase only three cartons each month. A Tom Collins drink could be purchased for five cents in certain bars, and "eat-out" food was extremely reasonable.

Upon presentation of their identification cards, airmen from Nichols Field could have a short-time-only girl at the Old Purity Bar and several other neighborhood places for only two pesos (one dollar). Along toward the end of the month when almost everyone was broke, the price was reduced to half that amount. We concluded that was because business was slow, and the girls needed to keep in training.

We hadn't been in the Philippines long before men began checking into the hospital with venereal disease of one type or another. After the counsel we had received from the medics, I couldn't understand why this happened, but it became clear there were some who believed they would be immune from catching anything unpleasant. They were wrong and suffered the severe consequences.

By Christmas of 1940, the majority of the men had settled in reasonably well. Almost all of us had become acclimated and were enjoying our work and life in general. There was one exception.

One of the enlisted men didn't want to come to the Philippines. On the voyage over he had threatened to jump overboard but failed to do so, even when he was shown the location of the deepest part of the ocean. Once in the Islands the fellows took pity on the play-dumb soldier and tried to involve him in their activities. The cheapskate would drink their drinks and enjoy the association with women, but he would continue to make his life and everyone else's miserable. Shortly before the holiday season, he was confined to the guardhouse for drinking and disorderly conduct.

On Christmas Day the officers and men met together for an early dinner. The CO, feeling sorry for the guy, negotiated his temporary release from the guardhouse so he could join the rest of us for dinner.

He was escorted to the squadron mess hall by two MPs who seemed happy to release him into the custody of the CO. Instead of eating his meal, he promptly proceeded to get exceedingly drunk. The more intoxicated he became, the more friendliness he expressed so he could join the rest of us and stay out of the guardhouse.

Once he made the rounds of the enlisted men, he went to the table where the officers were seated and sought out the squadron commander and made a complete fool of himself. He was so offensive to all assembled that the CO reluctantly concluded that he and all of the rest of us would be better off if the guy were returned to the guardhouse.

By New Year's Day the guy was on his way home, where he received some sort of discharge from the service. The following June the squadron received a postcard from him. On it was scribbled, "Potatoes and beets lookin' fine, you dumb suckers!"

During the spring I was promoted to corporal, and the squadron traded its P-26s for P-35s. The fellows who held out to become airplane mechanics finally were sent to school on the base and were graduated with airplane mechanics ratings. The rating gave them a larger income than I received, but no increase in rank. They continued to be privates. I would rather have had the increase in pay.

The seven-plus months at Nichols Field passed rapidly. The work was interesting, and I learned a great deal from Sergeant Kearney, our supply sergeant. In fact, he was training me to replace him because he was hoping to become material supply sergeant down on the hangar line when the person who currently filled that position returned to the States. Airplane parts were more stimulating to him than were sheets, shoes, and coveralls, I suppose. And there may have been the possibility that in the other assignment he might be eligible for a pay increase. I didn't know the details. He had met a beautiful English girl in Manila, and they had fallen in love. He confided in me they were making marriage plans. But again, I didn't know all of the details.

Food in the squadron mess was most attractive to me. It was plentiful and prepared very well. Among the cooks there were several miserable fellows, but all were competent in their assignments. Hotcakes were reserved for Sunday mornings, and I always enthusiastically anticipated Sunday evenings because then we were served cold cuts, salads, and baked beans. I genuinely appreciated both meals as I did the others throughout the week.

Papaya, mangos, pineapple, and bananas were always in ample supply. Huge bowls in the day room were kept full of freshly roasted peanuts. The mess sergeant said that because of the peanuts he always had ample money for other food items. The more peanuts the fellows ate, the less of the more expensive food they consumed, I learned.

Sometime during the spring Major Grover was assigned as group commander and Lt. Joe Moore was appointed as our new commanding officer. He had made the trip to the Philippines with the squadron and, although young, was among the senior officers in the outfit. Everyone in the squadron was fond of Lieutenant Moore. He was respected not only for his skill as a pilot but also for his competence as an administrator. His "open-door" policy with the men was greatly appreciated, and almost immediately he enjoyed the full support of all of the troops—officers and enlisted men.

Our supply office was located next to the squadron administrative office, so I became well acquainted with the CO and was reasonably well informed concerning most of the activities that took place in both offices. Besides, my friend Dick was senior clerk in the administrative office and that didn't hurt a bit.

On July 1, 1941, the squadron was transferred bag-and-baggage to Clark Field. It was located about eighty kilometers north of Manila. At that time the only outfits on Clark Field were a bomber squadron flying Martin B-10s and B-18s, a material squadron, and a headquarters squadron. There were no housing or office facilities for any of our men.

I was instructed to issue folding cots to everyone, and we were housed in one of the three hangars bordering the airstrip. I established my supply operation in one corner of the same hangar. Conditions were bad but not nearly as bad as they were going to become.

All of the men were good sports about our living arrangements. After provisions were made for properly supporting the mosquito nets over each bunk, all of them slept fairly comfortably. Latrine facilities were overtaxed somewhat, but we survived.

At Clark Field our squadron began flying P-40s. These were about the latest development in pursuit planes. They had plenty of firepower, carrying two .50-caliber guns in the nose and four .30-caliber guns in the wings. They gained altitude slowly because of their tremendous weight. However, according to our pilots, once they attained their proper flying level, they were bear cats in a dive.

Life at Clark Field was routine and fairly dull. After the move, the squadron members were on duty all day long. There was much to be accomplished, and the weather was considerably cooler, closer to the mountains. Not far from the hangar was a small post exchange, and a bit farther up the road toward Fort Stotsenburg was the NCO club. When we were free from duty, generally on Saturdays and Sundays, we could go to Fort Stotsenburg and ride cavalry horses, if they were available. The horse cavalry people wanted their horses ridden regularly and were most willing to have the mounts saddled for us. We were then free to ride on trails throughout the beautiful mountains that were near the fort. This activity was especially enjoyable for me because of my earlier experiences. Horses I loved and knew well, or so I thought.

On one of my visits to the stables I was informed all of the horses were out at the moment. "I can have a remount saddled for you if would like," the stable attendant informed me.

I didn't know what a remount was, but I responded enthusiastically, "Sounds good to me!"

It wasn't until I mounted and was thrown higher and harder than I had ever been before that I learned a remount was a horse only "green" broken. That is, he had only the rough edges taken off and was then turned loose to be fully gentled and trained at a later date. It was clear he hadn't been ridden before, or at least not recently, and knew very little about carrying a person. One thing for sure, he didn't have to worry about carrying me because I made no further attempt to ride the critter. And I didn't ask for or accept remounts on future occasions.

Clark Field was nearly twenty kilometers from the nearest town, Angeles, and that place wasn't up to much. In Angeles there were a number of bars and whorehouses and one good place to eat called Chicken Charlies. All of us were eager for the opportunity to return to Manila on weekends and were able to do just that on occasion. To do so we had to plan carefully because funds to cover the cost of travel, food, entertainment, and a hotel were necessary.

By October there was some talk of a possible war with Japan, but we didn't pay much attention to the chatter. We did make a few minor preparations, like digging foxholes and trenches. A half dozen Lewis .30-caliber machine guns were issued, and those, along with our sawed-off shotguns and a few 45s, constituted the squadron's ground defense weapons.

Two or three bomber squadrons flying B-17s were flown in from the States during the fall, and two tank outfits from Salinas, California, and Kentucky, and an antiaircraft outfit from New Mexico had also arrived.

I believe the general impression was that the Japanese would never attack the United States nor any of its possessions. We also felt, although our troops were few in number, they could be counted on to perform well. Guards on the planes were increased, and the CO did stress the importance of keeping always alert and especially while on guard duty.

# 7

# CHRISTMAS 1941

"GET THAT HULK OF A TRUCK movin'! We gotta be on Bataan before daylight!"

This order by the first sergeant abruptly brought me back to the present, and I instinctively maneuvered the truck around the city center and followed the convoy on the road to Bataan.

It was still pitch dark when we learned early on the morning of December 25 that our convoy had arrived on the Peninsula of Bataan. The night driving had been extremely difficult and tiring, and it was a group of exhausted men who moved off the road and into a bamboo thicket to sleep out the rest of the early morning hours. In spite of our weariness and the pressure from not knowing what was facing us, we had little trouble falling asleep.

By nine o'clock in the morning the cooks had been able to unscramble the items in the mess truck and served coffee and gasoline-soaked bread with jam for Christmas breakfast. That was a poor substitute for the hotcakes, sausage, eggs, orange juice, and coffee that we had ordered. However, compared to nothing, it was greatly appreciated.

During the morning there was no exchange of gifts, and no one would have dared to be in a festive mood. Nevertheless, by midafternoon the supply truck arrived, and the squadron was served a good Christmas dinner. In fact, it was surprisingly good when one considers that we were in a flea-infested bamboo thicket in the midst of a troop movement under fire.

Shortly after dinner we received word that dessert was obtainable in a grass shack a hundred yards or so from where we were bivouacked. There were other troops in the area, and several enterprising Filipino women had proceeded to set themselves up in business. The price quoted was ten pesos, which was five times the going rate in Manila and Angeles, but then it was wartime and the commodity could have already become scarce.

It was reported to the squadron men that the line in front of the shack was long. Reported also was the information that the women were not attractive nor were they responsive or exciting. They were merely accommodating.

As I sat leaning against one of the wheels of the supply truck, I couldn't help but think again of much happier days. Because there had been ample diversion in the Philippines, I hadn't spent much time thinking about women or, for that matter, about home. By disposition I had always been a rather happy, carefree person—one who could and would accentuate the positive. Now, I too readily recalled memories of home.

When I first met Barbara, she was only eleven or twelve years old but pretty and extremely interesting. We were classmates through junior-high-school years, but it wasn't until our junior year in high school that I really began to know her well. Prior to that time my world was one devoted primarily to work, fishing, camping, and swimming. I couldn't imagine anything more enjoyable than those activities, and I asked Barbara for a date to go swimming only because the fellows had said that I couldn't go with them and their dates unless I had one myself.

After that date, life was never the same for me. I fell madly in love with Barbara, and she and I were steadies during the rest of our high-school days. She got prettier as she got older, and by high-school graduation time, she was really something!

After completing high school she went to college, and I devoted my time to nonsense. Our paths crossed occasionally, and we dated once or twice during the year. After she went to the university, it wasn't quite the same, though. It seemed to me that she became almost a different person from the girl with whom I was in love during high-school days. Things just didn't seem to go right for us when she returned from school to be with her family. She had many new and interesting friends at school, and I had other attractions. Our last date ended less than pleasantly, and I told myself that relationships with her were finished forever.

The following year I heard nothing from her and practically nothing about her. Now, here on Bataan, I couldn't help but think of her and of the many good times we had together.

Those memories, or just plain good common sense, caused me to refrain from any interest in those Filipino prostitutes. Later, I was pleased with myself and the guys in the squadron because it was reported that one or more of the prostitutes had a venereal disease. The cost to an infected person would be far greater than ten pesos!

That evening just before sunset the squadron commander ordered us back to the vehicles and directed us toward the town of Orani. We were to join others moving farther down the peninsula at a bivouac site identified for us for the night.

The person sent to guide our squadron apparently didn't know the Bataan Peninsula well. Before we realized what was happening, he had the entire convoy on a road that took us to a small fishing village directly on the beach without the benefit of any kind of cover. Not only were we concerned to find ourselves out in the open like sitting ducks, the Filipinos living in the village were almost frantic with fear and encouraged us to leave promptly. They didn't want a military target such as the convoy to attract the attention of those flying Japanese airplanes As quickly as the mistake was realized, the convoy turned itself around and made a hasty retreat for the protection of the lush vegetation offered by much of the peninsula.

Just before dark we pulled off the road into a huge mango grove. The mango trees provided complete cover, enough to serve the needs of the entire squadron. There we spent the night.

Early in the morning, but after daybreak, Japanese planes bombed and destroyed three Norwegian freighters that were anchored in the bay just off our mango grove. The affair was completely one-sided because the freighters were not armed. It was a good thing for the Japanese that this was the case, because the accuracy of their pilots left a great deal to be desired.

The squadron had no food, so there was no reason for us not to be on the move. The commanding officer called me to him and informed me our squadron would be more or less permanently bivouacked on the southern tip of the peninsula, somewhere close to the new airstrip that was being constructed close to the port of Mariveles. He directed me to drive the heavily laden truck down to the southern tip of the peninsula, find a suitable bivouac area for the squadron, unload the truck, and return promptly to help convoy the troops to our new living area. He invited me to select one man to go along to assist in the mission and to guard the supplies while I returned for the men.

Without hesitation I asked Sad Sack if he would be willing to accompany me, and without hesitation he agreed. Sad was an old-timer compared to most of us in the squadron. He had been in the Air Corps for more than eight years and had been promoted to the rank of corporal more times than anyone else in the squadron. In fact, Sad had established for himself quite a few records.

During peacetime Sad had been given a variety of assignments around the squadron, the main one being to supervise the care and maintenance of the squadron day room. This he did with considerable enthusiasm because it also gave him the authority to run the poker, blackjack, and crap games there. And, while his income as a private wasn't enviable, his day-room activities supplemented his income to probably about the level of a one-star general.

Everyone in the squadron liked Sad. All the guys kidded him. He was, in a sense, the squadron roustabout. No one had ever taken him very seriously. However, when the war broke out, Sad immediately was a changed man. Life instantly became serious, and he began to demonstrate his real qualities as a soldier. But nothing, not even the war or the shortages, caused him to lose his good sense. Sad, along with his close friend, Norm Lonon, was the squadron news reporter, prophet, and all-around morale builder. He was the most fantastic GI on Bataan and the most formidable enemy of the Japanese. Had the Japanese killed him, the squadron might have folded. He could easily have been elected to replace MacArthur when he left Corregidor had a vote been taken. The courage, the wisdom, and the insights that he demonstrated were nothing short of magnificent.

Sad and I boarded the truck and moved slowly down the dusty road toward Mariveles. The heavily traveled road was never far from the bay but wound in and out of mango and coconut groves and huge stands of tropical vegetation. Most of the traffic was going our way, and the dust hung over the road in dense clouds.

The Americans had begun three airstrips on the peninsula—one at Bataan Field, the second at Cabcabin Field, and the third at Mariveles. We encountered no opposition from the Japanese as we lumbered along the road until we had passed through the burned-out village of Mariveles on the bay and had started west down the newly constructed airstrip. The area was a beehive of activity. Heavy construction equipment was moving about in all directions as workers hastened the completion of the field.

"Sad, it must be lunch time. Look. All of the men have stopped their equipment and are getting off."

"Lunch time, nothing! Look at the Jap planes coming down the strip!"

As quickly as I could, I stopped the truck, and we jumped out and crawled under it as the planes passed over, flying almost at ground level.

Sad then scampered to the top of the truck to survey the damage. He found only one bullet hole in the canvas that covered the supplies. This was a relief! Now, we had the impression that even if a person was caught in the open and attacked by Japanese planes, his chances of avoiding being hit by the gunners were good.

The road at the far end of the runway took us into the jungle area. We hadn't gone far when we observed a small side road that led to a beautiful, grassy, open area shaded completely by the branches of huge trees.

As we drove into the area, I quoted Brigham Young in saying, "Sad, as Brigham Young once said, 'this is the place!' We couldn't have found a more attractive one if we had searched forever. And, look at the way these trees protect the entire area."

We drove a bit farther and came upon a field kitchen that was in full operation. After parking the truck, we walked over to the fellows who were cooking and learned from the mess sergeant that the area had been taken over by a company of Marines who were serving on beach duty. The sergeant told us the Marines would be stationed in that area for some time, and it would be impossible for us to settle our squadron there.

We were disappointed, as can be imagined, but our spirits soared when the sergeant said, "As long as you're here, you can just as well have some food. You both look like you could use a good meal! The men will be coming off beach duty in a few minutes, and if you pitch right in, you can have your dinner before they arrive."

Of course we were most agreeable and were completely overwhelmed when we were served mashed potatoes and gravy and huge slices of ham with hot biscuits and vegetables. It was just unbelievable! We hadn't had good food like that since before the war broke out.

No sooner had we started to eat than swarms of Marines, accompanied by their officers, emerged from the thick jungle brush.

"Bring a bag of coffee and something to brew it in and move out!" their CO instructed the mess sergeant.

The Marines paused only long enough to grab their gear and then moved on through the camp. They had been ordered to Corregidor.

The mess sergeant approached Sad and me with a bag of coffee under one arm and a kettle under the other saying, "Men, it's all right for you to remain here. The place is yours. Not only can you have the area, but you can have the field kitchens as well!"

"How about the food?" I asked, hopefully.

"The food remains with the kitchen equipment."

Those poor devils didn't even have time to stop and eat. All of that beautiful food was ours!

Sad and I were just plain gleeful. We piled into the food with great gusto, knowing that not only did we have plenty of good food for all members of the squadron, but that we had a great bivouac area as well.

"Hey, Sad, maybe the old man will promote you to corporal again now that this mission has almost been completed so successfully," I said.

"I'd rather be a damned magpie or crow so I could fly out of here!"

"Would ya' take me with you?"

"Hell, no! Everyone knows ya can't run an army without a supply sergeant. Besides, I expect they'll make you a second lieutenant any day now. They can do that in time of war, you know."

"You don't believe that nonsense and neither do I, Sad."

After a leisurely dinner we looked about for a spot to unload the truck. Just then a green, dirt-covered command car pulled up, and a first lieutenant stepped out. My heart sank. Here was the much-disliked officer who had earlier been transferred out of our squadron to the headquarters squadron.

"What are you men doing here, Sergeant?" he asked.

"Our CO sent Sad and me down here with the truck to find a place for our squadron. We are to unload the truck; Sad is to remain as guard, and I am to go back up to the place where our people are presently located and return with a load of men."

"Sergeant, I have the responsibility of identifying an area for the headquarters operation. This looks to me just like the place we need. It isn't large enough to accommodate both squadrons, so I am going to claim it for the headquarters operation."

"Lieutenant, I already told you that we have selected this for our squadron. We came into the area earlier in the day and found it occupied by the Marines. They were ordered from here to Corregidor and turned the place over to us along with the field kitchens. While you are here, Lieutenant, why don't you and your driver stop and have some food? There is plenty of food in the ovens."

"I don't have time to stop and eat, and I don't have time to argue with you. Now you men just climb into your truck and go find another place for your squadron!"

"Lieutenant, I told you . . .!"

"Sergeant, do you want to make an issue out of this?"

"If our CO were here, he'd damn sure make an issue of it, for sure!"

"Well, he's not here, and you better not be much longer, either!"

With that, Sad and I got into the truck and watched the command car move out of sight into the jungle.

"The little sawed-off phony," said Sad. "I'd rather have a shot at him than I would at Tojo. Now, what are we going to do?"

With that, I drove the truck back out to the road and farther up the narrow, winding road. About three miles later we came to a small creek. The undergrowth was heavy on both sides of the road. As we investigated the area carefully, we concluded that it might serve our purposes well if we located the squadron supply, the administration tent, and the medical tent on one side of the road and placed the field kitchens and bivouacked the men on the other side of the road.

Once the decision was made, we proceeded to unload into a huge pile all of the items that we had earlier loaded onto the truck. That finished, we covered the pile with the huge tarps and went to sleep in the bed of the empty truck, rolled up in blankets.

Early the following morning Sad, with his World War I Springfield rifle, climbed to the top of the heap. There, like the king of Bunker Hill, he waved farewell to me, counseling me to return posthaste with our buddies. As I drove away, I wondered where he got the rifle. We didn't have any of them in the squadron. "I'll have to ask him about that when I return," I said to myself.

The trip back up the peninsula to the mango grove was uneventful, and I arrived there early in the afternoon. The men were anxious to move out because of the continual bombardment from Japanese planes. The enemy, observing the heavy troop movement onto Bataan, attacked the main road and the adjacent areas time after time.

The Peninsula of Bataan stretched along the west shore of Manila Bay, almost directly across from the city of Manila and north and a bit west from Corregidor. The northern part of the peninsula was cultivated and produced rice, vegetables, and a variety of fruits. South from Orani, along the east coast of the peninsula, were the towns of Abucay, Pilar, Orion, Limay, and Cabcaben. In some places, the road ran fairly close to the edge of the bay. At times it was some distance from the water at a much higher elevation. Much of the southern part of the peninsula was covered with dense tropical forest. As the road stretched toward the southern tip of the peninsula it was fairly high above the sea and wound back and forth along the sides of the mountains.

The field hospital had been established in a mountainous area, near the ammunition dumps, of all places. It was near the road and could be clearly seen from the road. Other than the construction on the airfields and the hospital and ammunition dumps, one couldn't see that much pre-war preparation for war had been made. As the war progressed, we were to learn how pitifully little attention had been given to preparing the peninsula, in general, as a strategic battle area.

Mariveles Bay and the town of Mariveles, which was completely destroyed by the bombs of the Japanese, were situated on the southern tip of the peninsula. Situated nearby, close to the bay, was a U.S. Navy tunnel, and a bit farther down the beach were red-brick buildings that had once housed a contingent of U.S. Marines.

The island fortress of Corregidor was located approximately two miles from the Bataan Peninsula at the entrance of Manila Bay. Near Corregidor were Forts Frank and Drum, both small, but extremely useful because of their strategic location at the mouth of the bay.

As we proceeded down the Peninsula of Bataan to Mariveles, we didn't travel in convoy but spaced the vehicles at least a mile apart to avoid the enemy and, almost as troublesome, the thick and stifling dust of the well-traveled road. Because only I knew where the bivouac area was to be, I led the group. During the entire trip of several hours, we had to evacuate the truck only once because of fire from enemy planes. All of us hastily abandoned the truck for the safety of the jungle and thus again avoided any injury to personnel. Even the truck came through unscathed.

The war had been in full swing for nearly three weeks by this time and, although we weren't nearly as cocky and self-assured as we had been just prior to the Pearl Harbor fiasco, a great deal of self-confidence had returned to most of us and we were eager to make a good accounting of ourselves. Those who had been injured during the air raid of the first day had been transported to Manila where they were placed aboard a ship that was to take them south toward Australia. We learned later that they did get away from the Philippines safely and were returned to the United States.

It was early evening by the time all of the troops assembled in the bivouac area. The squadron commander was not overly elated with my selection of the site but understood well the necessity for giving the lieutenant the more attractive area. He did, however, move to the upper side of the road the tent that we had pitched as his headquarters. He chose to be among the members of the squadron.

After surveying the area carefully he said, "This bivouac will serve our purposes satisfactorily. Most of our time will be spent working down at Mariveles Field, and, consequently, we will be using the area here primarily for sleeping purposes."

The following day each man selected for himself a sleeping spot and dug a foxhole adjacent to it. The entire area was completely covered by the limbs and leaves of the huge trees that grew all around us. If our position were bombed or strafed by the Japanese, it would be because action on the road had attracted their attention to it. Our pilots assured us that from the air the entire area was just one mass of jungle.

The two medics who were assigned to the squadron were helpful to us and undoubtedly were responsible for keeping us as physically fit as possible under the circumstances. They promptly convinced us the water in the small stream that ran through the camp was polluted. Thus, all culinary water had to be either boiled or treated chemically. Everyone gladly received and accepted their counsel. They also advised us concerning the need to continue with malaria prevention because the disease was rampant on Bataan. Other advice pertained to the necessity of being on the alert to watch for scorpions and snakes of any kind. These, too, were plentiful on the Bataan Peninsula.

It took several days before we were properly dug in, but once this was accomplished, we felt reasonably secure from the observation of the enemy and were of the belief that we could probably survive the rigors of sleeping on the ground rolled up in a blanket.

# 8

# THE BATTLE FOR BATAAN

EARLY ON THE MORNING OF December 30, the CO assembled the men and informed us that our assignment was to go to Mariveles Field to build revetments in the undergrowth near the field where planes could be completely concealed from the enemy. He advised us he was informed our squadron was to get fighter planes from the States and we could expect them at any time. Consequently, it was imperative we build the revetments as quickly as possible to enable us to accommodate the planes when they arrived. It was his opinion the planes would be flown in because the Japanese by this time had undoubtedly gained complete control of all sea lanes in the areas around the Philippine Islands.

To avoid being seen on the road as we went to and from Mariveles Field each day, we struck off through the jungle. The first trip was a difficult one because it was necessary for us to chop out a trail through the various sections of the terrain. We later estimated that the distance from camp to the field was approximately three miles. Once the trail was established, the hike to and from the airstrip presented no real problem. The more serious matter was that we were hungry all of the time. As soon as we arrived on Bataan, we were restricted to two meals a day, both of which were of poor quality, and the quantity was far less than we would have liked. Our daily calorie intake was estimated to be less than one thousand.

We couldn't understand why there should be such a pronounced shortage of food this early in the war because it was common knowledge there was ample food stored by the army quartermaster in the port area of Manila. We also knew of huge caches of rice stored in various warehouses throughout the country. What we didn't know then was that General MacArthur, or those accountable to him, failed to have food moved to Bataan between the outbreak of the war and the occupation of Bataan by the American forces.

The Hawaiian fiasco set the stage for the incompetence that followed. Throughout the months spent on Bataan we were to continue to learn of more inefficiency as we attempted to engage the enemy with poor or unusable equipment and ammunition, much of which was old and useless. The record established thus far by the U.S. military was nothing that could impress anyone, especially the Japanese. We recalled Theodore Roosevelt's earlier advice for those seeking to impress the world with the prowess of the United States to "Speak softly and carry a big stick!" So far our country hadn't displayed any big stick, and we American soldiers, so confident of our abilities to walk all over the Japanese, were learning our lesson of humility, also.

When we returned to camp that evening from working on the airstrip, December 31, New Year's Eve, the squadron commander called all of the men and the officers together and produced from somewhere a jug of rum. I thought of passing, but then decided, "What the heck," and along with the other single men toasted the married men in the squadron by singing to them the song, "I Wonder Who's Kissing Her Now."

Those of us who were single sang loudly. The married men didn't think we were too funny, although we tried our very best. There wasn't enough rum for anyone to get drunk but enough to warm our insides, and everyone felt a little better for the experience. In fact, a few jokes were told.

Sad described a Japanese as a "Slap-happy-Jappy with a clappy pappy."

The last few days of December and most of January were hell. Hell, not only because of the constant harassment from the Japanese planes, but because of the scarcity of food and the lack of involvement in anything that seemed to be at all productive. Each morning we would tread our weary way slowly along the narrow, winding jungle path to the airstrip. During the day and without any lunch, we would work building airplane revetments in which to conceal the planes that daily were to arrive shortly from the States. By the end of January no one really thought we would get planes. All of the talk resulted strictly from wishful thinking on our part. We were so eager to get back into the war with planes that could and would, we were sure, help to richly enhance our chances of driving the Japanese out of the Philippines. Our faith in our country was constantly challenged. Our feelings, derived from the evidence at hand, were to the effect that no one in the United States really did care about us on Bataan. We had a terrible time believing that America would sell us down the river, but the evidence was daily becoming more convincing.

It was at that time that someone on Bataan wrote

> Oh, we are the battling bastards of Bataan,
> No mother, no father, no Uncle Sam,
> No aunts, no uncles, no nephews, no nieces,
> No ammunition nor artillery pieces,
> And nobody gives a damn!

The few P-40s that had survived the Japanese bombing raids on Clark Field had been assigned to Bataan and Cabcabin Fields located somewhat farther up the peninsula. Several of our officers and a few of the mechanics were assigned to work with the planes. The rest of us continued to spend our time digging revetments.

As the days passed slowly, the morale of the men worsened. The futility of digging away at the revetments was increasingly obvious. The tools with which we worked were of native quality and were in short supply. Although we hoped and prayed, no planes were flown in from the States in spite of constant positive rumors. The possibility of getting replacements for those lost earlier seemed to become more and more remote. This concern was accompanied by the fact that the food supplies were rapidly diminishing. Our squadron had no food to bring to Bataan and consequently had to rely totally upon the army quartermaster corps on Bataan for supplies.

As supply sergeant, it was my responsibility to go each evening to the supply dump that was back up the peninsula ten or so miles. There, along with other representatives from various outfits on Bataan, I would meet the supply truck and receive our food allowances for the following day.

Our squadron's share of food would perhaps be a dozen or so round loaves of bread, fifteen to twenty cans of salmon, and approximately thirty pounds of rice. Each day the amount was reduced, and it wasn't too long before there was no bread. Shortly afterwards, the supply of canned food was also exhausted.

When I registered concerns about the skimpy food rations, I was told that little food had been moved to Bataan between the outbreak of the war and the occupancy of Bataan by the American and Filipino forces. To make matters worse, hundreds of civilians also fled to the Bataan Peninsula and had to be given consideration. Absolutely no provision had been made to support this additional unanticipated burden.

During the forty years preceding the war with the Japanese, several studies had been made, we later learned, of the possibility of successfully defending Manila Bay and retaining a foothold in the Philippines should the Islands be attacked by the Japanese. One after another, these studies had revealed that the Orange Plan, as the strategy for the defense of Bataan was named, was impractical and should be abandoned completely. When named commander of all forces in the Philippines, Douglas MacArthur maintained that he could defend the islands of the Philippines on the beaches and communicated that information to the President and military leaders in the United States. He apparently clung to the position until shortly before Christmas of 1941, losing valuable time during which food, medicine, and ammunition could have been moved to the peninsula. By the time he reverted to the Orange Plan, it was too late to transfer much-needed war materiel. We had earlier been informed there was stored in the tunnels on Corregidor ample food for all forces on both Bataan and Corregidor during the time that we would be there. It turned out that the Bataan forces had to rely almost completely upon their own resources.

To supplement the meager amount received from the cooks twice daily, the men engaged in numerous activities to generate additional food. The efforts to catch fish in the bay, using hook and line and even dynamite, were not overly successful. The jungle was scavenged for any kind of edible plants, including banana stalks, bamboo shoots, and roots of several kinds. Monkeys were shot, skinned, cooked, and eaten by individuals, and daily searches were organized to hunt for the aggressive wild caribou that were reported to range in our part of the Bataan Peninsula.

Once American and Filipino troops were secured on the Bataan Peninsula, the Japanese began to give higher priority to neutralizing other areas of the Pacific. A Japanese fighting force perceived large enough to conquer Bataan was left, and the Japanese pushed south from the Philippines to northern Australia and west through Indochina, Borneo, Malaysia, Burma, Singapore, and the Dutch East Indies. Singapore radio reported the progress of the Japanese troops and assured the world the British would never permit the occupation of Singapore by the Japanese. That also turned out to be a joke as the Japanese proceeded to sink two of Britain's largest naval vessels and move on Singapore from the jungles of Malaysia to the north.

In the Philippines were left ample Japanese planes to constantly harass American and Filipino troops on Bataan and carry out day and night raids upon Corregidor. American and Filipino infantry troops made a good accounting of themselves, and there were times when the Japanese were pushed back and lost ground was recovered.

Fairly early on Bataan we began to experience harassment from Japanese soldiers, individually and in pairs or small groups who had infiltrated perimeter boundaries. While we were fortunate that Bataan Peninsula was bordered on three sides by Manila Bay and the South China Sea, there was the problem of the Japanese being able to land small raiding parties on stretches of beach too vast and isolated to be patrolled effectively by our troops.

The fighting forces on Bataan consisted of the Philippine Army troops, some of whom were led by American officers, including Sergeant Matthews from our squadron. He was badly needed because of his technical savvy in communications and was commissioned a second lieutenant. In addition were what was left of the Philippine Scouts after their efforts to repel the Japanese invaders on the beaches of Luzon and a relatively small handful of Americans who were infantry, tank, artillery, and Air Corps troops. The Philippine Scouts proved to be some of the most capable and bravest soldiers found anywhere in the world. A total of approximately twelve thousand American troops served on Bataan with another six thousand based on Corregidor. This included Army, Navy, and Marine officers and men.

The Philippine Army, supported by Scouts and American tank, infantry, artillery troops, and some Air Corps men, was responsible for maintaining the front line that would keep the Japanese from moving down the Bataan Peninsula. Air corps personnel, with limited support from other military groups, were charged with the responsibility of maintaining the three airfields and defending the southern beaches.

During the second week in February, we moved from our jungle bivouac area into large, abandoned, and unprotected Marine barracks at Mariveles. While it was realized that we would be sitting ducks, we were assigned to the barracks because it appeared that finally new fighter planes were to be delivered to the squadron. It was important that we be close at hand where we could give proper attention to the planes when they did arrive. In this new location the harassment from Japanese planes, which had complete freedom of the skies by this time, was continuous.

The efforts of the men to secure food increased as the days passed. Practically all non-duty daylight time was devoted to catching fish and killing monkeys or other animals that could be cooked and eaten. A skinned monkey looked much like a newborn baby but didn't taste too bad if one could forget what he was eating.

In some areas of the jungle the soldiers and the monkeys waged war against each other. The monkeys, once aroused, would collect in large groups and scream and throw branches and twigs at the soldiers. As the torment increased, they would charge en masse. It was then that the riflemen would shoot as many as possible.

Occasionally, bombs from the Japanese planes would kill a domestic caribou or a horse, and for one meal there would be enough food for all.

Although not many casualties were suffered from the constant enemy air raids on the Marine barracks, we all suffered considerably from the constant harassment of the Japanese planes. The lack of undisturbed sleep and the constant bombing, which often restricted us to foxholes, kept us exhausted physically and mentally. Contributing to increased strain was the constant hunger and depression resulting from the increasing helplessness of our situation.

There was sufficient quinine of the powdered type to protect us from malaria for the time being, but other problems, such as beriberi resulting from the inadequate diet, were beginning to emerge. Beriberi was caused by severe vitamin deficiency, primarily from a diet of polished rice deficient in thiamin, a B-complex vitamin. This, accompanied by severe pain, caused the feet and legs to swell.

Also encountered by some were pellagra, constant diarrhea, open sores, and a variety of skin infections.

Then a situation developed that gave our morale a boost.

When the Japanese had made one of their earlier attacks on Mariveles Bay, a small seaplane lying at anchor had been badly crippled but not destroyed. Captain Joe Moore, our squadron commander, the gutsy person he was, one day announced to the squadron that he would fly the plane to the Island of Cebu at night in an attempt to secure food if the men would salvage and put it in flying condition.

Filled with hope and enthusiasm, the airplane mechanics, encouraged and assisted by others, beached the plane and in an unbelievably short time had it ready for flight. It carried no armament and, being slow and awkward, anyone flying it took great chances for his personal safety.

Good to his word, the squadron commander made several night flights to Cebu and other islands and on each trip brought back as much food as the plane could carry. Then, the Japanese discovered and destroyed the plane.

After several weeks of sheer hell in the Marine barracks at Mariveles, we received orders to vacate them because of the constant bombing by the Japanese and the word from the United States that it was unlikely that planes would be supplied to the Philippines. The war in Europe had been given higher priority for airplanes than had the struggle in the South Pacific. That information had a devastating effect on us, but the disappointment was partially offset by the knowledge that back in the jungle bivouac we wouldn't be quite the open target for the Japanese that we had been while in the barracks on the beach.

While the move reduced the pressure on us, Corregidor continued to be bombed daily by large flights of Japanese bombers. It seemed to us only reasonable that, unable to withstand the constant barrages, Corregidor would be forced to capitulate. The prospects were not at all encouraging.

When it finally appeared definite that air corpsman would not be needed to work with the airplanes, we were issued more Enfield rifles, divided into squads, and assigned to the Philippine Army. Most of us had absolutely no training or experience as infantry soldiers, so we began spending time becoming familiar with the Enfield and its use and operation and with learning infantry tactics. Our teacher was one of the cooks, a sergeant who had previously been an infantry soldier. Earlier, when the squadron had been so badly in need of cooks, he had been recruited from an infantry organization. He was a decent fellow and seemed to be knowledgeable enough.

Barely had this training begun when all troops were called together late one afternoon by the squadron commander. He advised us that he had received information to the effect that from six to seventeen Japanese had been secretly landed on the beach adjacent to our bivouac area. Increased concern was expressed to the effect that all Japanese infiltrators be found and captured or eliminated.

Our squadron was ordered to the beach, and within a matter of minutes, we were on our way to the section of the shoreline that we had been assigned to us to guard and defend.

My squad had the responsibility of encircling a small hill near the beach. As squad leader I had instructions to move the men single file down a path toward the hill that was adjacent to the beach. I was to post one man on the east side of the hill near the beach and then spread the balance of squad members along the side of the hill facing the ocean. The men were to be placed fifty yards apart, and I was to be the last one posted near the beach on the west side of the hill.

All squad members were keyed up, nervous and frightened and not overly enthusiastic about being separated from their colleagues. Being squad leader didn't automatically make me any more courageous than anyone else. I was both frightened and concerned and, after posting the other nine men as directed, searched for a safe place from which to watch for enemy movement.

By the time I had settled myself against the shore-side base of a huge tree, the night was pitch black. I had carefully selected a tree large enough to offer complete protection to my back. A member of the enemy forces might be able to slip up on me unnoticed, but no one could reach around the tree without exposing his body to me. One thing for sure, I wouldn't be caught napping and would be constantly sensitive to any movement whatsoever. I settled down, uncomfortably, to what I knew was to be a long and lonely vigil.

Throughout the long night I saw no one, but during the slowly passing hours, I was constantly sure that I heard men skillfully infiltrating the jungle, each having been assigned the mission of disposing of me.

After what seemed like forever, morning came. Along about eleven o'clock a messenger from the CO came to me with the report that all squad leaders were to report promptly to the command post. My squad members received word to remain at their posts.

Near the edge of a large clearing across which ran the path that we were following, we stopped. I was advised by the CO's messenger that we would have to cross the clearing and would likely come under enemy sniper fire. We couldn't avoid the crossing, as I would have liked to do, because the clearing was bordered on the left by a murky swamp and on the right by a steep cliff.

"Stationed in a tree," the messenger explained to me, "is a Jap with an automatic rifle.

"I made it across before," he said, "so will go first and then you follow at a respectable interval."

I wasn't opposed to that arrangement and tensely watched as he, running fast, was nearly across the other side of the clearing before the firing from the sniper began. The gunner was too late.

With my heart pounding in my chest, I took two deep breaths and then was off like a professional halfback on a football field dodging those attempting to tackle me. The sniper, this time set and ready, began shooting, and I tensed for the impact of a bullet. Again, he had reacted too slowly for the target under consideration, and I reached the safety of the jungle on the far side of the clearing without harm. The speed and agility of my performance must have been magnificent! Right then I enjoyed a brief feeling of triumph.

When all squad leaders had assembled with the commanding officer, we learned that our squadron had been joined by members of two other pursuit squadrons, by men from the corps of engineers, and by a number of Philippine Scouts. In brief, we were to pull our squads back out of the beach area to the road where we were standing. We were then to form a long line and together make a drive through the brush to the coast, clearing out all of the Japanese whom we encountered. The plan was to place two men five yards apart, and then fifteen yards farther down the line, to place two more men five yards apart, and so on.

We were instructed to keep the line straight and move as quietly as we could, probing the brush with our bayonets and making every effort to completely cover the terrain. The plan sounded orderly and completely efficient, but it wasn't implemented quite the way intended.

My first challenge was to return to my squad, again across the open clearing guarded by the Japanese with the automatic rifle, to instruct squad members in the necessary tactical maneuver to enable them to assemble at the designated meeting location.

All crossings were made successfully without injury to anyone but with determination someone should be assigned the objective of removing the Japanese sniper. He just had to be the first short-range goal of those assigned to his strip of jungle.

Assembled together on the road once again, each squad was assigned its section of the jungle to comb, and we were again instructed to keep the long line straight, to move as quietly as we could, and to probe the brush with our bayonets, making every effort to completely investigate all aspects of the terrain.

Once the drive through the jungle began, the plan as designed and explained was followed faithfully for about fifteen minutes. Then the men, separated from each other in the thick underbrush, began to shout for directions in an effort to keep the line straight. Within a short time, we were openly challenging the Japanese to come out into the open and make a stand. We must have looked and sounded like fools. The shouting and the expressions of bravado somehow seemed to relieve tensions, and we progressed through the jungle with considerably more self-confidence than we had when we first approached this assignment the evening before.

The drive, which lasted most of the afternoon, yielded only one Japanese soldier, as far as I know. He was an unarmed fellow who refused to be taken prisoner when given the opportunity, and when he demanded to be shot when he was approached, one of our men complied with his wishes. It was clear to us the Japanese soldier had been brainwashed into believing he must refrain from ever being captured by the enemy.

Late in the evening we returned to our camp completely exhausted, starved, and disillusioned. This wasn't the kind of war we as Air Force personnel had been trained to fight, and we were not technically competent as infantry soldiers, nor were we emotionally prepared for hand-to-hand combat. Our battle equipment was to have consisted of fighter planes, which we no longer had, and we had little confidence in our abilities to defend ourselves against trained infantry soldiers, let alone contribute much to the defense of the Peninsula of Bataan. Troop morale was at a low ebb that evening, and the small amount of food each person received for his only meal of that day didn't do much to help our spirits.

The following day each squad was assigned the responsibility of guarding a specific section of the southwest portion of the Peninsula of Bataan beach. That area was called the Points, and the struggle with the enemy intensified; the Battle of the Points was continuous and stretched along a large section of the beach.

My squad had the duty of assuring the defense of a point that jutted out into the South China Sea. This we named "Little Corregidor." On this point we had an air-cooled .50-caliber machine gun that had been salvaged and a number of British Enfield rifles. Barbed wire was strung along the sand near the water, and from our strategic positions we felt we were truly in complete command of all activities that might or could take place within our assigned section. It was our understanding the entire beach in the vicinity was equally well protected.

Initially, we had instructions to post men in two-hour shifts, two hours of duty followed by two hours of sleep. This plan was followed for several days and then discarded when it became clear that men could not function effectively under that schedule. When they were off duty and sleeping, they would doze off only to awaken abruptly, thinking they should be on duty. Then, on duty, they were so tired and sleepy they were almost helpless.

The new plan of six hours on duty and six hours for sleeping served the needs of the men much better. One thing for sure, there were few distractions from the two activities of beach patrol and sleeping.

We maintained our battle stations on the beach until nearly the first of April, and while the Japanese made constant efforts at the loss of a great many of their soldiers, they were never able to successfully land troops from the sea. In the area where it was first believed there was only a handful of Japanese soldiers, hundreds were finally routed out of caves along the rocky beach and killed or captured. This was accomplished only with the assistance of small U.S. Navy ships, which shelled from the sea the Japanese-occupied caves along the beach, and skilled artillery batteries on Corregidor, which directed mortar fire across the coastal areas.

Finally, the Philippine Scouts had to go into the caves occupied by the Japanese before the war had begun, and in hand-to-hand combat clean out the Japanese. The soldiers had fortified the caves well and were equipped for a long war.

From time to time we would encounter individuals or small squads of Japanese soldiers, and these would have to be dealt with. Different squads of men carried out routine patrol missions, some of which were productive and yielded both prisoners and information. One of our major problems all during the Bataan effort was the lack of dependable ammunition and hand grenades. Much of that issued to us was completely unusable. The problem of not knowing which was good and which was bad was extremely troublesome, and often we were confronted with frustration and serious concern over faulty equipment.

By this time we had experienced nearly four months of constant bombardment from Japanese planes and from the harassment of Japanese snipers and other enemy troops. We were suffering terribly from the lack of proper nourishment and from the environment, which created serious problems with disease.

From radio news we learned that the war was going poorly for the Allies and that the Japanese were moving rapidly south toward Australia. It was almost impossible for us to understand why our troops were not supported from home with equipment and much-needed food and medicine. I am extremely grateful we didn't know then the decision had been made in Washington to forfeit the Philippines and us to the Japanese and direct Allied resources to the war in Europe. However, had we known of that decision, it might have been possible for us to fade into the jungle and spend the war years supporting the Filipino guerrillas who so effectively continued to harass the Japanese occupation forces and thus contribute to the impediment of the achievement of long-range war plans by the Japanese.

# 9

# SURRENDER

BY EARLY APRIL, after having been subjected to the constant bombardment and strafing by the Japanese planes, we withdrew from our beach defense positions to our original jungle bivouac area. The men were at the point of complete exhaustion. While our frontal contact with the enemy had not been heavy along the beaches, we had almost reached the limit of endurance because of enemy aircraft attacks and the lack of food, medicine, and sleep.

Much earlier most of us had given up hope of actually getting planes or troop reinforcement from the States. The fellows in the radio department kept us informed of Japanese regional advances. We knew that the Dutch East Indies had fallen and that the Japanese had taken Singapore and were moving south toward Australia. We also knew they had drawn a large number of troops back to the Philippine Islands in an effort to seize complete control of the Island of Luzon. Manila Bay was a most strategic and useful piece of real estate, and the Japanese wanted it badly.

The news of General MacArthur's departure from the Philippines didn't concern us much. There was little evidence that "Dugout Doug" had made much of a contribution to the war effort thus far. In fact, it was our belief that he had been a serious impediment to the effective utilization of military resources at the beginning of the war and was really the one who was responsible for the improper planning for an effective defense of the Bataan Peninsula. We didn't blame him for getting out of the Islands when he did. No one that I knew would have turned down the opportunity to leave Bataan right then. In more rational moments we knew that MacArthur was perceived to be too valuable a resource to the United States for him to remain in the Philippines.

From among us had emerged the common feeling that our country had betrayed us. Not only were we not receiving equipment with which to fight, but there was practically no official communication concerning our situation and prospects for the future. I believe that we could have handled bad news much better than no official news at all. The morale of the men had sunk to an unbelievable low.

It was during this period that Tokyo Rose was the most active, and during the day and each evening, she kept all of us informed concerning the status of wives and sweethearts back home. In her sultry voice she did all that she could do to tempt men to give up the fight and surrender. To the best of my knowledge, she wasn't the least bit successful as far as the troops on Bataan and Corregidor were concerned. As bad as conditions on Bataan were, we were to learn shortly that they were much better than those as prisoners of war under the Japanese forces.

We hadn't been off beach defense long when the Japanese made their big final push to take the Bataan Peninsula. On April 8, 1942, Sad Sack and I had taken the pickup truck for supplies as we did each evening. We had driven from our bivouac area above Mariveles up the peninsula past the hospital area to the rendezvous area where we regularly met the supply truck to draw our allotment of rice. The allocation of bread had been discontinued long ago, and the supply of canned food had also been exhausted.

We had driven the truck off the main road to the meeting place and had been there only a short time when American and Filipino forces began an artillery attack on the Japanese. The roar was almost deafening as the shells passed overhead. And, to make matters worse for us, the Japanese were returning fire. If it hadn't been for the protection of the huge trees, some of us would have been killed or seriously injured. The heavy jungle provided helpful protection from the exploding shells and other debris resulting from the shelling.

Sad and I waited until nearly ten o'clock, at which time we concluded that there wasn't much chance of the supply truck coming that night. We agreed we should promptly get out of there and return to our squadron bivouac area. However, when we attempted to drive on to the main road, we found that it was completely congested with Filipino troops and equipment moving away from the front lines toward Mariveles.

I approached one Filipino officer and asked him the status of the situation.

"The lines have broken, and we have surrendered," he told me.

When I asked him why the lines had broken, he only kept repeating,

"The lines have broken, and we are retreating. The war is finished, and we have surrendered."

Neither Sad nor I would accept the report that we had surrendered. That sounded to us like nothing but nonsense.

"Filipinos, perhaps," Sad said to me, "but never would American troops surrender to a bunch of Japs."

It was a long and hectic struggle before we were able to squeeze the truck into the mass of humanity jamming the road. By midnight, we had gone only a few kilometers. By the time we reached the hospital area, the ammunition dumps, not far from where we were walking, were blown up by our troops. The sky in the area around the hospital was brilliantly lighted. Had the Japanese seized upon the opportunity to come in with fighter planes to bomb and strafe, they would have had a field day and would have taken the toll of thousands of Filipino troops with a few Americans thrown in for good measure. We finally had to abandon the truck and make our way through the jungle and over the mountain to our bivouac area.

When we arrived at the camp, it was nearly morning. Although the members of the squadron didn't have any information concerning what had happened, they were confident that something unusual was taking place because they had heard the heavy shelling. It wasn't, however, until Sad and I described our experience to them that they realized the seriousness of the situation.

While we had discussed the possibility of the Japanese completely overrunning the Philippines, we had never seriously considered being taken prisoners. We knew the Japanese had taken control of many of the southern islands, and from news reports we received information concerning the fall of Malaysia, Singapore, the Dutch East Indies, and other adjacent countries of Southeast Asia. However, we still had the conviction that we could hold Bataan and Corregidor in spite of the serious problems with which the American and Filipino troops were confronted. The confidence that was characteristic of us prior to the war surprisingly continued somewhat right to the very end of our confrontation as an organized force against the Japanese. We seemed to cling tenaciously to the conviction that America could never be defeated, especially by the Japanese.

That morning, April 9, several of us took the squadron's ton-and-a-half truck and went down to the Navy base at Mariveles. Until this time the Navy had shared none of its food and other supplies with us, although those troops always appeared to us to be well fed. As a squadron we had never really made an issue of trying to get food supplies from those people. On the other hand, however, the Navy had never volunteered to offer us any assistance in spite of the fact that they knew the seriousness of our condition.

When we arrived at the tunnel, the attitude of the men in charge was that of humility, and they willingly parted with whatever we could find that we could use. Their stores weren't nearly as plentiful as we had imagined them to be, but we found a good supply of white navy beans and gallon cans of prunes (a humorous combination), and a few other odds and ends that we knew would be useful. While we weren't able to get any cigarettes, I did find a carton of chewing tobacco.

The food items we turned over to the mess sergeant, who had the cooks pitch in and prepare as much food as they could. By the middle of the day the food was ready. Everyone dived in and ate as we had not been able to eat for several months. And while the food wasn't the quality that one might have wished, after months of near starvation, to us it was like a king's banquet.

By two o'clock in the afternoon everyone had eaten his fill, and the balance was reserved for a later meal. At this time I produced the carton of chewing tobacco and was just announcing to the men the availability of the plugs when all of a sudden machine-gun fire from the road below sent bullets flying through the trees into our bivouac area. From habit we all dived for the ground or into foxholes until the machine gunning stopped.

A day or two earlier, our squadron commander had been ordered to fly one of the last P-40s we had on Bataan to Mindanao to implement a plan that was to enable us to get several boatloads of food into Manila Harbor. Before he could return to Bataan, the peninsula had fallen to the Japanese, and we heard nothing more from or about him. We all hoped he was able to get to Allied forces because he was a great squadron commander and pilot and could continue to serve at a time when pilots with combat experience would be in extremely short supply. His absence left the administration of the squadron in the hands of a lieutenant.

The acting CO and I walked down the trail that led to the road and the direction from which the machine-gun fire had just come. There, parked in the road, was a Japanese tank with the turret open. Standing in the turret was a young Japanese officer who spoke English like an American. He informed us Bataan had been surrendered to the Japanese forces and the

Japanese had now conquered all of the Philippines with the exception of Corregidor, which he predicted would fall momentarily.

He ordered us to stack all of our guns and ammunition and by noon the following day to assemble in an area not too far away, which he described. We knew the place well because it was the one that had nearly become our camp upon our first arrival on the Peninsula of Bataan. He also warned us that none of the men should attempt to escape because they would be found and executed.

"Your commanding officer has surrendered all of the troops on Bataan unconditionally," he said. "The Japanese army could have killed all of you but dealt with you kindly. If any escape now, the men on Corregidor will all be killed. Surrender of them will not be accepted, and none of the men there will be left alive." Following that heartwarming statement, the turret of the tank closed, and the vehicle moved on down the road.

When we had returned to the squadron and the lieutenant had relayed the information we had just received from the Japanese officer, no one seemed to be in the mood for chewing tobacco. The whole camp took on a terrible mood of depression. Up until now there had continued to be hope.

During the balance of the afternoon and the night that followed, we were filled with apprehension, and very few of us had much sleep. We finished off the beans and the prunes and took some satisfaction in knowing that at least we would surrender with full bellies. There was considerable speculation concerning what might happen to us as prisoners of the Japanese, but we assumed or hoped that they would be civilized and humane in their treatment of us. We soon were to find this was no more than wishful thinking.

Most of the casualties that the squadron had suffered had resulted from the first-day bombing at Clark Field, with some additional loss of life from the bombing and strafing of our men while on Bataan. Now, we were prisoners, having no voice whatsoever in the action taken by the commanding officer of American and Filipino forces on Bataan. Nor had we received information from American authorities concerning behavior expectations as prisoners of war.

We were at the mercy of an enemy that had been trying its best to kill us, and we had been making the same effort toward them. There was also the agony from the humiliation of surrender. We asked ourselves if this weren't the first time in the history of our nation that Americans had ever surrendered to the enemy in large numbers. Would we, we asked ourselves, be considered as cowards or traitors by our people back home?

It was in this frame of mind we launched into a discussion of the futility of war. It is quite likely this subject would never have arisen had we been the conquerors, but as the conquered we felt completely hopeless and helpless. The helpless feelings were not strange to us, but never had we had them in the context of the vanquished.

Next to Sad Sack, the greatest morale builder in the squadron, had been the Methodist chaplain who constantly mingled with the enlisted men. He went on more patrols than did anyone else, and when we inquired of him concerning the appropriateness of his carrying arms, his response was "The Lord tells us that He helps those who help themselves!"

I wasn't a member of the Methodist Church but felt strongly that if all Methodists were of the same quality as this chaplain, the organization was worthy of careful investigation.

Now that the Japanese officer had notified us we were to surrender our arms and assemble in a designated area, we needed direction from the acting squadron commander concerning certain courses of action. The counsel we hoped for was not forthcoming, because he didn't have the necessary information needed to respond properly to the questions raised. Consequently, about all we could do was to get together with our closest friends and attempt to determine what course of action was in the best interest of our country and of ourselves.

Prior to the war we had, from time to time, assembled as a squadron for the purpose of hearing read certain articles of war that pertained specifically to us. The information contained in those documents was to the effect that, if taken as prisoners of war, all we were required to provide the enemy was our name, rank, and serial number. We were also expected not to aid the enemy in its war effort and to escape if at all possible. Now, we had been advised by a representative of the Japanese army that we had been surrendered unconditionally, and that the men still holding out on Corregidor would be slaughtered if those surrendering on Bataan attempted to escape.

Although we had been on the Bataan Peninsula for three and one-half months, we were familiar only with the area in which we had served and knew the jungles and mountains of the Bataan Peninsula could be treacherous. The other problem was our total lack of information relative to the present placement of Japanese troops. As I now contemplate the situation in which we found ourselves, I am of the belief we should have tried to escape into the jungles. And then we should have done our best to become part of the underground movement. Some did exactly that, although most were eventually caught by the Japanese or reported to them by the Filipinos. They were executed or confined with other POWs in one of the many camps that were later established throughout the Islands. At least they did try to do something besides meekly submitting to the Japanese as most of the rest of us did. But at the time we did what we were told to do because we were fairly confident the Japanese would have taken revenge on the troops on Corregidor.

The questions were raised of how the Japanese would deal with the officers and noncommissioned officers as compared to the other men, and we debated whether or not we ought to wear our rank insignia or whether we all ought to strip off all indications of rank and present ourselves as privates.

After considerable unenlightened discussion, we decided we should wear whatever rank and insignia we were entitled to and to assume our relative positions and responsibilities as much as we were able to. As it turned out, it didn't matter much anyway because the Japanese military treated everyone about the same, and that treatment was brutal.

I still had a large store of coveralls and other pieces of clothing and pairs of shoes in the supply tent and encouraged the men to take whatever was needed to get them properly clothed. As a result of this, everyone surrendered to the Japanese with good clothing. I selected for myself a new pair of coveralls and shoes, and into a new green mosquito head net I placed three extra pairs of shorts, several pairs of socks, bars of soap, and a safety razor. On top I dumped the plugs of chewing tobacco. All others were invited to select anything they found that would be helpful to them. Most chose to carry a minimum load.

We placed all of our rifles in a pile by the side of the road and threw side arms in a separate location. Ammunition was sorted and stacked apart from the guns. Tents and all squadron gear were left standing in place. Personal items not needed or wanted were tossed into the brush or buried by the more energetic. In anticipation of being searched, we burned all money, Filipino and American. No one wanted the Japanese to enjoy the benefit of that. While it was almost impossible to buy anything of value on Bataan, this was the first time I had ever seen absolutely no value placed on money.

By noon of the day following the formal surrender of Bataan, we were ready to move to the area designated for assembly. Most of us still wore our ancient World War I steel helmets, which were by far the heaviest of any items carried. Each also had a canteen, a cup, and a mess kit.

Within the hour we met with men and officers from the other outfits in the area. There was much conversation and many questions. While there was much speculation, no one had collected any reliable information concerning the actual surrender or what we could expect when the Japanese troops arrived.

We knew that the Japanese were in the area because they had set up artillery pieces on Bataan in large numbers. The firing of these huge guns was so rapid that they sounded like machine guns.

# 10

# DEATH MARCH OUT OF BATAAN

ALONG TOWARD LATE AFTERNOON Japanese troops began to be spotted on the road moving toward us. The first Japanese to approach were small scrubby-looking fellows who carried heavy field packs and rifles and in groups pulled heavy infantry pieces. They looked more like beasts of burden than human beings, and shortly proved themselves to be almost inhuman.

While there were Japanese officers with the soldiers, no attempt was made to control the dirty, ragged, unshaven looters who pounced upon us like a pack of wolves. They swarmed over us, searching each man roughly and thoroughly, slapping, kicking, taking whatever they wanted, and destroying items they couldn't use. Within a matter of minutes they had stripped us of our watches, rings, pens, and anything that looked at all valuable. We had abandoned anything that looked Japanese, and it was a good thing that we had done so because they were looking for evidence that we had any previous contact at all with any of their soldiers.

These men were angry, greedy savages. Dick Watts made an effort to keep his glasses, which he needed badly, and was severely beaten for his efforts. What humiliation and abuse we suffered in that short time following our initial encounter with them! Little did we realize that this was nothing compared to what was in store for us.

During the next several hours hundreds of Japanese troops moved into the area and began setting up additional heavy artillery pieces. There was no doubt in anyone's mind these troops meant business, and they gave every evidence of being able to carry their part of the war to their enemy on Corregidor. It was clear none of them intended to miss an opportunity to take revenge on their captives. When along toward evening we were ordered to move down the road toward Mariveles, we did so with considerable relief.

The distance from our gathering place to Mariveles Field was not great. We earlier had walked it twice daily, as we made the trip to build revetments for the security of the planes promised but never delivered. However, because of the activities of the Japanese soldiers along the road, it took us nearly three hours to reach the large open area at the upper end of the unfinished Mariveles airstrip. As we approached, I wondered what had happened to the airfield construction crew from Boise, Idaho.

We were herded into the field and ordered to lie down. There was ample space for all of us, and after the afternoon-long experience with the Japanese soldiers, we were badly in the need of rest. There was very little conversation among the men. Rather it was a time for personal contemplation of the terrible situation that confronted us. No longer was there any question concerning the treatment of POWs by the Japanese. They had already exhibited their feelings and their willingness to vent their anger upon those of us who continued to represent the enemies of Japan.

As I lay on the ground thinking, I recalled the feelings that I had experienced in high school as a boxer. My dad loved boxing and encouraged me to become involved in boxing in high school and in the smokers that were sponsored in our community from time to time. I didn't enjoy boxing, and for several days before a scheduled event, I had serious reservations about getting into the ring with an unknown opponent. When the bout began each time and I made contact with my opponent, the apprehension and fear promptly left me and I was able to perform to the best of my ability. I didn't always win, but I managed to keep Dad reasonably happy with my performance.

Now that we had made the initial contact with the Japanese as their prisoners, my fear of them and the apprehension vanished. They were tough and were mean, but I was convinced with the help of the Lord and each other and by using good judgment we could all survive whatever they imposed or inflicted upon us. While that feeling helped me then, I was shortly to be proved wrong. The Japanese had demonstrated themselves to be capable soldiers, and shortly they would introduce to us their talents as vicious torturers of men who were in no position to defend themselves in any way. We learned from them atrocities that we had never even dreamed of, let alone witnessed.

In the barren field we remained for three days without either food or water. Filipino troops intermingled with American soldiers during those days, and Japanese officers and enlisted men constantly wandered leisurely through the gathering trying to find something of value that might have been missed by those who had gotten to us first.

The Japanese advised us we were being held at Mariveles until trucks to transport us out of the combat areas could be secured. From time to time men were taken from the group to serve as truck drivers for the Japanese. The Japanese talked with many American prisoners, trying to find out who could drive a truck. While many of us could, most of us denied the fact. We wondered afterwards whether we had done the right thing, but at the time very few of us were in any frame of mine to assist the Japanese in any manner unless we were forced to do so.

The battle between our forces on Corregidor and the Japanese on Bataan Peninsula raged furiously all during the three days we were waiting for transportation out of the war zone. Fortunately, we were not in the direct line of fire, but we did have serious concerns about the possibility of being shelled by the Corregidor guns. We had earlier noted with considerable pride the effect of Corregidor artillery, which had been able to keep Japanese naval vessels from shelling Bataan and which so effectively sent mortars over our heads as they dislodged those Japanese who had established a beachhead on Bataan prior to the beginning of hostilities. Those mortars rumbling over our heads sounded like huge trucks rolling over a long rickety bridge. The noise was eerie, but the results were reassuring.

On the evening of the third day we were ordered to move out, and under heavy guard we were marched down the airstrip to Mariveles Bay. The retreating American and Filipino forces had assembled their trucks and field pieces of all types on Mariveles Field. Some were badly damaged as a result of the recent battle for Bataan, and some had been partially dismantled by drivers who didn't want the Japanese to profit any more than necessary from our failure to hold the peninsula.

When we reached the shores of the bay, we found that no trucks were waiting for us, but angry, excited Japanese guards with fixed bayonets urged us up the road in the direction of Manila, constantly insisting that trucks would arrive at any time. It was not easy for us to walk in the ankle-deep dust of the road, and crowded together as we were, it was almost impossible. In utter blackness of the night, we stumbled over ourselves and each other until what must have been nearly midnight. We weren't able to know the hour of day or night from the time the Japanese took command of us because they had stripped us of all watches. The road wound up from the level of Manila Bay to the top of a fairly high range of mountains, so the first part of our forced march was almost entirely uphill.

Finally, the Japanese directed us to move off to the sides of the road and stay there until daylight. Hungry, thirsty, and completely exhausted, I lay down and for the first time gave serious thoughts to slipping off into the jungle. After careful examination of the pros and cons of that course of action, though, I concluded I didn't know exactly where we were or how many Japanese soldiers were guarding us. One thing for sure, there were thousands of Japanese soldiers in the immediate vicinity waging an all-out offensive against Corregidor. I finally fell asleep.

As soon as daylight broke the following day, the Japanese guards came crashing through the brush and shouted us into motion again. They seemed to be in special haste to get us moving, and before long we were even more anxious than they to get off the Peninsula of Bataan.

By midmorning we had reached that area of the peninsula that was directly across the bay from the island fortress of Corregidor. A strip of water only two miles wide separated Corregidor from the Bataan Peninsula at that point. It seemed to us that the Japanese had artillery stationed almost everywhere, and the guns were firing as rapidly as possible. There was no question but what Corregidor was receiving a terrible pounding.

What was puzzling and terribly frightening to us was that Corregidor continued its relentless shelling of the Japanese while we were still in the area. But this it did, and the consequences to us were disastrous. A number of our men were either killed or, worse yet, were severely wounded, leaving them at the complete mercy of the Japanese troops, who had demonstrated absolutely no mercy whatsoever. Sadly, we concluded that Corregidor's troops were showing us no more consideration than were the Japanese.

The Japanese officers and guards who were in charge of the prisoners were visibly frightened and ran around like excited children insisting we move faster and faster to get out of the area. While they appeared to be concerned about keeping us from getting killed, it seemed clearly evident their major concern was saving their own necks.

The dead were left where they had fallen, and the injured were initially assisted by those who hadn't been hit by shell fragments. As tired as we were, we found it difficult enough to keep ourselves moving down the road without the extra burden of trying to carry another person. Consequently, the injured were finally abandoned, and I never did learn what happened to them. The only evidence we had as to what might have later taken place were the subsequent atrocities committed by the Japanese guards on those in the marching group.

During the morning we observed again, this time from very close range, the accuracy of Corregidor's guns as time after time they made direct hits on Japanese gun emplacements and upon Japanese troops and equipment. Had we been in a safer place, watching the battle would have been sheer pleasure. Of course, we had no way of knowing how much damage the Japanese were inflicting on Corregidor.

Corregidor fortress had been established much earlier to serve as the defender of Manila Bay. Her huge guns had effectively kept the Japanese navy vessels a long way away from Bataan, and had they been mounted in such a manner that they could be swung in an arc to fire up the Peninsula of Bataan, the Japanese might never have been able to secure that peninsula from Allied troops.

All during the day the areas through which we passed were littered with debris from battle, and the bloated bodies of Filipino soldiers were to be seen all along the road. The Japanese apparently suffered few casualties, or else they had been able by this time to clear their dead from the battle area. They had made no effort to pick up the Filipino dead. On several occasions we saw headless bodies, only to see the heads perched on a fence post or hanging from a tree. It was obvious the Japanese had beheaded these troops, perhaps after they had been killed, and had left the evidence of their brutality to warn those who passed that there was no doubt they weren't in the Philippines on vacation.

It wasn't until late afternoon that we cleared the battle area. By this time we were so exhausted and hungry and thirsty that when the Japanese assembled us in a field at the edge of the bay, we dropped to the ground in sheer exhaustion.

After dark we slipped out into the bay, and even though the water was salty, it was refreshing, and we were able to enjoy a great amount of relief from it after the torture of the day.

We had no food, and the Japanese made no effort to give us either food or water. They did, however, permit us to rest in the field until late in the night. Then, they hurriedly reassembled us on the road to continue the march off Bataan.

This, then, became their pattern of operation. Beginning in the middle of the night, we would be jammed together on the road and would be marched until the hot Filipino sun was high in the sky. When the day became very hot, the Japanese would move us off the road into a field. There, they would crowd us together standing, as close as we could possibly get to each other, and then force us to sit down. Jammed on top of each other, we would remain in the scorching heat until late afternoon. The sun beating down upon us was bad enough, but to have to put up with the continuous harassment of the Japanese soldiers was almost more than we could bear. They taunted us continuously and seemed to delight most when men fainted—and many did—from a combination of heat exhaustion, fatigue, hunger, and the lack of water.

The Japanese gave us neither food nor water, and the only times we had anything to eat or water to drink were when we could steal a stalk of sugarcane from an adjacent field or a cup of water from one of the many flowing wells along the road we were traveling.

The water or sugarcane was secured under the constant threat of brutal punishment or death if a guard could get to us with his bayonet before we could get back into the group. The Japanese thought it was great fun to run someone through with a bayonet or shoot someone through the head. Both were common sights as we made slow progress toward our unknown destination. There was by this time absolutely no doubt in our minds the Japanese were seeking revenge and were looking for the least excuse to get it.

Ordinarily, the area through which we marched was one of beauty. Now, nothing seemed to us to be beautiful as we trudged along the dusty road that had earlier supported the innumerable vehicles of both the Allied forces as they had moved back and forth, first with equipment and supplies for the Americans and Filipinos and more recently with war materials to support the Japanese in their final and successful effort to conquer us.

As we marched, we continually encountered Japanese troops moving in the direction from which we had just come. As before, each new group of soldiers seemed to feel a personal obligation to search us and to inflict as much brutality and humiliation on us as possible. It was difficult for me to understand why officers of any army would permit troops to behave toward captives as those soldiers did.

After several days we reached the town of Limay and moved on toward Orion and Abucay. The farther we walked up the peninsula, the more often we came upon bodies of dead Filipinos and Americans. These were not battle casualties, they were bodies of men who had died from exhaustion, starvation, and disease, or who had been bayoneted or shot by the Japanese guards as they made their way off the peninsula. By this time we had become used to the idea it was highly possible any one of us might be killed at any time for any reason or for no reason at all. It appeared clear to us that we were fair game to any Japanese soldier, and they clearly enjoyed their status. None showed any mercy toward us at any time.

It was during this period, more than ever before in my life, that personal discipline was required. The easiest thing in the world would have been to give up completely, and some of the men did this. Others, suffering terribly from the lack of water, plunged headlong into horribly polluted roadside pools to drink their fill, only to die shortly from dysentery. One had to be on guard all of the time not to do anything that would anger the guards or attract their attention. While we tried to encourage each other and help when we could, it became apparent each person would have to be responsible for himself and for his own behavior. This seemed to be a purely selfish attitude, but it was a grim fact of life.

By this time the Japanese had stripped me of everything I had put in the mosquito net except the plugs of chewing tobacco. My watch, class ring, pen, and razor had gone first, followed by the articles of clothing. They hadn't taken my mess kit or canteen and cup. The knife and fork went early, also, but I was able to keep the spoon. Many times different Japanese had closely examined the chewing tobacco, had smelled it, felt it, and then put it back in the mosquito head net in disgust. I tried to explain to them how it was used, but they seemed not to know anything about chewing tobacco. I really don't know why I kept the stuff; I wasn't a tobacco chewer, but I lugged it along.

About halfway up the peninsula, hungry and thirsty, I took a bite out of one of the plugs of tobacco, out of sheer boredom. To my surprise, the tobacco tasted good, and I found that a small piece of it in my mouth would stimulate saliva and keep my mouth from getting so dry.

I tried to persuade other fellows to take a piece of the black stuff but was unable to convince anyone else of its value. It should have been obvious to them that I was suffering considerably less discomfort than were most of the others. There was no question the chewing tobacco helped me to control my craving for water and, perhaps, may have saved my life. By the time the march was completed, I had used the entire carton of chewing tobacco.

Late in the afternoon of the sixth or seventh day of the march, we straggled into the town of Balanga under the prodding and insults of the guards. There we were again crowded into a small field and left to rest. One man, digging around in the loose soil, found a turnip that hadn't been harvested. The word passed like wildfire, and within the next few minutes, the field was completely gleaned, the effort yielding a fairly large number of turnips. Almost everyone got at least a bite. The digging, I am sure, did not go unnoticed by the Japanese, but for some reason or other, they made no effort to stop us. At the same time neither did they make any effort to supplement the turnips with other food or water.

It was at Balanga we watched, horrified, as the Japanese guards forced four American soldiers to dig their own common grave. The soldiers were then beaten and abused in other ways and finally shot as they stood in the grave. One American soldier, only wounded by the volley of shots, struggled to claw his way out of the grave. He was beaten senseless by a shovel-wielding guard. Atrocities like this became more common as the march continued.

Just before dark on the same day, we were moved into a compound already partially occupied by Filipino soldiers. A tin-covered shed in the compound was filled with men. I found a vacant spot by the side of the tin building and sat with my back against it. That felt good.

All of a sudden I felt something warm and wet against my back. I turned around to see a Filipino army officer urinating on me through a hole in the building.

"What in the devil are you doing?" I demanded, looking through a tiny glassless window.

His response was, "What do you care about a little thing like that? The Japs are going to kill you, anyway."

"You dumb idiot!" I growled at him. "Aren't things bad enough without you making them worse? I'd rather be killed by the Japs than be urinated on by a stupid Filipino officer. With officers like you, it's no wonder that we lost Bataan!"

It was a good thing for both of us that we were separated by the shed wall. The Japanese would have been thoroughly delighted to see two prisoners banging away at each other. In our hopeless physical condition it was doubtful that we could have injured each other but it would have given the Japanese an excuse for punishing us severely or even killing us.

During the night the Filipinos were ordered out and down the road. By early morning, however, we had caught up with them again. Unfortunately, marching at the head of the American group, I witnessed over and over again during the day what happened to those too weak to continue the march off Bataan. Clearly, this was a death march!

Pistol-wielding Japanese walked along behind the Filipinos and shot through the head those who dropped out of the ranks from exhaustion. Such inhumanity was unbelievable, but each execution was enjoyed greatly by the Japanese, who laughed with each other as though they were playing some innocent game.

After that day I made sure that I was never again at either the head or the rear of our group of marchers, because we learned that our dropouts were receiving the same treatment being administered to the Filipinos. This could be verified by us as, from time to time, we spotted white men among the Filipino dead. Those who had been injured earlier by Corregidor's guns had been hauled away never to be seen again by us. The Filipino dead included officers as well as enlisted men.

During the entire march, the Japanese changed their guards at regular intervals, keeping fresh troops to watch us at all times. These well-fed men badgered us constantly, insisting that we move along rapidly, yet constantly making it difficult for us to walk at all. Crowded together as we were and in our poor physical condition, it was almost humanly impossible to keep up the pace they demanded. The thing that kept most of us going then was our hatred for our captors and the feeling of assurance that the Yanks and tanks would arrive shortly and avenge this terrible wrong.

As we continued our march off Bataan, our numbers daily grew fewer as those too sick or weary could go no farther. Dysentery and malaria, not new diseases to us on Bataan, had been reasonably well controlled, but now they began to take their toll in large numbers. While we were on Bataan, the medics furnished quinine pills, but now on our own and without preventive medicine, the malaria-carrying mosquito was able to effectively take its toll.

At the time of surrender, one of the medics assigned to our squadron had given me a tiny aluminum can in which he had placed fifteen five-grain quinine pills.

"Don't let these get away from you," he warned strongly, "and don't use them until it is absolutely necessary for you to do so."

As the days passed, I saw many sick with malaria, but none of my close friends, so I continued to heed the counsel the medic had so forcefully given me. Each time we were searched by the Japanese, I placed the small can in the top of my shoe and removed it only when I was sure that it would be safe in the pocket of my sweat-caked coveralls.

Water and sugarcane were two items over which there was a constant contest between us and the Japanese guards. The rules seemed to be that we could have both if we were willing to take the chance of being bayoneted or shot or severely beaten, if caught. However, if we could get water or cane and get back into ranks before a guard could get to us, we seemed to be safe for the moment. The guards were always on the alert and taunted us with fixed bayonets, daring us to make attempts for water or food.

In spite of the threat of death, or worse, some men gambled and won. Those who did get stalks of the cane found that while the juice did help to sustain them and give them energy, their mouths quickly became raw from chewing on the coarse cane fibers.

Because all of this was like an unreal horrible nightmare, it was difficult for us to keep track of the days. No one cared about the time of day. Our thoughts were constantly on food and water and hatred for the Japanese. There was little conversation among the men, each saving his strength to carry him through the ordeal. Adding to the depression was the gnawing fear the Japanese might execute all of us. We had ample evidence they were capable of doing just that.

One morning as we sat bareheaded in the blazing tropical sun to take our daily punishment, several Japanese soldiers from a nearby camp approached and struck up a conversation with us. The interpreter for the group, a noncommissioned officer who spoke English well, asked why we came to the Philippine Islands. He said we had no business being in that part of the world.

This was the first calm, halfway human Japanese I had encountered thus far. So, with as much bravado and conviction as I could muster, I told him we were professional soldiers and the Philippine Islands had been under the control of the United States for more than forty years. As professional soldiers it was our obligation to go where our country sent us, and we had been assigned to Philippine Islands duty.

My colleagues confirmed this.

We also reminded him he probably wouldn't be in the Philippines now, either, had he not been brought here by the military of his country.

He solemnly nodded his head in agreement and said he would rather be in Japan. However, he did tell us emphatically that Asia is for the Asians and we should have refused to come. The Philippine Islands are a long way from America, and the Japanese people didn't want war with America. "We do not hate the American people. We hate only one person and that is your President. He is the one responsible for all of us being here. You and we have only him to blame for all of this. He is the enemy of all of us, including you American soldiers. But, on Bataan you have killed many Japanese soldiers, and for that each of you will have to pay."

He didn't elaborate on just how he expected the Japanese to collect their debt from us, but if this march was an introduction to the treatment that was to follow, none of us needed to have a picture drawn for us.

After days of walking, exactly how many miles I do not know, those of us who survived the rigors finally arrived at the town of San Fernando. That was the little community where we had stopped on Christmas Eve to rest and listen to the church bells on our way to Bataan. How conditions had changed for us in the short period of three and one-half months! It seemed like years ago.

In San Fernando we were all crowded together in buildings, and the following day, for the first time, the Japanese gave us each a canteen cup full of cooked rice and some water. We wept for joy. Although we were kept in the building for two nights and days, we were given no more food, and the suffering continued.

About noon of the third day we were ordered out of the buildings into the street, where we were marched through the community to the railroad tracks. As we passed through the town, the Filipinos waved to us and carefully gave us the V for victory sign. This was the first time we had observed any type of positive emotional behavior by the Filipinos on our behalf. We had begun to believe that they had completely forgotten their friends, the Americans, and had gone over to the side of the Japanese. We knew this wasn't the case; the reason they had given us little recognition was that they feared for their own lives. Here in San Fernando, though, the Filipinos were open and very frank about their feelings for the American soldiers.

At the railroad we were jammed into oven-like boxcars and were forced to stand, pressed closely against each other. The heat was almost suffocating, and to make matters worse, the doors to the boxcars were jammed shut. After considerable delay while the Japanese ran around frantically shouting and yelling at each other, the train began its slow way toward Clark Field. We wondered if the Japanese were going to take us right back to our original home base. It turned out this was not to be.

Late in the afternoon we reached what appeared to be our destination and were permitted to get out of the steaming boxcars. The heat inside had been unbearable, and some, already completely dehydrated, suffocated. In some cases it wasn't until we got out of the boxcars we realized that there were dead soldiers among us, held in standing position because we had been pressed so closely together.

## 11

# CAMP O'DONNELL

ONCE WE WERE OUT OF THE BOXCARS, the guards promptly organized us into columns of two and started us marching up a dirt road away from the small town, which we later learned was Capus. The pace was brisk, but after the boxcar ordeal, the hike was a welcome relief.

After several hours of walking, we reached what appeared to be a rather large camp of some sort. Inside the camp, we were marched into a section occupied by Japanese troops and were assembled before a high platform.

Within a matter of minutes, a short, stocky Japanese officer mounted the platform and began screaming at us. Finally, he slowed down enough to enable an interpreter to explain to us, "You are prisoners of the Imperial Japanese Government!"

After giving us numerous instructions, he told us, "You will be severely punished for what you did on Bataan, and if anyone attempt to escape, he will be found and promptly shot to death!"

The Japanese officer continued by informing us that the Americans had always been enemies of the Japanese. "Japan is prepared to fight the Americans for one hundred years if it takes that long! In the end, America will be ours!"

"It will be a cold day in hell when America belongs to the Japs!" I wanted to shout back at him, but for obvious reasons I didn't.

The officer said a lot of other things, including "You Americans are nothing but cowards! Japanese soldiers would never surrender to America. You have dishonored your country, your parents, and yourselves. Japanese soldiers would take their own lives before they would surrender! You have shown yourselves to be cowards, and you will be treated with contempt and dishonor!"

None of his pronouncements earned him applause from the audience. But then no one booed, either.

We learned shortly that we were in Camp O'Donnell, a former Philippine Army training camp, earlier abandoned and in a sad state of repair. The camp was large and divided down the middle by a road.

On one side of the road were the Japanese soldiers and the Filipino prisoners of war, separated by a high barbed-wire fence. The other side of the camp had been divided into four areas: one for the Navy and Marines, one for the Army, one for the Air Corps personnel, and the fourth area reserved for the sick and wounded. This latter space was called the hospital area and included a two-story wood building. However, there was neither medical equipment nor medication of any kind.

Later, we learned that the purpose for dividing the American servicemen into the three designated areas was to provide a list of prisoners for the Japanese and to determine for the American officers in camp the names of the men who had survived the battles on Bataan and the subsequent march from the peninsula.

After the enlightening but thoroughly depressing speech by the Japanese officer, we were individually assigned to one of the three areas indicated. All were large, and for the first time in what seemed like eternity, we were able to stretch out on the ground without being herded together like animals.

Stretch out on the ground I did, all alone and by myself, and although I was terribly hungry and thirsty, I immediately went to sleep. The hot sun beating down on my face the following morning forced me awake only long enough for me to seek out a place in the shade. I promptly went back to sleep.

By midafternoon I awakened and realized I was starved. There would be food, I learned, but not until later in the evening. Given this information, I wandered around our section of the camp to become familiar with the place. Hopefully, I would be able to find some of the members of my squadron, many of whom I had not seen since leaving Bataan.

Before chow time I had found two of my best friends. One, a fellow from Oregon by the name of Norm, had clerked with me in the squadron supply. He was a couple of years older than I, but we had been in the Air Corps for about the same length of time. He wasn't the most technically competent fellow I had known but was a plugger and a delightful person, eager to be of service to those with whom we worked. The other fellow, Dick, a Mormon from Utah, and I had a great deal in common and had enjoyed each other's association immensely prior to getting ourselves into the present mess. He was a clerk in the first sergeant's office and was much sharper than was the first sergeant. Everyone liked him because of his personality and his effectiveness in his assignment. He was in a position to help squadron members and seemed to derive a great deal of pleasure from doing so.

The three of us entered into a solemn agreement that we would make every effort to stay together and would help each other as much as we possibly could. This agreement and the fact we were together as friends helped to give us the reassurance we needed at that particular time.

When it came time for us to eat, I learned the amount of food provided was adequate. In fact, the amount was much greater than we had received on Bataan, and after the long period of time without food, it tasted much better. The menu consisted of steamed rice and boiled eggplant. Many men in our living area were too ill to eat, and others, because of the trauma of the Death March and the overall depression, just couldn't get the food down. Being among the fortunate few, I was reasonably well off physically and mentally and was extremely hungry. Never had I been quite so happy to get a meal! The rice and eggplant, we soon learned, were to be our regular fare twice daily. For breakfast we received a watery rice served as cereal.

After our meal we walked around our area in search of other members of our squadron. Some, we located. From them we learned the sad news that others had died on the Death March, and some, too ill for placement in our Air Corps area, were placed in the area reserved for the sick. It wasn't long before we learned that rarely did anyone recover once he was placed in the filthy hospital area of the camp.

After some searching we located and staked out a place for ourselves on the ground underneath an abandoned building. We had nothing to place on the ground to sleep on, but we didn't complain about that. It still felt wonderful just to have the luxury of room enough to enable us to stretch out.

We learned water was scarce in camp. In fact, there was only one spigot on the American side of the camp. It was in the Navy and Marine area, some distance from where we lived. Drinking water was secured from this one tap for all men in camp. A long line of men could be seen day or night waiting for a turn at the water tap. Each took with him as many canteens as he could carry back to our area. By doing this, he wouldn't have to return to the water tap until each person for whom he had secured water had paid him back by bringing a canteen of water for him. Conservation of drinking water was practiced religiously by everyone within the prison camp.

The water for cooking was obtained from a small pond some distance from the camp and brought to the camp in half gasoline drums carried on poles on the shoulders of men. As the water detail set off, it would go through the Japanese part of camp, where it would pick up a Japanese guard to accompany it to the pond. On the return the guard would drop off, once the camp was reached. He would then wait for the next detail. The water detail was a difficult assignment, but men willingly served on it realizing the cooks needed lots of water if we were to have cooked food.

Camp O'Donnell was surrounded by barbed-wire fences, none of which served the purpose of keeping men in or out. The low fence just marked the boundaries of the camp. Guard towers were located at intervals around the entire enclosure. It was not, however, the intention of the Japanese to assume full responsibility for guarding the prisoners. There is little doubt the soldiers would have happily shot anyone attempting to escape had they seen him. However, to the American officers had been given the assignment of keeping our own troops inside the wire enclosure. Undoubtedly, the Filipino officers were given the same responsibility relative to Filipino prisoners of war.

Our officers assigned enlisted men to walk the inside perimeter of the fence. We were told if any person escaped, those on guard duty at the time would be shot. This announcement was taken seriously and made everyone standing guard attentive and cautious.

Instructions from our officers were that no one was to attempt to escape at this time because of the retaliation against those of us in camp and those who were still holding out on Corregidor. It was not difficult to understand how the Japanese would have known whether or not a person had escaped because the names of newly arrived prisoners were given to the Japanese. While stragglers continued to enter O'Donnell, the list of internees daily became shorter as men died from the terrible diseases of dysentery and malaria. Other serious medical problems took their toll, also.

I couldn't understand why the Filipinos remained. It seemed to me they could easily disappear and not be detected, while a white man could be spotted without difficulty. But then, Filipinos could have been slipping out regularly and not confiding in me. More barbed wire separated us, so we didn't have much of a chance to talk with any of them.

The Japanese ordered daily work details. Others were scheduled by the

American officers. First priority was given to the rice and wood details. Those assigned to the rice detail would go to either the towns of Capus or Tarlac on trucks to load rice in boxcars for shipment out of the country or to load rice on trucks to feed the Japanese troops in O'Donnell and elsewhere on Luzon. Some of the rice was distributed to the prisoners of war. What a tragedy it was that this rice, stored so close to the battle area, couldn't have been trucked to Bataan before the Japanese moved into the area.

Details of POWs labored for many days hauling rice from warehouses to railroad loading stations. The work was terribly hard because of the weight of the rice sacks. It took two men to lift a heavy sack onto the back of a third, who would often fall to the ground, unable to bear the weight.

On occasion it was necessary for men to unload trucks bringing rice into camp. Prisoners assigned to work on rice details all hoped they would be sent on a truck to load the rice. While the work assignment was demanding, there were potential rewards for those who were able to get out of camp. The Filipinos sometimes gave them food items when the Japanese guards relaxed their vigil. The generous Filipino givers risked a severe beating or even the loss of life if they were caught giving food or cigarettes to POWs.

Next came the problem of keeping the gifts out of sight of the Japanese guards. Over a period of time we became rather skilled at outfoxing those miserable creatures. It wasn't unusual for one to be caught and severely beaten, but the reward was worth the risk.

The wood detail was another sought-after work assignment. While the rice detail required a great deal of heavy work, those on the wood detail rode in the trucks to the town of O'Donnell, where they would load the trucks with small bundles of wood stacked for them by the Filipino workers who were in the wood-selling business. Once the trucks were loaded with firewood for the kitchens, those with half-decent guards were permitted to accept gifts from the Filipinos. Back in camp the men would often be searched by a different group of guards, who would confiscate items received and would beat the men for having the goods in their clothing.

Each day after the more able-bodied men were chosen for Japanese work details, others not too ill to work would be assigned to guard duty or to the burial detail. Never were the burial details able to dig graves as fast as they were needed.

Early each morning the burial detail went to the hospital area and all helped to dig a large square hole. The ground was hard and the men were in weakened condition, so the progress was slow. By midafternoon the men would stop digging, and groups of four would shoulder rickety wooden litters and head for the large hospital building.

This was a horrible experience for those involved. The building was nothing but an empty shell filled with stink, filth, swarms of flies, the dead, and the dying. Once placed in this building a man was most surely doomed. With no medicine and flies crawling over everything, recovery was practically impossible. One thing for damned sure, these men were never bothered by the Japanese, who completely avoided the place.

Inside the building men were lying on the wooden floors with barely room to walk among them. The wooden litters were too large and cumbersome to go through the doors, so they were stacked outside while the workers went inside to separate the dead from the dying. This was no simple task because so many, while not completely lifeless, were near death.

Although the detail members were reluctant to touch the dead because of the filth and the consequent possibility of becoming ill, they had no alternative. Bodies pulled from the filth in which they had been lying, many for days, were dragged out of the building and each placed on a litter. They were then carried to the newly dug grave and piled in. When the hole was filled to capacity, the workers covered the bodies with the dirt that had been shoveled out of the ground earlier. The dead of the day who wouldn't fit into the hole had to be put on the waiting list for another day.

The next day's detail on arriving at the burial site would find that roving dogs had dug into the grave during the night to eat their fill. That was almost more of a terrifying experience than to go into the hospital building, and one that left the workers shaken and terribly angry.

There were times when we were angrier at the American politicians for permitting this terrible tragedy to happen than we were at the Japanese for not providing help to those who were so sick and needed it desperately. We wished we could have taken pictures of the Death March and the subsequent conditions in Camp O'Donnell to show to the Americans back home. There were times when those responsible at home for allowing these horrible tragedies were perceived as the greater criminals. No government, and especially not ours, should have ever forfeited the lives of thousands of soldiers. Theirs was a crime committed against us and against our families at home. We felt we had served our country as well as we possibly could have under the conditions imposed upon us by those in authority in the United States. While we prayed that the Japanese who so horribly mistreated us would be made to pay, I included in my prayers a request for an accounting by those in our government who had, in effect, turned us over to the Japanese to do with as they pleased.

One of the first men whom I helped bury at O'Donnell was Corky. He was the guy at Clark Field who hit the foxhole with both fists full of cigars when it was being attacked by Japanese bombers. Dysentery had been the cause of his death. Sergeant Nyberg, from Boise, Idaho, who survived the first attack of Zero fighters with me behind the sandpile, died a few days later, also from dysentery.

Litter bearers carrying Filipino dead out of camp seemed to be on the road twenty-four hours of each day. Our forty to fifty deaths daily were few compared to the numbers of Filipino soldiers dying.

While the burial detail was a terrible work assignment, the bodies of our men had to be cared for. No one was willing to deny colleagues of war a resting place, even though it was a totally unacceptable one.

After nearly two weeks of in-camp details, Norm, Dick, and I were assigned to the rice detail and went on trucks to Capus. Each of us climbed on a different truck, hoping that at least one of us would be lucky enough to get extra food.

In Capus we carried the fifty-kilo bags of rice from a warehouse to boxcars for shipment out of the area. Normally, the work would not have been difficult, but in our weakened condition we suffered greatly. None could pick a bag of rice off the ground, so two men boosted a bag to our backs. Unless the one-hundred-and-ten-pound rice bags were properly balanced on our backs, we would be thrown off balance and would fall, often with the bag of rice on top of us. This would anger the guards and often earn us a kick as we struggled to our feet.

At noon on this day when we were given a short break to eat our cold rice and eggplant, a Filipino lady gave me a bottle of catsup. Someone else gave Norm a can of corned beef. That night back in camp we had a banquet of rice and corned beef, covered with catsup. We ate all of the corned beef but limited ourselves on the catsup, thinking of future meals. The meal wasn't as good as hamburgers smothered in onions, pickles, catsup, and mustard, but it wasn't bad after just rice and eggplant. We weren't experiencing any hunger pangs right then, that's for sure.

A few mornings later I was again assigned to the rice detail. Norm was to walk guard, and Dick was too ill to work. Neither of us had been infected with either dysentery or malaria to date. Dick just had a bad cold. There wasn't water for use in washing our mess kits so we just stood them in the sun whenever that was out, hoping that the heat would sterilize them after the morning and noon meals. We knew it was imperative we take every precaution possible against contracting dysentery. There was little we could do to prevent mosquitoes from biting us.

When the rice-loading detail arrived at the Japanese guardhouse, I, unfortunately, along with about twenty other men, was assigned to remain in camp to unload the trucks as they arrived. We were all terribly disappointed that we weren't able to get out of camp, because there was absolutely no chance for securing many sought-after items within camp.

We had been working at our assignment for several hours and were standing among the storage buildings waiting for more loads of rice to arrive. I was in the shade, leaning against a building. One of the fellows, sitting on a step of an adjacent building, after looking carefully in all directions, got up and slipped inside the shack. In a matter of seconds he emerged from the building and sat down on the step again. His companion then arose and walked away. The step sitter was then joined by another fellow who shortly ducked into the building.

When he reappeared, I walked over and took my place on the step when it was vacated.

"Back in the corner in a pile of straw are some sugar cakes. When I give you the word, slip inside and get yourself some. Don't be inside too long. If I see a Jap coming, I will give you the word."

I needed no more encouragement, and when the word "go" was given, I went. I cinched up the belt on my dirty coveralls, and with hands shaking from fright, I stuffed sugar cakes inside the coveralls against my skin. I could have taken more, but good judgment directed me to get out of the building before a guard spotted me.

Back on the step I scouted while one more fellow got his quota, and then I walked over behind another building to examine my loot.

The sugar cakes were flat on one side, about four or five inches in diameter, and oval on the other side. They consisted of raw, brown, only partially refined sugar molded into cakes for shipment by pony-back into areas difficult to reach by truck. They were also placed in the feed bags of small horses to give them quick energy. We had seen them before the war, but until now we had never paid serious attention to them. Now, they were a valuable commodity.

Breaking off a piece of the sugar, I stuffed it into my mouth. It didn't look clean, but it surely tasted good.

"What do you have?"

I spun around to confront a Filipino officer standing on the other side of the fence separating the Filipinos from the Japanese living area.

While I wasn't overly excited about the prospects of getting caught by the Japanese guards and punished for talking to Filipinos, I told him that I had some sugar cakes.

"Sell them to me," he said. "We don't ever have a chance to get anything like that, but we can get money."

"I don't want to sell these sugar cakes. We haven't had anything sweet for a long, long time, and I want to keep them."

"You'll get caught, and then you'll be in real trouble for stealing from the Japs. Just look at what your companions are doing now."

I turned to look and saw the guys had thrown off all caution and were boldly walking into the shack in numbers.

The Filipino officer was right, so I promptly sidled over to the fence and passed the sugar cakes to him. In return he passed to me a number of bills that he extracted from his shirt cuffs.

Quickly counting, I said to him, "Twenty pesos is a lot of money for sugar cakes."

"Money is nothing to us right now," he responded. "We have no trouble getting money into camp."

As the officer had predicted, we were in for trouble and shortly we were lined up and searched by angry guards who had learned of the loss of the sugar cakes. They gave severe beatings to those men with sugar cakes. Then we received a lecture on the seriousness of stealing from the Imperial Japanese Government. It was, we were told, a crime punishable by death. Thanks to the Filipino officer I had not only avoided a beating, but now I had twenty pesos to spend if I ever got out of camp on another work detail.

When we were finally released from our rice-unloading detail, I hustled back to Norm and Dick and divided with them the money I had acquired in hopes, if we ever did get on an out-of-camp work assignment, we would be able to buy from the Filipinos food that would supplement our diet of rice and eggplant. We felt extremely optimistic about the prospects.

At the same time we were counting our blessings over our good fortune, we couldn't help but recall with some sadness the great amount of money we had destroyed just prior to the take-over by the Japanese. Had we kept it, the Japanese would have taken it from us and perhaps we would have been punished. We concluded we should not be greedy and just hoped the money we now had could be used to good advantage.

The following day the opportunity came for all of us to be assigned to go together on the wood-hauling detail to the town of O'Donnell, which was some distance from our camp. We all assembled as usual in the area of the Japanese guardhouse, where we were assigned to trucks. For some reason there were more trucks involved than usual, but that meant there would be more wood to load. After the usual delay, our convoy moved off in the direction of the mountains to the west.

On reaching our destination, we merely had to load the trucks with bundles of wood that had been cut into small pieces and tied together by the Filipinos. Once the trucks had been loaded, we were seated on the load for the return trip. I don't know what agreement the Japanese had with the Filipinos for paying for the wood, but no money changed hands while we were watching. The Filipinos, however, seemed not at all reluctant to furnish the wood to the Japanese. Apparently, prior arrangements had been made.

While the Filipinos made no effort to communicate with us verbally, they would give us an occasional smile or a wink as if to tell us that they understood our situation fully and that we were still on the same side of this international conflict.

It had been the custom of the Japanese to stop their trucks in the town to enable them to purchase items for themselves. In the past there had been reported instances where especially generous guards permitted some Americans to negotiate with the Filipinos for a variety of useful items.

On this particular day the trucks did stop in town, and the guards on several of the trucks immediately authorized the POWs to make purchases. Our guard, however, only shook his head at our request. Down the line of trucks we could observe our colleagues getting sugarcane, canned items, and cigarettes. Luckily Norm, Dick, and I had been wise enough to get on different trucks, and it appeared that this pre-planning was going to pay off.

Finally, I was able to persuade the guard on our truck to let us purchase cigarettes. He reluctantly agreed that each of us could buy two cartons. The other fellows on my truck appeared to have money, which was by this time becoming fairly plentiful in camp, thanks to the Filipino prisoners.

At that time Filipino cigarettes were selling in town for two pesos for a carton of twenty packages of the long, brown smokes. In camp they were selling for two pesos a pack. I was overjoyed we were able to make these purchases because I knew cigarettes were much more sought after in camp than were other items. I would be able to use the cigarettes well for barter.

When our wood convoy finally arrived in camp, the Filipino prisoners, as usual, were crowding the fence separating the Japanese area from their own and making every effort to buy from us everything we had purchased. Because of their antics, our Japanese guards were becoming restless and feared they might be punished by their officers for permitting us to purchase items.

I moved over as close to the fence as I could. A Filipino asked me what I had, and I told him. He immediately offered to buy the cigarettes, and I hurriedly passed them through the fence to him and received the money, which I tucked safely away inside my dirty coveralls. It was a gamble on the part of both of us, because he didn't know I was selling what I said I had, and I didn't know how much money I would receive from the transaction. Everything had to be done hurriedly.

While those of us who were permitted to go out on work details took advantage of the Filipino soldiers in camp, they, in turn, had the money we so badly needed to buy items on future work details. It helped our consciences when the Filipinos assured us they had plenty of money. However, the peso was beginning to lose its original value because the Japanese had begun to print Filipino money.

When we returned to our camp area, I learned that Dick and Norm had been more fortunate than I and had been able to secure a few cans of food. One had bought several bottles of catsup, a much-sought-after delicacy that helped to make the rice much more palatable. They had spent what money they had, so I divided my cigarette money with them in hopes we would all be able to put our funds to good use later.

Several days of grave digging and guard duty passed before I was again assigned to the rice detail. This time I had the opportunity to go to Tarlac to help load the trucks. I was sure now I would be able to buy food, because this detail had the reputation for being the most sought-after of all of them.

While we were standing in the Japanese area waiting for trucks to assemble, large flights of now-familiar Japanese bombers flew over the camp. The Japanese guards with big grins on their faces looked at the bombers, then at us, and gleefully muttered, "Corregidor."

It was apparent the word had been passed to them, and they were enjoying a great deal of satisfaction knowing that Corregidor was being bombed by Japanese airplanes. We had no idea how the war was going, but one thing we knew for sure: we never saw any American planes in the skies over the prison camp.

I was heartbroken.

As we left the rice-loading area, I found myself on the last truck in the convoy. When we pulled onto the main road, a Filipino on a bicycle approached the back of the truck. The guard on the truck was looking ahead and paying no attention to me, so I asked the Filipino on the bike what he had in the basket. He told me that he had candy bars that he wanted to sell to me. When I asked him how much he wanted for them, he said he would have to have ten pesos for each of them. That was outrageous!

In prewar times these candy bars, which were made of melted brown sugar and large chunks of coconut and wrapped in banana leaves, could be purchased for just a few centavos. We never did buy any as we traveled through the countryside because we had been advised that they were not clean and we shouldn't take a chance of becoming ill from eating the stuff. It was now highly prized by the Filipino soldiers, who constantly asked us to try to find some for them.

I pulled my money out of my pocket and showed him I had a number of bills. On the outside was a ten-peso bill. Riding alongside the truck, he handed the candy to me as the truck began to pick up speed and told me to hand him the money. I reached it out to him and fully intended that he should have it. But, as the truck went faster, he dropped way back. He shouted me to drop the money, but I said he should catch up and take the money from me. Unfortunately, he was never able to overtake the truck. So, I returned to camp with several huge candy bars and my money also. Feeling absolutely no guilt whatsoever, I asked myself if I were beginning to behave like the Japanese whom I despised so thoroughly.

Upon our arrival in the unloading area, I immediately sensed that I should not have purchased anything. The Japanese guards, completely unpredictable always, today were angry over something. They were threatened by their NCOs, and the lowest ranking officer had the authority of the Emperor himself as far as the Japanese soldiers were concerned.

We were ordered to line up to be searched, but in the confusion I quickly moved over to the fence separating the Filipinos from the Japanese area, shoved the candy through the fence, and took the money that was pushed into my hand. The money I quickly put out of sight and moved over into line in time to be searched. By now the searching didn't bother me quite as much as it had earlier, but I wasn't eager to be battered about if it could be avoided. It was becoming somewhat routine to most of us, and we chalked each experience up as being another reason for getting our revenge, hopefully, in the not-too-distant future.

The money I pushed down in the shoe that didn't contain the can with the quinine pills. As often as I had been searched, not once did any guard give attention to my shoes.

When I arrived back in our section of the camp, I found this new money, added to what I already had, totaled nearly one hundred pesos. Norm and Dick had ample funds for purchases they might be able to make, so we felt we were about out of the woods as far as financial transactions were concerned. By the time we used the funds we had accumulated, the war should be over.

Because of our activities on the work details, the three of us were able to bring in various items of food almost daily and were able to share some of this with fellows from our squadron who were too sick to work. By this time rice had become an enjoyable part of my diet, and I found myself gaining strength daily. For sure, I could handle sacks of rice with much greater ease than when we first arrived in O'Donnell. The constant carrying of loads of rice and serving on the water detail were beginning to impact negatively on my back and my knees. At times they were so stiff and sore from the work that the pain became fairly intense. However, there was much work to be done, and the Japanese weren't about to show any consideration for their coolies. That is what we had become.

Six or seven weeks had passed since our surrender, and during all this time none of us had been able to take a bath or to have our hair or whiskers cut. We were filthy beyond belief from the dirt and the sweat, and our hair and beards had become matted. Why I didn't become ill, I'll never know. This was proof that one had to be more than just dirty to feel ill.

We finally heard that Corregidor had fallen but had no way of verifying that rumor. It didn't come as a surprise to us because of the intensity of the shelling of that small island even as early as the time of the fall of Bataan. Sooner or later the troops on Corregidor would have to turn the fortress over to the Japanese.

I had been able to trade food items for one-half of a pup tent, but there weren't any other clothing or bedding items for trade. I still had the pair of coveralls, but by this time my socks were worn out. My clothing consisted of shoes, coveralls, and a khaki hat that I had received earlier in trade for my steel helmet. My other possessions were a canteen, a cup, the bottom part of a mess kit, a spoon, and the small can of quinine pills.

Norm and Dick and I made arrangements with one of our squadron members, too sick to work, to guard our few food possessions and the other items while we were on work detail. For the service rendered, we divided our food supply with him at mealtime.

By late May there was so much sickness in camp that anyone who was well enough to do hard work was required to go on an outside work detail for the Japanese each day. By this time hundreds of Americans had died and had been buried at O'Donnell. Prospects of our surviving as prisoners weren't too good, so there wasn't much to be happy about except the fact that we were still alive. We had been so sure that the Americans would retake the Philippines and liberate us within a few months, but it now appeared the Japanese had little concern over having to do battle again with the Americans in the Philippines in the very near future. They had become more demanding and more difficult in general and clearly demonstrated they had little respect for us or concern for our welfare. The more deaths, the fewer they would have to feed.

It was our impression they were stripping the Philippines of everything they could use, so we gave the Filipinos credit for providing the rice and eggplant for us. The adequate servings of rice and eggplant we were given following our arrival in camp had by now been reduced dramatically. So, we had to scrounge more and more for additional food every time we were out on work detail.

*(Opposite above)* Clark Field, 1941

*(Opposite below)* Officers of the 20th Pursuit Squadron. Commanding officer, first Lieutenant Joseph H. Moore, middle row, fourth from left. Courtesy Harold Poole

FORT STOTSENBERG

Post Exchange

Bachelor Officers' Quarters

CLARK FIELD

AIR STRIP

Operations Shack

New shacks for enlisted men

Mess shack

H

H

H

H

H

S

Supply shack

H = Hangars

Officers and men of the 20th Pursuit Squadron. Staff Sgt. Jacobsen *(note arrow)* at left edge of right-hand portion of photo. Courtesy Harold Poole

*(Opposite)* Military port area, Manila Bay, 1941

The Philippines

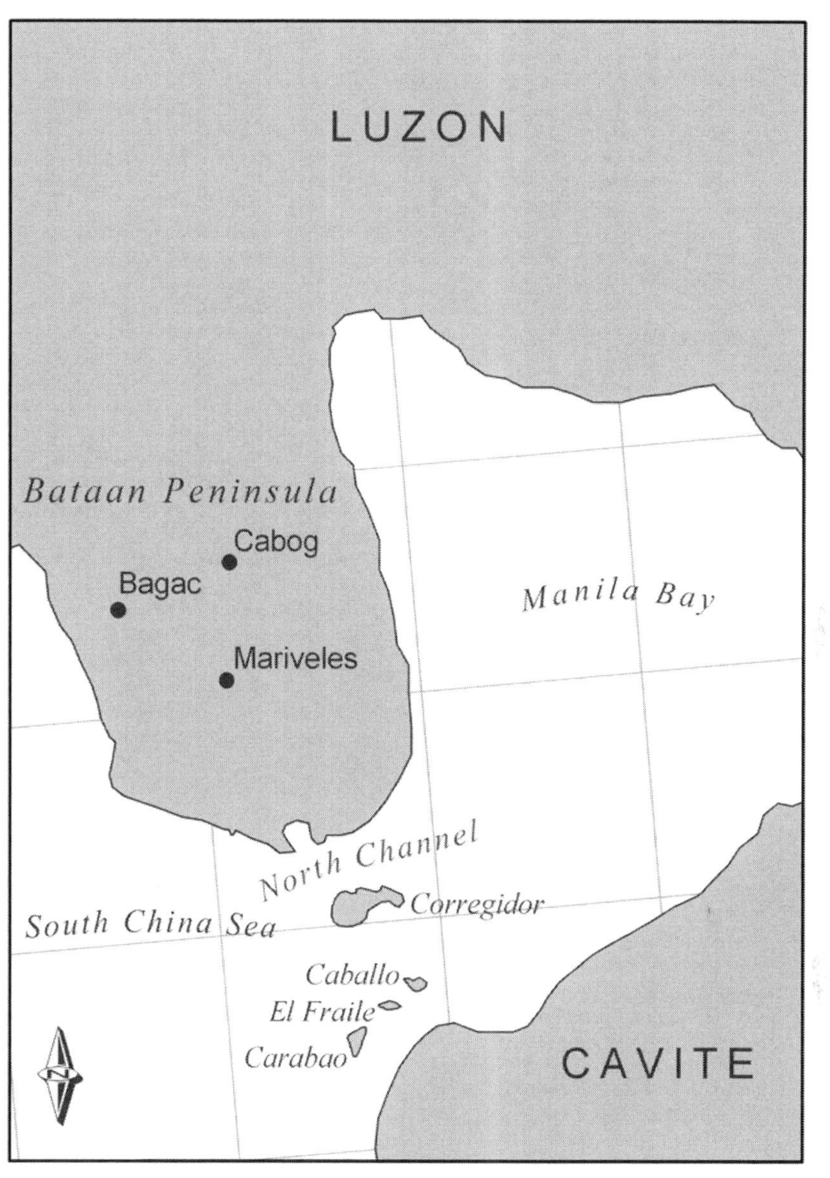


Bataan Peninsula, Philippines

CAPTURE

Many American and Philippine fighters are captured individually and in small groups before they reach the southern tip of Bataan at the mouth of Manila Bay. Two are forced to kneel along an ammunition trail while Japanese soldiers kick dirt on them, signifying that the prisoners are as low as dirt. By Benjamin Steele.

Beginning the March

After capture, 8,000 American and approximately 40,000 Philippine troops begin the march back up the Bataan Peninsula, staggering along the road for ten days to two weeks. A Japanese soldier wipes his bayonet after killing a POW who has fallen out. By Benjamin Steele.

Death march. Courtesy Roger Mansell.

Death Marchers Drink from Mud Holes

With temperatures around 100 degrees, many men die from thirst. The Japanese have made no provision to supply water on the march. In desperation men lie on the ground to drink from a mud hole. By Benjamin Steele.

THE STRAGGLERS

Men unable to continue the march are killed by guards. Fellow prisoners dare not intervene. By Benjamin Steele.

Eating Sugar Cane

When Japanese guards are not too close, marchers break off into the cane fields for food. If caught with any cane, a prisoner might be beaten or killed. By Benjamin Steele.

Some were forced to march with bound hands. Courtesy Roger Mansell.

Rules and Regulations
Death march prisoners go to Camp O'Donnell, a former Philippine Constabulary camp. They are told first by a Japanese officer, then an interpreter, what they must do to survive in the camp. By Benjamin Steele.

C A M P   O' D O N N E L L



Camp O'Donnell

His Own

Approximately 2,300 Americans die and are buried at Camp O'Donnell the first six weeks of internment. A soldier is forced to dig his own grave. Perhaps he tried to hit a Japanese guard or he possessed Japanese currency. By Benjamin Steele.

TAYABAS ROAD

With conditions so bad at Camp O'Donnell, prisoners volunteer for work details. On the Tayabas road detail, men walk twenty-six miles in from the railroad. The sick are carried on doors. The road is built during the rainy season, July through August, with no shelter or blankets and twelve-hour work shifts. Of the 325 men assigned to the project, only about fifty survive. By Benjamin Steele.

Tayabas Road Hospital

Prisoners too weak to make shelters for themselves lie on neap leaves on the wet ground. Rain and typhoons add to the misery. At the end of the two-month road detail only five or six "workers" can walk. By Benjamin Steele.

Burial on Tayabas

Tayabas Road created countless "unknown soldiers." The dead are placed in individual graves with their dogtags tied to crossed sticks. The graves are on a floodplain, and many bodies wash away or are covered by the jungle.
By Benjamin Steele.

INCENTIVE TO WORK

The Japanese are hard taskmasters. Sick men are beaten for not working fast enough to suit the guards. By Benjamin Steele.

Tayabas Trenches

Straddle trenches are used as latrines on the detail. Some of the men are so ill from the effects of rain, hard work, dietary deficiency, and tropical diseases that they fall dead in the trenches. Lean-tos of neap palm leaves form the only shelter. By Benjamin Steele.

*(Opposite above)* Bilibid Prison in Manila. Courtesy Roger Mansell.

*(Opposite below)* Cabanatuaan Prison Camp

FARM AREA

CABANATUAAN PRISON CAMP

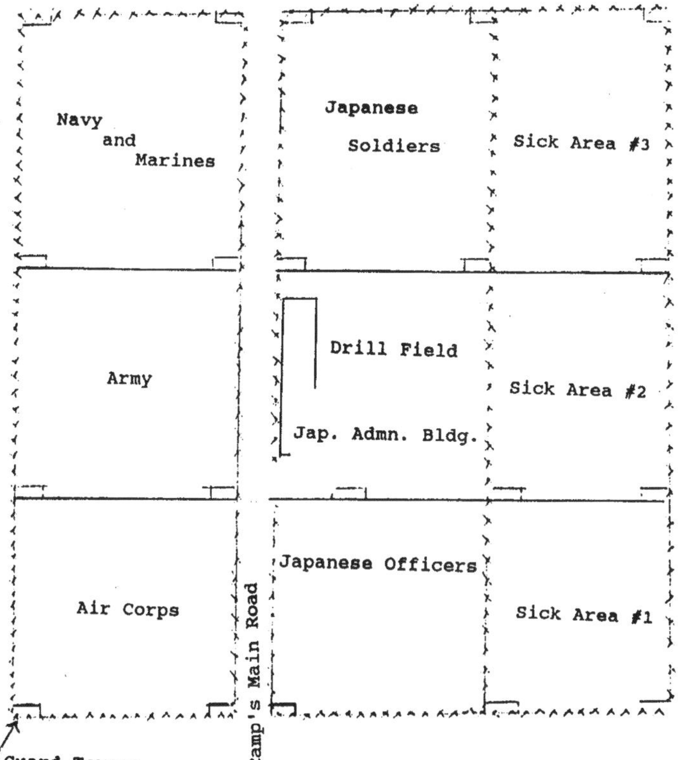

CHOWLINE AT CABANATUAAN

Men line up to receive their rations of rice and soup. If they are lucky, there will be fishheads in the soup. Sometimes they are given green fish that is rotten. Once in a while the soup contains kelp. By Benjamin Steele.

# 12

# THE TAYABAS WORK DETAIL

ONE MORNING, AS WE FELL OUT for work I was told to assist with guard duty for the day. I didn't mind the assignment, although it denied me the opportunity to purchase the additional food we so badly needed. Norm and Dick went, however, and I knew they would do well without me. I did hate to see us separated even for the day because we had become so dependent upon each other for moral support. We talked with each other a great deal and made every effort to be optimistic, even in spite of our predicament.

Shortly after twelve o'clock Japanese officers came to our section of the camp and directed the American officers to select from among the prisoners three hundred men to go on a special work detail. The Americans informed them that all of the able-bodied men were already on assignment and the only ones left in camp were those who were really too sick to do hard work.

The Japanese were insistent, and the American officers in charge were able to comply with the demand only by gathering together three hundred of the oddest assortment of men ever assembled. I was one in the group selected, and although I did everything I could do to convince the officers that I couldn't leave Norm and Dick, I was forced to go. This was most depressing for me. I didn't realize it then, but I was never to see either of my two buddies again.

The Japanese gave no information concerning the nature of the detail, but they did tell us that we would be out overnight so we should take with us our canteens and other personal belongings. Most of the men had nothing more than their canteens and mess kits. I did have the shelter half.

I sadly gathered my things and along with the other men walked down to the Japanese area. Before departing, I did leave word for Norm and Dick that I would probably be seeing them shortly.

One American officer accompanied us to the guardhouse where we always assembled for out-of-camp assignments, and right up to the time we were loaded into trucks, he pled with the Japanese not to take us out on detail. By this time many of us were suffering from beriberi, and he pointed to the swollen feet and legs. Most of us were thin, and we and our clothing were filthy. The long hair and shaggy beards didn't help our appearance, either.

The officer did his very best to impress the Japanese we were in terrible physical condition and assured them that if taken away to work, many of us most surely would not survive. All of his words fell on deaf ears. The Japanese could not have cared less.

After an hour or so of delay, we moved out and down the road toward San Fernando. Had Norm and Dick been with me, I would have felt good about leaving O'Donnell because most of the memories of that place were anything but pleasant. Now, I was alone again and found myself becoming terribly depressed when I should have been happy for the ride through the beautiful Filipino countryside.

By nightfall we had reached the city of Manila, and there we were put into an old civilian prison in the heart of the city. We were not given food, not unusual for the Japanese.

It was dark when we arrived at the prison, and in the morning we left before it was daylight. Thus, we had little opportunity to observe our surroundings.

In the trucks once again, we rode south of Manila to a school in the vicinity of Nichols Field that was used for housing prisoners of war. The men there informed us that theirs was a death detail. They were also suffering from dysentery, malaria, and beriberi, and the Japanese were demanding work from them completely beyond their ability to produce.

They were working as coolies to assist in the enlargement of Nichols Field, and each morning the work details were assigned a quota of work to complete.

Food was as scarce as it had become in Camp O'Donnell, and the treatment was brutal. If possible, the men in this camp were in even more serious condition than were we. We became alarmed that this was going to be our place of work.

We remained in the small compound all the rest of that day and one night and until noon on the following day. Those of our group who were too sick to go on were left there and were replaced by more able men from the Nichols Field work detail. Our work assignment apparently took precedence over that one, and many from the Nichols Field group were eager to go with us. In fact, they were eager to go anywhere to get away from the terrible situation in which they found themselves.

From the school yard we walked to the railroad station, where we were put on flatcars. Here we sat until late afternoon, when the train finally got under way and headed south. Our train rattled along during the rest of the day and all night and most of the following day. It stopped often, however, for unexplainable reasons.

The second night the three hundred of us were grouped together in an old lime-kiln area. There, each of us received a serving of rice and a can of corned beef. I located in the group two other men who were from my squadron, a fellow by the name of Lloyd from Montana, and one named Ed. The latter was from Wyoming. Although we had never been close friends in the squadron, the three of us felt a common bond and enthusiastically agreed to be buddies and to help each other as best we could.

We ate our issue of rice and divided one can of corned beef among the three of us. After the long fast we found this meal to be unbelievably good and most satisfying.

The following morning we again climbed aboard the flatcars and continued our journey south. During the day the train stopped out in the jungle somewhere, and while we didn't have any rice, the three of us shared the second can of corned beef. That evening we reached the end of the railroad. There, we were given a small ration of rice, and together we finished the third can of meat.

None of us had any idea where we were, and the Japanese didn't seem at all inclined to discuss with us our location or the type of work in which we were to be engaged. After dark, around nine or ten o'clock, the Japanese led us out of the field where we had been assembled and grouped us together on a road. Then we had to move south once again.

We were in no physical condition for another forced march, and while conditions were not nearly as difficult as they had been on the Bataan Death March, we suffered considerably throughout the long night. During the march we had an occasional rest break, but these were short. Almost all of the entire night was spent marching.

Some of the men who were too weak to continue the walking just dropped out. What happened to them, I don't know. My feeling was their chances of survival were much better then than they had been earlier during the march off Bataan when we were with guards just fresh from combat.

Those of us who were in better physical condition had the added misery of carrying the heavy field packs belonging to the Japanese guards. They hadn't been directed by their superiors to have us carry their gear, and when the Japanese commander, an older officer with advanced rank, became aware of what was going on, he harshly reprimanded his men. From that time on, they carried their own field packs.

By morning it was an exhausted group of men who reached the end of the road. There, immediately in front of us, was a huge mountain of something covered with heavy sections of canvas. The Japanese officer in charge, who spoke very good English, directed several prisoners to remove the canvas from the pile. In this heap of goods were sacks of rice, many cases of American corned beef, corned beef hash, salmon, and sardines.

We couldn't believe our eyes!

"If we only could have had this food on Bataan!" I thought, and once again felt a surge of anger toward MacArthur.

After the chatter of the men subsided, the officer told us we would be on this work detail for one month only. Our job, he explained, was to extend through the jungle to the coast the road on which we were standing. We also learned we were in the Province of Tayabas.

"There is more food here than you can possibly eat during this month. The Japanese are being very good to you because this is such is a very, very important assignment which you have. The distance to be covered isn't far, so you should be able to easily finish the work in the time assigned. Then, when the road is completed, you can return to your friends back in Camp O'Donnell."

Even though we were completely exhausted and bewildered, the sight of all the American canned food thrilled us. We just couldn't believe the Japanese were really going to be that generous. Before us was far more food than we had seen since before leaving Clark Field and managed properly it could sustain us and perhaps even help us to recover some of the strength and energy we had long since lost.

"Don't kid yourselves about them being generous," counseled one spokesman. "This stuff all came out of supplies left in the port area in Manila by the Quartermaster Corps. It's food we should have been getting on Bataan. Instead, MacArthur left it for the Japs. That's consistent with every other stupid thing that our great leaders have done since the outbreak of the war. Why they ever got us into war with the Japs without being prepared will always remain a mystery to me. Now, we are payin' for their stupidity, and they're home free and clear. It just ain't right! They ought to be forced to change places with us. Then they just might learn what the real world of war is like and not be so damned cocky. They play big shots, and we pay the penalty!"

There was considerable agreement among those close enough to hear the speech.

The Japanese officer further informed us that Japanese soldiers would be working on the road where we were presently standing, and we were to be assigned to a section farther along in the jungle.

With that introduction to our new temporary career, we were instructed to each take a case of canned food or half a sack of rice and proceed through the jungle to our new campsite. Those of us who were able to carry that much weight—fifty to sixty pounds—picked up our loads and started down the winding jungle path with the rest of the men following. The trail was only wide enough to accommodate one man at a time so, at least for a while, we were free from the babbling of the guards. With the exception of a few in the lead, the guards were the last along the trail.

The jungle through which we struggled for the next few hours was dense. Mammoth trees and heavy underbrush of many varieties of plants almost completely blocked out the sun, leaving the air close to earth heavy and damp. With frequent stops for rest, it wasn't until the middle of the afternoon that we arrived at our destination—a small clearing along the side of a shallow river. This, we were told, was to be the site of our bivouac.

No one within our group was assigned or offered to take charge. The several Japanese officers along seemed to want as little to do with us as possible, and we were not at all opposed to that relationship. It was quite apparent that little planning had gone into this work detail; it was more like one planned by American politicians in Washington or MacArthur in the Philippines. We began to be filled with doubts as to what the final results of this undertaking would turn out to be.

Within the group we finally reached consensus that all of the food should be stacked in a pile for the time being. It seemed we were not to make a return trip for more supplies that day, and while we were happy to have some free time for ourselves, we were concerned over the possibility of losing the balance of the food supplies designated for us.

Not having had a bath for over two months or the opportunity to wash my coveralls, I headed for the river. From a distance the water had looked clean but as I walked out into the stream, I could see pollution in the water and could feel the pollution once I had stripped off my coveralls and had begun to wash myself. The water felt slick and slimy. I wondered if I would be getting the river dirty or if the river would add to my already miserable and deplorable condition.

Without the benefit of soap, it took considerable scrubbing before my clothing and I looked and smelled more acceptable. Not having a change of clothing, I spread my coveralls out on low bushes and then went back into camp to get Lloyd's coveralls for washing. He was ill but with great effort accompanied me into the water where he sat and washed himself as I scrubbed his clothing. Ed was able to take care of his own needs.

In spite of the humidity, the sun fairly quickly dried our coveralls. Before putting mine on, I turned both Lloyd's and mine inside out, remembering vividly a time on Bataan when I pulled on coveralls that had been drying on the bushes only to be stung several times by a scorpion before I could grab it. The problem was compounded by the fact that I had one leg in the coveralls and was halfway into the second leg when the scorpion struck. I was able to hold him away from my leg but had to call for help to extract myself from the coveralls to enable me to turn the coverall leg inside out and extract the vicious beast. While the poison had not been strong enough to put me completely out of commission, for a few days I had difficulty walking because of the swelling and pain caused by the poison.

My long hair, daily getting longer, and my beard, bright red and curly, was way past the itching stage. My mustache was so long that it hung down over my upper lip and required constant effort to keep it out of the way of food at mealtime. The hair was the least of our worries, though, because we knew that the prospects of a shave and haircut in the very near future were not good. And we knew of no one who had died because of long hair on any part of his body.

Having no large vats or kettles in which to cook rice, each person did as best he could that evening to cook in his canteen cup or mess kit. Few knew much about the art of cooking anything, let alone rice. That much the Japanese could have taught us because each Japanese soldier on that detail was responsible for his own cooking. Their mess gear was properly designed for cooking rice. Right then they would have had receptive and appreciative students.

Lying under a huge tree, we didn't have any trouble falling asleep. However, during the night the rain soaked us, and by morning six men had died. We were instructed to bury our dead but had no shovels. The task had to be delayed until later.

Our high-priority responsibility that day was to move the balance of the food to the camp area. Everyone able to work walked back through the jungle to the supply dump. There, added to the pile of food, were shovels, picks, and iron-tired wheelbarrows. Each man selected his load, and we returned to camp.

Had all of our men been well, we could have easily made two trips each day, but as it was, one trip completely exhausted us. And, in spite of the fact we were told our project was most important, the Japanese seemed inclined not to exert much pressure on us. Perhaps they didn't want to make the second trip either. By the time we had the holes dug to bury our dead of the night before, two more men had died.

That evening we attempted to cook rice in one of the wheelbarrows. We washed the rice in the river, covered it with river water, and pushed the wheelbarrow over the fire. The results were disastrous. The rice on the bottom was burned black. That in the middle was gummy and horrible, and the rice on the top was still raw. Among all of those men present, no one had any experience cooking rice. The Japanese witnessed the revolting affair but at no time offered to provide any assistance. During the months the detail lasted, our rice-cooking efforts were almost totally unsuccessful.

By the end of eight days in the jungle, we had all of the food and work equipment moved into camp. Because several expressed concern the food would not be cared for properly if left in a general stockpile, another conference of the men was held. It was decided then the canned food should be divided equally among everyone, and everyone would have the responsibility for caring for his own supply. The rice was to be left in a common dump.

We formed a long line and marched by the food pile, each person taking four cans. The process was repeated until all the food had been distributed. Each of us had between seventy-five and a hundred cans of the various items. I initially avoided the corned beef hash and the sardines, but as everyone else seemed to have the same preferences, I ended up with a fair supply of these two food items, along with the salmon and the corned beef.

The three of us from our squadron had earlier selected a sleeping area under a huge tree, so we stacked our canned goods there along with our mess gear. During the day I covered the pile with my shelter half.

On the ninth day, under the watchful supervision of the Japanese guards, we took picks, shovels, and wheelbarrows and began to build a road. A Japanese engineer supervised the project and advised the guards to keep us working steadily. The ground was wet and soft, and the digging wasn't difficult. It was not intended that the road would be wide, so much of the dirt, once loosened, could be tossed off to one side or the other.

As our work progressed during the first day, we learned there were going to be obstacles. The ground was infested with huge roots, some supporting heavy vines and shrubs, but the tough roots from the enormous trees were like iron, and seemed to extend in all directions. Clearing out these troublesome tentacles by hand would have been difficult under the best of circumstances, but we had absolutely no cutting tools.

Had it not been for the roots, we would have built some road during that first day. However, because of the impediments, progress was extremely slow in spite of the continual prodding of the Japanese guards and the constant complaining of the engineer.

As a work force we were divided into small groups of from four to six men and assigned to various sections of the road-building project. Once the Japanese got the program organized to their satisfaction, they assigned two guards to each working group. One Japanese would actually stand guard while the other one directed our activities. Working for these Japanese who had fewer talents than most of us wasn't easy. They were extremely rigid, and everything had to be done their way. In addition, they constantly bullied us about the inferiority of the Americans and the fact that we were sick and weak while they were well and strong.

As the days passed, we found our supply of canned food was dwindling rapidly. At first the blame was placed on the more than one hundred sick men left in camp. Careful investigation, however, revealed they too had lost food. Filipinos, wise in jungle living, slipped into camp while we were away and were stealing all of the canned items. They were finally seen doing this, but the sick were too weak to protest or to prevent the looting. Soon, with nothing left but rice that we didn't know how to cook, the future once again looked almost completely hopeless.

In addition to all of our other problems, we found ourselves right in the middle of the rainy season. During the day the ground was slippery, and sticky mud was not only heavy but also was extremely difficult to move. At night we would return to camp only to be faced with the prospects of half-cooked rice and the knowledge we would be rained on more during the night as we tried to sleep.

The three of us tried to tie the shelter half up over us to shed the water, and while it did help, we were soaking wet most of the day and night. Each day we all grew weaker and more despondent. By the end of the second week twenty-one men had died. The following week seventeen more men had to be buried.

The work of the burial detail was extremely difficult. The Japanese, insisting that all able men report for work on the road, left burial work to those remaining in camp. Sick men were too weak to carry the dead bodies to the burial area and too weak to cut through the tangled jungle roots and vines as they tried to dig graves. Consequently, most of the digging and burying was done in the evenings by the working men as they returned from the day's work on the road. That placed an additional burden on them when they so badly needed good food and rest.

Lloyd, one of the three of us from my squadron, dropped out of work after about a week. He had earlier suffered from dysentery and was again struggling with the problem from which he had really never recovered. He would have had little appetite for the best of food in his condition, and what was available, he just couldn't eat. We did all that we could to cheer him and were able to keep him clean, but there was absolutely no medical assistance available to him or anyone else.

Prior to captivity I hadn't heard much about dysentery, but on the Tayabas work detail I observed firsthand how it claimed its victims. Initially, one who became infected would be plagued with diarrhea and the constant urge to have bowel movements. As the disease progressed, the person became deathly sick to his stomach and would become nauseated and dizzy and unable to eat. In the final stages, he would vomit blood and pass bloody pus-filled substance from the bowels. When we observed a man passing blood and pus, we came to know that death would not be far off.

One evening when we came into camp from working on the road, Lloyd talked with me about his parents and how he wished he could talk with his dad. He said, "I know that you are a member of the Church of Jesus Christ of Latter-day Saints. Some time ago Dad joined your church and was called to be Branch President in the area where we lived. On a number of occasions he tried to talk to me about his church because he felt so close to it and desperately wanted me to become a member, also.

"It was bad enough that I didn't have the courtesy to listen to what he had to tell me. I even made fun of his newly found religion. I am so sorry now I behaved that way. I know I am not going to survive this work detail and will be buried here in the jungle. That means I never will have the opportunity to tell Dad I really do love him and how sorry I am for not listening to him when he wanted to talk to me.

"I want you to promise you will do two things for me because I have a feeling you will get back home. First, I want you to personally bury me and make sure that I am buried deep in the ground where dogs or wild animals won't get to me. Then, when you get back home, find my dad and tell him how I feel about him. Don't describe to him the condition I am in but tell him you saw to it that I received a proper burial. Will you promise you will do those two things?"

I promised him I would find his parents in Montana if I lived through prison camp and would make it a point to deliver to his dad the message that he had given me for him. I also assured him I personally would bury him if he preceded me in death. Right then I wasn't overly optimistic concerning my chances for survival in this jungle hell.

The following morning as I left for work I placed him in a sitting position with his back against a large tree. By his side I left a canteen of water that I had boiled the evening before. He attempted a smile, but the effort seemed almost too great. That evening when I returned to camp he was dead, still sitting against the tree. His eyes were wide open.

I moved him to lay him down and found that, by pulling his coveralls tightly to one side, I could completely encircle his leg just below the thigh with my hand. He was just a shell of a man, and although he was fairly tall, he weighed far less than a sack of rice. He wasn't heavy to carry to the burial area where Ed and I laid him to rest in the damp, root-infested dirt of the jungle. While we were a long way from anywhere important to us, this jungle, far away from anyone or anyplace that we held dear, was the proper place for him to be buried. In death he would no longer suffer the insults and the abuses of the Japanese and would now be free from the pain of imprisonment. From the dreaded disease that was killing so many fellow prisoners he would also be safe. Just before covering his body with dirt, I gave a short prayer asking the Lord to protect our friend and this sacred piece of the jungle.

Convinced we had been completely abandoned by our own country, I felt it was proper that his final resting place should be in this foreign land. At least the Filipinos had joined with us in making an effort to save their country and each other, and that is far more than America had done.

Nearly half of our original three hundred men had died from dysentery and malaria during the first month in the jungle, and many of those still living were not far from death. Burying the dead had become an increasingly burdensome task. It took so much of our strength we seemed to have little left over for road work. The tough jungle vines and roots were terribly troublesome, and we weren't very strong any longer.

Daily the Japanese reminded us of our responsibility to complete the road. As the progress became slower and slower, they became more difficult. There was no doubt that pressure was being applied to them, and they merely passed their fears and frustrations on to us, compounded by their contempt for us as prisoners of war. Not having anticipated our loss of food, they had made no plans to provide more. Finally, they secured eggplant to supplement the soggy rice, but there was no longer any meat.

Each morning as we left our sleeping area, the guards joined us and made the entire day miserable for us. When we returned to camp in the evening, however, they went to their own camp, and we were left almost completely alone.

One night, to the amazement of those of us who were left, sixteen of our men escaped. No one remaining in the camp had heard of their plans. Or, if they had heard, they were not admitting as much.

The situation was almost funny. It wasn't until the work squads were formed that anyone realized men were missing. Even then, I don't think that it occurred to the Japanese that some might have left intentionally. To the best of my recollection, we had never been counted since arriving in the jungle, and to my knowledge, the Japanese had never posted guards during the night. Had we been smart enough and well enough, more of us could probably have joined those who were missing.

Once convinced the men had really left, the guards became very angry and sullen and rough with the rest of us. That day we didn't go to work but spent most of it being counted over and over. They had kept records of the number of deaths, so they knew how many live men should be left. My hunch was their greatest concern was what might happen to them for permitting so many men to escape, all at the same time. We were really pleased over the situation and hoped they would be seriously punished. We also hoped those who had left would be safe and would be able to contribute to the work of the underground. I personally hoped the loss of our canned food was in no way connected to their escape. I suspected Filipinos, many of whom were also suffering from food shortages, would have guided men to safety in exchange for canned food. Never once did I suggest there might be a connection, but I did give that possibility some thought. It was suggested by someone the escapees might even return with help and free the rest of us. That wasn't to happen, however.

Several patrols of Japanese guards went out searching for those who had left but never found the truant prisoners, as far as we ever knew. They never were returned to our camp, we did know. The Japanese divided those of us left in camp into squads of ten men each. They were supposed to have done this earlier, and promised to shoot all left in a squad if any member escaped. The situation was more serious because we really didn't know who the other members of our squad were. From then on, there was little talk of getting away, in spite of the fact that sixteen of our colleagues had apparently been successful.

We all tried desperately to avoid contracting dysentery. Flies were everywhere, and it was almost impossible to keep them from crawling over the soggy rice. We knew that these same flies had visited those who had dysentery. Some days the sun just didn't shine, so we couldn't sterilize our mess kits from its rays. Before eating, we held them over the fire until they turned black. While that didn't do much to improve the flavor of the rice, it was tough on the dysentery germs, we were sure.

Through constant care and effort, I was one of the fortunate ones who avoided the dreaded disease. However, I was suffering from a variety of other illnesses, as were others. Each morning I was terribly stiff and sore all over, and it was difficult for me to get the joints functioning. We worked in the rain and slept in the rain and on the damp ground. I also had contracted hepatitis, and my eyes and body had turned yellow. That would have been embarrassing if so many others had not been suffering from the same problem. My feet and ankles and my legs as far up as the knees were swollen, and daily it was becoming more difficult for me to stand and especially to walk. I had developed a deep cough and also suffered from pellagra, which caused sores to break out on the backs of my hands and on the backs of my knees. The pellagra blisters, purple in color when they formed, eventually broke and left open sores that became filled with dirt.

Malaria became my biggest problem and challenge. In its early stages I experienced mild chills and fever, but as the days passed, the chills and fever became much more severe, and I began to experience attacks daily. One morning, shortly after we had arrived on the road, I felt chills beginning once again. I had remembered well what the medic back on Bataan had said when he gave me the fifteen five-grain quinine pills.

"Keep these pills until you absolutely need them, and then take them!" he had said forcefully.

To myself I said that morning, "The time has come for me to take the pills."

I still carried the pills in the small round coffee can. This I had pushed down in the top of my shoe dozens of times when I had been searched. I had watched over them as though they were diamonds and felt just as strongly about them. Many times I could and probably should have given them to others suffering from malaria, but I didn't. I suppose I might have given them to a close friend but was never confronted with that decision because all close friends who had died to date had done so as a result of dysentery, rather than from malaria. In fact, I couldn't recall that anyone whom I had known had suffered from both dysentery and malaria at the same time.

Now, under the pretense of going to "benjo" (toilet), I dumped all fifteen five-grain quinine pills into the palm of my hand and, with a drink of river water from my canteen, gulped them down. I must not have been completely rational, or I would not have done such a foolish thing. As it was, I felt that I did exactly what the medic had told me to do.

I remember returning to the road work detail and beginning to work again. Then, all went blank.

When I awakened, I was lying on my back by the side of the road, the rain beating steadily on my face. I felt like I couldn't move, and not seeing anyone around, I called to the other fellows. Shortly, two appeared and helped me to my feet. By this time the road had become too muddy for the work to continue, so we left for camp. With help from the others, I made the short trip, but was terribly weak and dizzy.

After the death of so many of our men and as a result of much pleading, the Japanese had finally provided several large tents for us. After that, we each had our own spot of firm dry ground.

Sick and exhausted, I fell to the ground under the tent and promptly passed out again.

As if drugged completely, I slept through the balance of the day and all night. When I awakened the following morning, I was weak but was in good spirits. That was the last malaria attack I ever had, even though I spent several more years in areas thoroughly infected with the malaria-carrying mosquito.

The large dose of quinine I took must have not only destroyed the malaria I had in my system but also provided complete immunity from further malaria attacks during the following thirty-eight months of internment. It also could be that I had received a bit of help from a loving Lord on that occasion.

It became difficult for us to keep track of days of the week or the month but during the latter part of August, we were still plugging along. By this time we had lost somewhere between two hundred and two hundred and fifty of our men from disease. Then there were the sixteen who had escaped into the jungle.

We hadn't built much road, and it must have finally become apparent to the Japanese that we were a lost cause as far as being road builders. Scarcely more than a dozen men were able to report to work, and we were all sorry-looking individuals. Our clothing was dirty and ragged. My shoes had earlier rotted away from wear and from the mud. It hadn't mattered much to me. Because of swollen feet I couldn't have gotten them on anyway.

With our long, matted hair and beards, we looked more like wild animals than American soldiers. We were emaciated humans, most suffering from jaundice, with swollen feet and legs caused by beriberi, and made uglier by raw, infected sores.

From where the food was stacked originally, Japanese workers had completed the road to the river where we were bivouacked and were presently building a bridge across the river. Trucks were able to reach that point.

One morning of what was to become one of the happiest days of my life, we were informed by the Japanese that we were to be taken out of the jungle. We didn't believe what we were told, but a short time later trucks arrived for us. I have little recollection of exactly how many of us were still living, and the details of the trip back to Manila are extremely fuzzy in my mind. I do remember I was in good spirits in spite of the pain from the variety of medical problems. We were down but not completely beaten yet. It was helpful knowing that so far we had won out over disease, the jungle, the rains, and the miserable Japanese guards who served so effectively as our tormentors.

# 13

# BILIBID PRISON

BILIBID PRISON IN THE CITY of Manila was an old civilian facility abandoned by the government years earlier when the new prison was built some distance from the city. Completely surrounded by high walls and divided across the middle by another high wall, it was put into service once again, we were told, to serve as both prisoner of war camp and an internment facility for political prisoners. On arrival from Tayabas, we joined other POWs in one-half of the huge compound. What went on in the adjacent section, we never learned. Many rumors floated about telling of the brutality of the Japanese with the captured civilians. We had no way of knowing whether these were true or not, but to date most of the rumors that we had heard and shared proved to be less than accurate and true.

Sometime after our first visit to Bilibid Prison prior to the work assignment in the jungles of Tayabas, the American Navy hospital at Cavite was taken as a unit by the Japanese and moved with all of its equipment, medicine, and staff into the prison where we found ourselves once again. The Americans, by declaring Manila an open city, had saved the city from destruction by the Japanese and, by doing so, had also helped the fortunate American prisoners who later were to benefit from the expertise of the Navy medics.

To be taken as a prisoner to Bilibid in the early days of the internment period was a great stroke of luck for me. There, all of us from the Tayabas detail were given the best medical attention the Navy medics could extend to us.

My weight upon our arrival at Bilibid was slightly over one hundred pounds. I had lost sixty pounds since the outbreak of the war. Close examination by the doctors revealed I was suffering from malnutrition, in general, and beriberi and pellagra, specifically. By this time my feet and legs were terribly swollen. The swelling not only made it more difficult for me to walk and to work, there was also considerable pain associated with the disease. We later learned the beriberi resulted from a diet of polished rice and little else. Actually it results from the lack of thiamin. The pellagra caused purple blisters to develop on the backs of my hands and on the backs of my knees. The blisters eventually broke, leaving some scarring.

Hepatitis caused the yellowing of my skin and eyes and resulted in a damaged liver, which was diagnosed following the termination of hostilities. I was also diagnosed as having tuberculosis in its early stages. The deep cough that I had developed caused the doctors to be suspicious, and a skin test verified the problem.

We were assigned to buildings and bedded down on old mattresses on the cement floor. After sleeping on the ground for five months, I found the mattress wonderful, even though it was lumpy and damp resulting from the high humidity in the Philippines and moisture from the cement floor.

I was counseled to keep my legs elevated as much as possible. Twice daily we were visited by the Navy doctors and were given every consideration and courtesy. We began to feel almost like human beings once again.

My shoes were past history, and my coveralls were filthy rags. The medics found a pair of khaki shorts for me but no shirt. At night I suffered from the cold, but after Tayabas, I wasn't about to let a little cold weather worry me. For the time being I was still alive. And, looking about, I could see fellows who were in much worse physical condition than was I. One fellow, two mattresses over from me and also a survivor of the Tayabas work detail, was so swollen from beriberi that it looked as though he could burst at any moment. He was just one huge blob. I felt sorrier for him than for myself.

My turn to get a haircut and a shave came a few days after arrival in Bilibid. My hair and whiskers had been growing unbothered by soap for nearly five months, and they were in bad condition. Since my hair was blond and straight, I couldn't understand why my beard would be dark red and curly.

A Navy chief was serving as camp barber. As he clipped me bald and cut the whiskers on my face with a pair of hand clippers, he expressed disgust over the filth and scales he uncovered as the hair gave way. I was embarrassed over his rude remarks, but since he had not been subjected to either the war or the ordeals of Japanese work details, how could he have known what we had faced? He did give me a bar of soap and some encouragement, although I really didn't need the latter. I was well motivated, lacking only the water and equipment to get the much-needed job done.

After a thorough scrub and a shave with a sharp mess-kit knife, I looked skinnier than ever. My eyes had sunk deep into their sockets, and my cheekbones protruded. The humorous part was that those of us who had met after beards had grown didn't recognize each other once the long hair and beards had been removed.

In Bilibid the medicine wasn't plentiful, so it was administered sparingly and where it could do the most good.

We received three small meals a day. Although the diet consisted of rice and soup, the food was well prepared, and those of us who could mend began to recuperate. This camp, we learned, was a place where the sick and disabled were sent between work details to be patched up. Our chances of remaining in Bilibid very long were slim, for as soon as one was able to do hard work once again, he was taken by the Japanese to be assigned to one of the many work details in the islands of the Philippines. Some were also being sent to Japan.

Because of my weight loss, beriberi, and serious malnutrition, I was assured I wouldn't be leaving for a few weeks, so I made the most of the chance for rest. When given the opportunity, I hobbled around the camp to keep from getting too stiff, but I was grateful I was freed from hard work, at least temporarily.

During my confinement in Bilibid Prison I was able to assist a fellow who was too sick and weak to take care of himself. He was soft-spoken and very thin. I carried his food to him and fed him all that he would eat. He never had much of an appetite, and when he couldn't take more food, he motioned for me to eat what was left. I was always hungry but felt guilty eating his food when he needed it so badly. He seemed to get some satisfaction out of watching me eat with considerable enthusiasm and as I busied myself around him. And, although he didn't respond verbally, he liked to have me talk to him about home and about things in general.

In spite of the best efforts of the Navy staff to help him, he died. He just went to sleep one night, and in the morning he was dead. This was a difficult experience for me because, although by this time I had seen death come often and in many ways, this fellow had become something special to me, and the opportunity to be of service to him, even in a small way, was extremely satisfying. He had helped me to feel needed and good about myself once again.

I thought about him a lot and was lonely without him. Interestingly, I didn't learn much about him—didn't know what outfit he belonged to or where his home was in the States. He just didn't have the strength to talk about those things.

After his death, the Navy doctor who had been attending him gave me his shoes. They were good shoes but were small for me because of my swollen feet. By slitting them across the top of the toes, I was able to wear them later. So, I just tied them together by the laces and hung them up for use again when I was assigned to my next work detail. Around camp most everyone went without shoes or got along with wooden sandals fashioned out of chunks of wood lying around the prison. I greatly appreciated the leather shoes because they were sort of special.

Each person or group to come into Bilibid Prison brought new tales of atrocities and new rumors. We literally thrived on rumors. Some of them were so fantastic it was amusing, but nevertheless they were listened to attentively.

Rumors were divided into categories as follows: those that had to do with food packages we were to receive from home and from the Red Cross, those that had the United States winning the war in the Pacific and moving in on the Philippines momentarily, those having us go to work details in all directions, those dealing with the transfer of all POWs to Japan, those having Japan attempting to negotiate a surrender, and on and on.

From the men arriving from work details we occasionally learned of our friends and of the conditions on the various work details in the Islands. Some of those projects were to be avoided at any cost because they were mean. All were bad. Everyone could cite from firsthand experiences tales of atrocities and brutality on the part of the Japanese. Here in Bilibid I also learned the details of the fall of Corregidor, our last stronghold and our last hope of early repatriation.

After nearly four months of excellent treatment and care by the Navy doctors, I was declared to be as fit as could be expected under the conditions of the times and went to the building occupied by those ready for work assignment. From there I could only guess where I might go next.

Christmas of 1942 came and went like any other day with one exception, an incident that caused our morale to soar. During the middle of the afternoon word was passed quietly that there would be an assembly of POWs in the northern compound. That area, formerly death row and the location of the execution chamber, was rarely frequented by the Japanese guards. Quickly but quietly the men assembled, then just as quickly two fellows spread out before us a large American flag. Underneath was a large printed sign: "We'll be free in '43!"

A rousing cheer broke the stillness, and then all were immediately quiet and somber as guards raced to the area. All they found were men talking with each other. Where the flag came from and where it disappeared to, few of us knew. We did know, however, the owner or owners would be severely beaten or executed if the flag were found in the camp.

January passed by slowly, as did February and March. By some stroke of luck I was still at Bilibid Prison. I later learned I had been permitted to remain there longer than usual because I was helping a legless captain by washing his clothing and doing for him chores that he was unable to do for himself. He was a super fellow, an artillery officer who had lost his legs in the battle on Bataan. I never did find out how he was able to get off Bataan and into Bilibid.

By April of 1943 my weight was back up to about 120 pounds. I felt fairly good and had far more strength than I had anticipated I would ever have again. Almost daily those of us from the work barracks were sent out on details. Sometimes we would be taken in trucks; other times we would walk through the streets of Manila.

Our work assignments varied from day to day. One day we would be working at the Japanese general's house, perhaps mowing the lawn and trimming the hedges and shrubs. The following day we might be loading ships down at the docks or unloading trains that came into the city stacked high with loot from various parts of the country. As we came in contact with the Filipinos, they would occasionally give us food or cigarettes. On other occasions we would help ourselves to anything we could steal from the Japanese.

On one work assignment we were loading cases of canned peaches into the hold of a ship. These were American peaches shipped to the Philippines, which the Japanese had found stored in one of the many warehouses. Every time we carried a case of the cans into the ship's hold, we would gulp down as many peaches as we could. How many cans we emptied that day I have no idea. But I do know by the end of the day I had lost my appetite for canned peaches.

We learned to become skilled thieves and stole from the Japanese every time the opportunity presented itself. Many times we risked getting a severe beating by smuggling items into camp to other men. Occasionally one of us was caught and suffered the consequences. A broken arm or a whipping were bad enough, but long periods of standing at attention or holding our arms out were far more severe. The art of human torture must have been part of each Japanese soldier's training program.

Within Bilibid Prison we fortunately had a minimum of contacts with the Japanese guards. On occasion we would be counted, and at times we would be required to do strenuous exercises at their commands. It was when we left and entered the prison that we were scrutinized and questioned carefully. They seemed to have the idea that we could carry large amounts of contraband and secrets into camp. Why we were so thoroughly searched as we left camp each morning, we never learned.

The Japanese who guarded us while on detail were never friendly or relaxed. The lowliest private behaved as if he were our lord and master. The privates were the most severe in their treatment of us. Rarely did we encounter a friendly guard. We assured ourselves this was because they were losing the war and had nothing about which to be happy. We also came to realize that Japanese privates, the lowest of the low in the Japanese Army, were treated no better by their superiors than we were treated by the privates.

New American prisoners were admitted into the camp at any time of the day or night. Human skeletons, too weak to walk and suffering from starvation and disease, were a horrible sight lying alongside mountainous hulks of human flesh swollen and puffed from beriberi. All shared the terrible suffering of these men, having experienced firsthand the same hurt and misery. At times hatred for the Japanese was so intense it seemed we would surely swarm the guards and beat them to death. Only the futility of it saved them and us.

The sick, those not too far gone, slowly responded to treatment and survived to go out on work detail again. For many, the help came too late, and they died.

One day in April a group of men came in from Cabanatuaan Prison Camp. They were to be overnight guests on their way to a work detail in southern Luzon. Whenever any new men arrived, I inquired about fellows in my squadron and especially about Dick and Norm, my two buddies left at Camp O'Donnell nearly ten months earlier. From them we learned that Cabanatuaan Prison Camp, like Camp O'Donnell, had formerly been a Philippine Army training camp. Shortly after the beginning of the rainy season the year before, Camp O'Donnell had been closed. All who were physically able were moved to Cabanatuaan. The sick were left at O'Donnell to die and be buried alongside the thousands who, weakened from starvation, had already died from the horrible diseases of dysentery or malaria.

Only Americans occupied Cabanatuaan. The major work responsibility of the camp occupants was to farm the surrounding three hundred acres taken from the Filipinos. Apparently this enterprise was proving to be profitable for the Japanese camp commander.

During the first months of occupancy of Cabanatuaan, hundreds of Americans had died from dysentery. For a while it appeared that all in the camp would be lost.

Finally, deaths decreased, and while few recovered from the dreaded disease, those who hadn't been afflicted seemed to be getting along reasonably well. Work on the farm was hard and the hours were long, but there were opportunities to steal vegetables. And a few of the vegetables grown on the farm were occasionally being reserved for American kitchens.

After general news and rumors had been exchanged, everyone began inquiring about his friends. I located a fellow who had worked in the hospital area of Cabanatuaan, and from him I learned about Dick and Norm.

He told me that Norm, as a result of prolonged illness and starvation, had become a mental case. One night, without telling anyone what he was up to, he crawled under the fence that surrounded the camp. The Japanese guards caught him and beat him unmercifully. He was dragged back into camp, but because of the beating and his poor physical condition, he died later that night. Careful examination revealed that there were at least seven bones broken from the beating.

Norm's death was a terrible shock to Dick who, already sick and covered with pellagra sores, died a few days later. Both were buried at Cabanatuaan.

I thanked the fellow and walked away fighting tears. There were hundreds of men in camp, but right then I felt completely alone and helpless. It wasn't that I was feeling especially sorry for myself. It was such a terrible waste. Norm and Dick had been two great young Americans, and the loss to me was considerable.

As I sat reflecting on the past, I recalled seeing the Japanese bombs cut some of our best men down at Clark Field. I thought of Corky, and the time he hit the foxhole with both hands full of cigars. Then I remembered him lying in the filth and stench of dysentery at O'Donnell when he died. Then there was Lloyd, whom I had buried in the jungle of Tayabas. I had tried to find his grave for one last visit before leaving that death detail, but it was already lost forever in the tropical growth of the jungle.

Now Dick and Norm, two of the neatest guys in the world. And what tragic deaths theirs were. I wondered who would tell their parents and who would break the news to the girl back home waiting to marry Dick.

"This rotten dirty war! These filthy stinking prison camps! Are we all to die without ever learning of victory? If so, why couldn't we have been killed on Bataan or Corregidor like honorable men instead of rotting away or working ourselves to death for these miserable, vicious Jap soldiers who are so filled with hatred toward us!"

That night I thought a lot and asked myself how long I could last. I wondered if I would ever see my family again. I thought about the girl I had loved and doubted that I would ever again hold a girl in my arms. I quietly shed a few tears that night.

During the first part of May 1943, there were rumors in Bilibid that a large detail of men was to be sent to Cabanatuaan Prison Camp. I couldn't see how I could possibly miss this detail, and sure enough, when the list was posted, my name was on it.

On May 9 we walked for what we thought was the last time through the streets of Manila to the railroad station. My health was fairly good, but my morale was at low ebb. My only belongings were a blue Navy jacket, a hat, a pair of khaki shorts, a pair of GI shoes slit across the toes, and a blanket. The hat and the blanket were presents from the British and delivered by the Red Cross. The other things I had accumulated in Bilibid Prison.

At the railroad station we were crowded into boxcars. By midafternoon, after a rough and dirty ride, we arrived at the city of Cabanatuaan. From there to the prison camp was a long walk, but we were used to long walks by this time. It felt good to no longer be confined behind the high concrete walls of Bilibid Prison.

We were marched up the camp's main road and were halted before the Japanese headquarters building. Posted on this building was a large sign reading, "Anyone attempting to escape will be shot to death." I later had an opportunity to see that those who commissioned the sign meant what the sign said.

Here at the headquarters building the Japanese officially checked us in, and from there they marched us inside the camp to the American headquarters building. We were assigned to specific sections and barracks according to our affiliation with the various branches of the American military.

Just after I had received directions to a barracks in the Air Corps area and before I could go there, I heard someone behind me say, "Well, I'll be darned if it isn't old Idaho himself!"

I spun around and came face to face with a fellow by the name of Lewis Moldenhauer, with whom I had graduated from high school in Montpelier, Idaho, in 1939. I almost fainted from shock and was overcome with happiness at seeing someone from home. I felt as though I had spanned the entire Pacific Ocean in a second. Someone from home! I could scarcely believe what I was seeing. As I was rushed away, he assured me that he would find me that evening for a long talk.

## 14

# CABANATUAAN PRISON CAMP

CABANATUAAN PRISON CAMP was situated in an area of farms several miles from the city of Cabanatuaan. The unpaved road between the city and the camp had seemed to be heavily traveled with Japanese-manned check stations along the way. Every Filipino was required to present an identification card before being permitted to pass a check station.

A high, heavy wire fence completely surrounded the camp, and lookout shacks on stilts, only short distances apart, towered over the fence. It was immediately obvious that escape from this camp would not be easy for any who had that in mind.

I could see the camp was divided into three distinct areas. One area, I learned, housed the prisoners physically able to work. The middle section served as a housing area for the Japanese, and the third area was reserved for those prisoners too ill to work the farm.

Each of the three large areas was further divided into three sections. The workers' area was separated into spaces for the Air Corps, for the Army, and for the sailors and Marines. Each barracks was supervised by an American officer who lived with the group for which he was responsible. I don't know where the other American officers were housed.

The center section of the camp provided an area for the Japanese officers. Separating them from the Japanese soldiers were the administration buildings and the Japanese drill field.

The "sick" section of the camp, as it was so often called, was sectioned off to accommodate the seriously ill, those on the way to recovery, and those almost ready to cross the road back to the work barracks.

While walking from the headquarters building to our assigned barracks, we were definitely impressed with what we saw. Although most of the buildings were built out of bamboo strips and thatch, they appeared to be durable. And the buildings and grounds were clean. I wondered if this was the result of good American supervision or Japanese insistence.

The living area was almost completely deserted at the time of our arrival because most of the men were working on the farm. In the Air Corps area an officer in charge of the barracks assigned my colleagues and me each to a narrow space that we could claim for sleeping purposes and for storing our belongings. In most cases our possessions consisted of what we were wearing, a mess kit, spoon, canteen and cup, and a blanket. The barracks were built on stilts and had two sleeping bays on each side. Down the middle was a dirt walkway. The lower bay was approximately two feet off the floor, and enough space separated it from the upper bay to permit a man to sit up. The bays were nothing more than strips of bamboo stretched over and nailed to bamboo poles. The floor was of dirt. While we could see that the sleeping quarters were not going to be overly comfortable, they appeared to be clean. Looks were deceiving, I soon learned, for the bamboo slats were havens for bedbugs, body lice, and fleas.

We hadn't much time to wait until the men returned to camp from the various work details. While I didn't see any whom I knew well, there were a few whom I had seen somewhere before.

Each area of the camp had its own kitchen, and shortly the chow gong sounded. The men promptly got into the chow line. The food here didn't seem to be any more plentiful than at Bilibid, but there was a small piece of steamed sweet potato. Rice, of course, continued to be the main part of the diet.

We were told by the "old timers" not to expect anything more because the servings were regularly small and the diet routine. There would be opportunities, we learned, to steal food on the farm for on-the-spot consumption. We were also to learn that there were unattractive features associated with that activity.

While the food was being served, we were entertained by a three-member camp band. These fellows rotated to the three sections of the camp during the evening meal and provided entertainment. Since I had heard nothing like that for well over a year, the three sounded professional to me. I was amazed that the Japanese would permit anything like that to go on.

Shortly after the evening meal, my hometown friend, Lewis, came over and routed me out of the barracks. To my surprise he had with him another fellow from home—a Marine, by the name of Glenn. The Marine was a year or so younger than I, and I hadn't known him too well. I just couldn't believe that three of us from that little Idaho ranch town could have wound up in the same piece of foreign soil in the same miserable situation.

During the evening session I learned that both Lewis and Glenn had been on Corregidor. Lewis had been there for more than a year before the beginning of the war. He was with the field or coast artillery. Glenn arrived in the Philippines shortly before the war began and went immediately to Corregidor. Those two, much to my amazement, were in fairly good physical condition. Both were eager to talk of home, but no more so than was I. We had a great evening together.

After we had exhausted the subject of "back home," I heard from Lewis and Glenn the complete story of the fall of Corregidor. The last I had seen of that little island was when we were on the Death March out of Bataan. That was the day that many of our men were killed or wounded from the shells fired from Corregidor's guns. After that, the Japanese shelled and bombed Corregidor steadily for nearly a month.

When they had battered her almost into the bay, the Japanese attempted a landing across the narrow two-mile channel separating the once-proud island fortress from the Peninsula of Bataan. The American fighting men who had already suffered almost beyond human endurance continued to lay a barrage on the advancing Japanese. Guns of every size were in use. The men on the antiaircraft guns reportedly cut shell fuses so that their antiaircraft shells would burst over the advancing boats.

Several times they were able to drive the Japanese back, but finally the numbers were too great, and the Japanese swarmed over the island. A more thorough examination of the island by work details showed how exhaustive the Japanese were in their shelling of Corregidor. One of the fellows reported that one couldn't lay a GI blanket out anywhere without some part of the blanket falling into a shell crater.

The captured American and Filipino prisoners were put to work salvaging everything they could for the Japanese, and then most of the Americans were sent to Cabanatuaan. Fortunately for them, they were taken across the bay in boats and went from Manila to Cabanatuaan by train. Thus, their chances of surviving the rigors of the POW camps were much better than were those of us who had struggled to survive the Bataan Death March.

General MacArthur, having left the Philippines while we were still on Bataan, assigned to several different generals the command of the military forces in the Philippines. While it was General King who surrendered Bataan to the Japanese, it was Wainwright who surrendered Corregidor.

He, along with his officers and men, was taken prisoner by the Japanese. The proposal to award the Congressional Medal of Honor to General Wainwright for his gallant defense of Corregidor was vetoed by General MacArthur, who was angry over the surrender of the island. (This information we received after the war when that medal was awarded to General Wainwright upon his release from prison camp.)

The Japanese placed great importance on the surrender of Corregidor. It was a necessary victory for them, because as long as Corregidor held the Americans had command of the entrance to Manila Bay. I also learned that night that many soldiers from Bataan had crossed over to Corregidor when Bataan fell and were later captured there.

As we talked on and on into the night, I learned that most of the men in the camp worked on the adjacent farm on which many types of vegetables were grown. I was told the work was monotonous but not too hard. The prisoners were supervised by Japanese soldiers who were extremely severe and were guarded by young Formosans, new recruits into the Japanese army. I was warned to be very careful of my actions and not to get caught stealing. The punishment for stealing was extremely severe.

There were, I learned, a variety of different daily work details. Some were much preferred over others. Each day most of the men were assigned to do general farm chores. Each Japanese supervisor would be given six to fifteen men and one or two guards. Because there was a year-round growing season, there were always crops to be planted and harvested. There was weeding to be done, and weeds could be pulled from a kneeling or stooping position, depending upon how the supervisor happened to feel at the time. Crops had to be irrigated, and this was done by bucket brigades. Some groups carried water in buckets from the ponds to the fields. On other occasions fellows stood in ditches, dipped water, and poured it into adjacent fields.

In addition to the large farm detail, there were special assignments. One group went daily to bring wood from the nearby hills to the cook shacks in camp. Another select few men went with the oxcarts that hauled the farm products to the city to be sold. Another group was assigned to the corrals to take care of the prime herd of Brahma cattle claimed by the Japanese camp commander.

The assignment to be avoided, if at all possible, was the "honey" detail that daily cleaned the Japanese toilets and carried the contents to the farm to be spread around the plants. The work was bearable, but the humiliation was almost too great. Besides these regular details, there were also special ones to serve as orderlies to the Japanese.

The conversation might have continued all night, but rules were that every man had to be inside the barracks by 10:00 p.m. I turned in, as required, and although the bloody spots on me the next morning verified that the bugs had enjoyed a big feast, I had slept soundly.

Early in the morning we were routed out, and I, along with a lot of other fellows, got into the chow line immediately. The breakfast consisted of a mess kit of watery rice. I supposed it was meant to represent cereal, but there was no relationship between that stuff and the breakfast cereal prepared by Mother back home. The thin, gruel-like unsalted rice was hard to take. The cooks just had to use the worst and dirtiest rice for this meal. Daily, before we could eat what was served, we had to spend a period of time picking out the large white worms and the dirt and rocks.

There was the story around camp about the fellow who went to the dentist with a broken tooth. The dentist examined the tooth and asked the fellow how he broke it.

The guy answered, "I bit into a rock."

"You bit into a rock? You should have been able to see a rock large enough to break your tooth that severely!"

"Oh, I saw it," was the response, "but I thought it was a rat dropping and didn't pay any attention to it."

Before too many days had passed, I had sampled most of the work details. Nearly all of the work on the farm was done by hand. Manpower, as far as the Japanese were concerned, was cheap. At eight each morning we would march out of the camp where we were divided into small details. Once guards were assigned, we would check out tools and be on our way to our respective jobs.

The land was loamy and fertile, and the growing season was continuous. We might be planting a crop in one section of the farm while another group would be harvesting the same type of crop in the neighboring section. How different that was for me, coming from an area where we had nine months of winter and three months of really cold weather.

As we finished our work at noon and again in the evening, we would carry large vegetable-filled litters into camp with us. If the Japanese had given us for food all that we raised, we would have been able to get along fine. Instead, the Japanese camp commander sold nearly everything and pocketed the money or traded the produce for rice that he sold.

We POWs had special names for all of the Japanese overseers, and we soon learned which guards were the mean ones and which were just plain ornery and miserable. Donald Duck, so named because he was quacking around all the time, was one to be cautious around. When he "flipped his lid," he beat up everyone in the neighborhood. He was a noncommissioned officer and one of the farm big shots. Instead of being in charge of one small detail, he supervised one section of the entire farm. Other Japanese were called "Big Speedo," "Little Speedo," "Mortimer Snerd," and "Smiley." There were many others, and though their names I have forgotten, their deeds I remember vividly.

The camp, in addition to being one for prisoners of war, was also used as a recruit training center for the young Japanese recruits from Formosa. They were just as brutal and as eager to show their authority as were the regular Japanese. Some of them were even worse, I believe.

One day I was with a group assigned to pull grass around the edges of the Japanese drill field. One young Formosan recruit was having an especially difficult time executing the commands given by the Japanese NCO in charge. Finally, after cursing the recruit over several irregularities, the NCO in exasperation picked up a length of wood two-by-four and crushed the recruit's skull with it. He must have died immediately because he dropped and didn't move. When we returned to work in the afternoon, his body was still lying on the field in the sun. In wasn't until sometime during the afternoon that a Japanese detail came and hauled the kid away. If they would treat their own like that, it was easier for us to understand their brutality and savagery toward the prisoners of war.

Very few of the Japanese could speak English, and very few wanted to learn the language. There was one, however, who had made up his mind that as soon as America was defeated, he was going to the USA to live. So, he wanted to learn English. He was one of the dumbest Japanese with whom I had come in contact to date, and he learned very slowly. Somewhere he had heard the song "Maria Lena" and was determined that he was going to learn it. I unwisely told him that I knew the song, so whenever possible, he arranged for me to be assigned to his detail. He then not only remained with me while I worked, but also hounded me to death to teach him the song. He finally learned it, but what a struggle!

Whenever we worked in a section of the farm where the produce was edible, we would steal and eat all we could. Whether it was dirty potatoes or raw okra, it didn't matter a bit. We ate anything we could find that would help fill our bellies and do us some good. Some days we were able to steal quite a little extra food. It all had to be eaten on the spot because we were searched when we went through the gates into camp. Many times the punishment for stealing food would be a broken arm. And, in spite of the fact we knew that we would be in serious trouble if we were caught, the stealing continued. Regularly fellows were caught and punished.

While setting out little onion sets one day, one of the fellows emptied the water out of his canteen and filled it full of the onion sets. These he planned to carry back into camp. As the day got hotter, he took his canteen and belt off and laid them at the end of the row. Our Japanese supervisor, thirsty, picked up the canteen. I held my breath as he unscrewed the cap and tipped the canteen to his lips. Never before had I seen a Japanese drink from a POW's canteen. They weren't about to take a chance of infection from a POW. The look on his face when onion sets hit his lips instead of water should have been recorded for posterity.

I expected the Japanese supervisor to let out a roar, but he didn't. He called all members of the work detail over to him, and before us he dumped the sets out of the canteen. He then held the canteen up and asked who the owner was. I again shook my head in disbelief when the owner stepped up and claimed the canteen. He was ready for his punishment, but no punishment was dealt. The supervisor instead said he knew that we weren't getting enough to eat, but it was very bad to steal. He made the canteen owner promise he wouldn't attempt to steal again, and that was the end of the affair. We could scarcely believe what we had seen. It occurred to us the war must be winding down with the Allies winning.

Another incident almost as surprising took place one day in another section of the farm. For some reason, the Japanese couldn't get carrots to grow. My hunch was that the climate was too hot for carrots, but the Japanese supervisor seemed to have made up his mind he would make them grow or else. He had planted a small patch, and on that particular afternoon had put six of us to work weeding it. The carrots were very tiny, and the weeds were so thick that weeding was a tough and tedious job. Separating the weeds from the carrots was an almost impossible task.

After we had been busy for nearly an hour, the supervisor came back to see how we were getting along with the weeding. One of the weeders was a kid from New York who had apparently never in his life seen a carrot growing. Without seeking advice from the rest of us, he had done an excellent job of weeding and had pulled out everything green.

The supervisor, seeing what had happened, dropped to his knees and picked up a handful of the weeds and carrots. Though he couldn't speak a word of English, it was easy, from the expression on his face and from his voice, to tell what he was thinking and saying as he separated the carrots from the weeds. I know he must have been quietly sobbing, "My poor little carrots, my poor little carrots."

The New Yorker felt just as bad and was most apologetic.

"I have never seen a carrot growing," he said.

Without seeming to lose his temper a bit, the supervisor then very patiently showed the kid the difference between carrots and weeds. I thought the war surely must have ended with us as the victors.

Usually the Japanese stayed out of our camp areas so, once we were inside, the feeling of pressure was lifted somewhat, and we got along fairly well. In this camp the Japanese permitted the fellows to sponsor entertainment. Occasionally the three musicians put on a special concert, and during the year two plays were produced and presented. Although the actors were amateurs, they did a wonderful job, and with the band, they did much for the morale of all of us.

I remember they acted out the plays "Dr. Jekyll and Mr. Hyde" and "Uncle Tom's Cabin." The Japanese soldiers turned out in numbers to watch the activities, and on occasion we were honored by the presence of their officers. But as the war progressed, food became scarcer, and the work more tiring, the entertainment stopped. No one felt like watching, let alone participating.

The talk at spare-time bull sessions always focused on either food or home, but mainly on food. The guys would tell of meals they had had at home, or were going to have, until all mouths watered. Listening to the discussions, or entering into them, was pure torment. Yet we continued to torture ourselves. It now seems unbelievable when I think back of how grown men talked of recipes and concoctions like a group of female home economists. It wasn't funny to us then, though.

Very rarely did anyone, except the cooks, get enough food. Anyone getting a job in the kitchen had it made. Those guys always made sure that they got theirs first. I didn't blame them, either, because that's probably what I would have done, given the opportunity—although I am not quite sure about that.

One evening as we came in from the farm, we noticed a group of men walking up the main road toward camp. Naturally everyone was interested in hearing the latest rumors and news, so we hung around the gate waiting for them to come in.

As they came through the gate, I was overjoyed to see my two good friends from the squadron, David R. Carrier (Sad Sack) and Sgt. Norman Lonon. As soon as they were checked in and released, I hurried over and shook hands with them. Right off the bat I asked Lonon how the war was going. He answered, "'Old out 'till 'elp arrives!"

The Japanese had beaten, starved, and killed many men, but I could see that they hadn't taken anything out of those two jokers. Their morale was good, and their sense of humor still plenty sharp. Physically they were in bad shape, and Lonon could hardly walk. He was suffering terribly from dry beriberi.

After supper I spent one of the most memorable evenings of my life reminiscing with them. We talked of the good old days before the war and the escapades the two of them had been on together. As far as I was concerned, those two fellows just had to be among the greatest.

Shortly before Christmas 1943, the rumor began to spread across camp that we were going to receive packages from home. Many such rumors had boosted our hopes high only to drop them with a thud later. A package from home would be too much to expect, our better judgment told us—yet we hoped in earnest.

One day we saw the almost impossible: large mail bags full of packages unloaded from a Japanese truck. Excitement ran high in camp. It seemed like the day before Christmas back home when we were kids.

Some two or three days passed before the Americans, under the close supervision of the Japanese, were able to get the packages sorted and ready for distribution. Everyone was sure he wouldn't get a package, but secretly everyone prayed he would. Of course the contents of the packages would be appreciated but even more important were the thoughts of home and knowing the package would have been assembled by someone at home who really cared. While there is no question but what the war and prison experiences had brought out new feelings and more meaningful friendships, there was still the lack of the kind of love that comes from the folks at home. We were homesick, and we were terribly lonely.

For some reason or other, only a few packages were put out each day. The Japanese were always on hand to witness the opening of each box and carefully inspected each article. Each day we individually worried and sweated out our turn. Each fellow spent much time speculating just what his individual package might contain. I knew if I got a package there would be sure to be a box of gingersnaps included. Everyone hoped for food.

After about a week of waiting, my name was finally called, and my heart leaped. After the box was inspected, I carried it back to my sleeping area, carefully went through it, and handled and examined each article. I felt very close to home right then because I knew those things in the box had been packed by my mother and dad. I thought to myself, "I'll bet they wondered and worried about what to include. They probably asked themselves time and time again what I could use best."

Sure enough, there was a large box of gingersnaps. Also included were packages of candy and other food, several towels and washcloths, and an Autostrop razor and about a dozen packages of blades. That razor, during the balance of our internment, shaved thousands of men. Also in the package were several bars of soap, a toothbrush and toothpaste, three pairs of socks, and three pairs of shorts. The latter were ten inches too large for me around the waist. I couldn't see how the folks at home were able to cram so many items into the small box they were allowed to send.

The different fellows received all sorts of things from home. One guy's box was filled with five-grain sulfa pills. When he first saw those, he was disappointed, but when he realized he had actually received a gold mine, his attitude quickly changed. With that medicine he had it made. He swapped them, a few at a time, to the Japanese soldiers who would have taken them from him had they dared. From them, especially those with venereal diseases, he got food, cigarettes, clothing, and even special treatment. Those pills would have been put to very good use by the American doctors, but they wouldn't take them from him.

Surprisingly enough, many of those who received packages shared with those who didn't. Those unfortunate ones we tried to console with the counsel that their folks had sent a package and it had been confiscated by the Japanese. That could have happened.

At this time, too, after being interned for nearly two years, we received our first mail from home. I didn't get a letter from my parents, but I did receive one from a dear aunt of mine. She told me to stay in the ring and keep punching. The letter had been written nearly a year before, but it was wonderful. I read it over and over.

Shortly after Christmas the Japanese began smoking American cigarettes and chewing American gum. The rumor had circulated that we were to receive food and clothing from the Red Cross, but we hadn't as yet seen any. We questioned the Japanese about where they got the cigarettes and the gum, and they informed us that they had captured American supplies and were using them. This we didn't believe, but that didn't seem to bother them.

Finally, the Japanese actually broke loose with the Red Cross supplies. I don't have any idea how much the Red Cross sent, but I know we didn't receive very much. We were thankful for what we did get, though. The help came in the form of individual food packages and also large cases of bulk food, clothing, and medicine.

Each man was given a small box for himself. The boxes were compact, and the amount of food they contained was almost unbelievable. Each box held two chocolate bars, thirteen packages of cigarettes, a can of powdered milk, a can of corned beef, a package of cheese, a jar of jam, some sugar cubes, and a can of soluble coffee. We were really in the height of our glory with this new stuff. Many of the fellows used good judgment with their food and rationed it sparingly. Others just gorged themselves, and some even gambled theirs off. Within practically no time a few fellows had cornered most of the cigarettes and much of the food. Those who didn't smoke traded their cigarettes for food because, to some, tobacco was even more highly valued than was food.

The bulk food was turned over to the kitchens. Instead of letting us use the American chow to supplement the food that they ordinarily issued to us, the Japanese merely cut down on the amount of our daily issue. Because of that, we weren't much better off, even though the intentions of the folks back home had been the best. I must say, however, the quality of the food served was far better than the usual Japanese issue.

Most of the medical supplies went to the Japanese for their own use. We saw much more brought into camp than was ever made available to the American doctors.

## 15

# MOTHER'S DOOR IN '44

We weren't free in '43, so we had to come up with a new slogan for 1944. "Mother's door in '44" seemed appropriate for 1944. For some reason or other, the suggestion of "Frisco whore in '44" didn't stimulate much enthusiasm.

After the earlier experiences the camp had with dysentery, everyone got busy and nearly cleared it of flies. The Japanese had been especially concerned, not so much about the men dying but because they were living in the same area. They had their own safety to think of. It seems as though at one time there had been a dysentery epidemic in Japan that killed thousands of people. Our captors knew what the disease could do.

They had helped the cause along by offering a cigarette for every forty flies turned in. It wasn't long until it was almost impossible to find any flies. This was the best thing that could have happened. As the flies went, so went most of the dysentery. There continued to be a few new cases, and many in the hospital area were still suffering from the disease. It was, however, nothing like it had been.

After months of good fortune I was among those to come down with the dreaded disease after its spread had been fairly well controlled. I was always especially careful with my mess kit and tried to keep it as clean as I possibly could. Too ill to work, I was transferred to the hospital area, and for nearly two weeks, I thought that I was going to die for sure. Conditions over in that area were much worse than in the main camp section.

In the first place, the hospital compounds were on land that was partially swampy, and that in itself was unhealthy enough. The barracks were dirty and some were actually filthy. Some of the men couldn't take care of themselves and were in terrible shape. The morale of the men in the building to which I was assigned was at low ebb. Most of us knew from experience that chances of recovery from dysentery were slim.

The Japanese had the most unbelievable attitude toward sick men. They maintained that a sick man who couldn't work didn't need as much food as a working man. Consequently, to the ill, food servings were very small, even much smaller than the miserably dwarfish amounts served to workers. A person who was trying to recover had an extremely uphill battle attempting to do so.

During the first week, when I was too ill to pay attention to what was going on around me, my leather shoes were stolen. They were the ones given to me at Bilibid and were still in fairly good condition. I hated to lose them, knowing that there was very little chance of my ever getting another pair. Unable to wear them on the farm because of the swelling of my feet caused by beriberi, I had put them away and had gone barefoot. I couldn't imagine anyone being mean enough to steal a sick man's shoes. In fact, I had great difficulty accepting the fact they were really gone. I felt sick over the loss and was terribly angry because I was helpless to do anything about it. Some of the fellows in the building told me that having things stolen was a daily occurrence in the hospital area. I made up my mind to locate them just as soon as I got well enough to do so. They wouldn't be hard to recognize, I knew, because they were both split in two places between the tongue and the toes.

After the first two weeks in the sick area, I began to recover somewhat and happily moved to another section of the camp reserved for those improving but still too ill to be sent back on the other side of the camp for work. There the fellows were still not healthy by any means but were much better off than some. We didn't have anything to do to occupy our time, and, consequently, it hung heavily on our hands. We just lived from one scanty meal to another. The talk, as usual, was always centered around the subject of food. How we constantly tortured ourselves!

My buddy Lewis, from my hometown in Idaho, was assigned to regular guard duty in the hospital area, and occasionally he would bring me a little extra rice. I don't know where he got it, probably went without his own at times to give it to me. Thanks to his concern for me and his help, I recuperated faster than many of the other fellows did.

The lieutenant in charge of our building in this section of the sick area was a lover of poetry. He had written several poems and knew many more. I spent hours talking with him and learning many poems that he would write down for me. I must have learned dozens, some of which I still remember.

Several fellows, those who were Masons or sons of Masons through one means or another, were getting assistance from the outside. I don't know whether Filipinos were smuggling in the food or money or whether the Japanese were doing it. I thought that the Masons must be pretty much on the ball if they could help their members under such circumstances. Another group of fellows getting outside help were the Catholics. Catholicism was, of course, very widespread in the Philippines. The Catholic chaplains seemed to be the dispersing agents for the food smuggled in. I consoled myself with the feeling that the Mormons must be praying for their members because, in my case at least, someone was looking after me reasonably well under the circumstances.

As quickly as each of us recovered to the extent that we could walk, we were permitted to go to the kitchen to get our food. The first time that I went to get my chow, I spotted my shoes being worn by one of the cooks. My anger surged and I went up to the guy and shouted, "You are wearing my shoes! You have stolen them from me! You are worse than the Japs!"

He was a red-faced blond and a giant alongside of me. He just sneered and said, "Prove it, skinny."

I couldn't prove it, and both of us knew that I couldn't. I also knew there was nothing I could do right then to get the shoes back. He had taken them, I was positive, but I was helpless. All I could do was leave the kitchen biting my lip to keep from crying from anger.

After about six weeks I was sent back to the work side of the camp and was most happy to go. First, I was happy that I was well enough to go, and second, on that side of the camp we were forced to work, and keeping busy helped to make the time pass much faster. There the morale of the men was much better, also.

When I arrived back in the main camp area, I could see quickly changes had been made. Hundreds of men had been declared to be free from dysentery and had been sent to Japan. I found that both of the boys from my hometown and Sad Sack and Sgt. Lonon had been sent out. I hated not having them to talk with but knew they had no choice about whether they would go or stay. I was assigned to a sleeping spot in the old Navy and Marine section of the camp. This area was on higher ground and was the cleanest section of the camp. I was given a bunk space next to a young fellow from Texas by the name of Jasper Burkett. He turned out to be one of the finest fellows I had ever met. We became close friends and helped each other as much as we could.

During those months the Americans weren't the only ones suffering from disease. It seems as though the Filipino prostitutes were doing their bit for the cause. The Japanese soldiers who visited them apparently knew little about taking care of themselves against venereal diseases, and, consequently, many of them began suffering from syphilis and/or gonorrhea. They were afraid of turning themselves in to their own doctors for fear of punishment. Consequently, they asked us what they should do to cure themselves. We strongly recommended plenty of beer, gin, whiskey, or any kind of alcohol they could get to drink. I always wondered how many of them got cured that way.

Back at work on the farm once again, I found the Japanese guards and overseers had become tougher and were demanding more work. Because of the large exodus of men to Japan, there were now far fewer men to work the farm, and there was still the same amount of acreage to farm. There was very little opportunity to steal vegetables. The Japanese guards would allow us to pull a certain kind of weed and take it into camp with us, though. Boiled, this weed didn't taste any worse than some of the stuff they were feeding us and much better than the bean vines they had tried to get us to eat. The cooked weed was filling and must have been good for us because those of us who could stomach the stuff seemed to get along fine.

It was here, also, that I ate dog meat for the first time. A couple of the fellows had rigged up a dog trap over by the corrals and were quite successful in trapping the stray dogs that roamed the area. Earlier, the thought of eating dog meat was actually enough to turn one's stomach. In the Philippines prior to the war we had seen Filipinos in the Baguio area eating dog meat, and they seemed to relish it. Boiled, we found that it tasted something like mutton. It was greasy like mutton, anyway.

In the spring of 1944 we figured the war must be going badly for the Japanese, because they rounded us up one day and told us that we were going to help make a movie. We speculated they must be in serious need of some convincing propaganda with which to help assure the home folks that Japan was winning the war. Anyway, we were marched way back into the hills and given instructions. We didn't have to do much. I guess they thought we weren't smart enough to put on much of a show. They gave us white flags and rifles, with no ammunition of course, and then took us into a wooded area. They dragged some old wrecked trucks into the area and set them and the edge of the woods on fire with lots of smoke. We then came through the smoke waving the white flags. A handful of Japanese then easily captured hundreds of us and had us throw our rifles into piles. They then marched us down the road with our hands held high over our heads.

We were on the movie location for two days while they shot many scenes. They had a leading man and all. We were anxious to see the leading lady, but she never appeared. Later a small group of POWs was taken to Corregidor to shoot more scenes there. It appeared as though the Japanese were showing the surrender of both Corregidor and Bataan. They never did give us the pleasure of seeing the finished product, though. More disappointing, however, was the fact that neither did they increase the quantity or quality of food dispensed while that special assignment was imposed. Success for us in life during internment was measured by the amount and quality of the food obtained.

The farm work was not all a waste of time and talents, as far as we were concerned; at least that is what the Japanese continued to tell us. They were giving us the opportunity to learn proper farming procedures. I helped with one complete rice crop, and, who knows, this knowledge may still come in handy, although I am slightly dubious about that.

As rice farmers we first flooded the fields by standing in a ditch all day with a bucket, dipping water from the ditch and pouring it onto the field. On many occasions, I dipped water steadily for four hours at a stretch.

After the paddies were flooded, we would tromp around in the muddy water until the soil was slimy. If we were lucky, we had a couple of caribou with rake-like teeth to help us. A seed bed had been planted earlier, and as soon as the plants were large enough to be set out, we tied them into small bundles. With enough men to form a line clear across the field, we received our planting instructions. There is only one proper way to plant rice, we learned, and the Japanese wanted it to be planted that (their) way. So that we would keep the rows straight, they stretched a string. When we finished a field, it would be near perfect. The Japanese were great ones for show and were eager for the fields to look good when their inspectors came to see what was being done.

After the rice seedlings were planted, we had to keep the paddies flooded until shortly before the harvesting time. When the grain became ripe, we cut it with small sickles and tied it into bundles. The bundles were at once stacked, and later we thrashed out the heads with a hand machine. Then, the Japanese commanding officer sold the rice. At least, that is what the guards told us.

During the rainy season the roads around the farm became almost impassable. There were many rocks in the area, so the Japanese conceived the idea that the roads should be surfaced with rocks. For days we stood in long lines passing rocks from one person to another. Under the close scrutiny of the Japanese guards, the rocks came fast, even though many of them were large. Many of our guys suffered skinned and bruised legs and mashed feet. This didn't faze the Japanese one bit. Anyone dropping a rock could expect a hit from a guard. At times when the work was going badly, the Japanese made us all pair off and slug each other. If they thought that one wasn't getting hit hard enough, they would contribute with fists and rifle butts.

Sometime during April of 1944 the Japanese began constructing an airfield on a section of land about three or four miles distant from our camp. They needed all the workers they could get, so fewer men had to continue the work on the farm to release others to work on the landing strip. We didn't know the purpose for the airfield so we assumed hopefully it was to enable a Japanese plane to land and rescue Japanese officers and guards when the Americans repatriated the camp.

Our work assignments were finally rotated to enable us to work on the airfield for a week and then on the farm for a week. As usual, all of the work on the airfield was done with hand tools. We would knock down the high spots with picks and shovels and fill in the low places with dirt hauled in wheelbarrows. When completed, the field was to accommodate large planes. To pack the dirt we would form long lines all the way across the landing strip and walk back and forth, back and forth. In about three months the field was finished. We never did learn whether or not the Japanese got a chance to use it.

After the work on the airfield ended, I was given a politician's job inside the camp helping to clean the prisoners' toilets. As messy as the job was, I preferred it over work outside the camp because we didn't have to put up with the Japanese. We were furnished disinfectant, and each morning two of us would wash the wooden toilet seats. This helped to keep the flies down and also helped to prevent the spread of scabies. Once a week the toilets had to be bailed out and the stuff carried out and dumped into a ditch. The Japanese wanted the cleaning from their own toilets dumped on the farm. I guess they thought that theirs was "pure stuff."

While we were working on this job, my work partner confided in me that he had a Filipino wife and child in Manila. I asked him if he ever heard from his wife, and he said no. He said that he was afraid to try to get in touch with her for fear the Japanese would kill or punish her and their child. (After the war he contacted me to tell me that his wife had died while he was in prison camp and his daughter was cared for by a Catholic sister. He was able to get his daughter and take her with him to the United States when he returned from the Philippines.)

One evening when I had finished work I saw that there had been assigned to our barracks a certain blond, red-faced fellow whom I was interested in seeing. He was the person I had seen wearing my shoes. When I first spotted him, I walked over and asked him what he had done with my shoes. He looked at me with that same sneer on his face and came out with another wisecrack. I slapped him in the face as hard as I could with the back of my hand. All the hate for him that I had been carrying around inside me since I had spotted him wearing my shoes surged now that the day of reckoning had finally arrived. I wasn't quite as skinny as I had been, and besides being angry, I was in the right, and he knew it.

He hit back but didn't stand a chance.

No one tried to interfere, and I almost beat him to death. Only fatigue saved him, I feel confident.

I then saw to it that he confessed not only to stealing my shoes but to other thefts as well. The Americans had a way of punishing thieves who stole from their colleagues. For ten days he wore a sign around his neck for everyone to see. It read, "I am a thief. Watch out for me."

I think he was punished enough, even though he had worn out my shoes.

With the exception of the time I spent in the sick area of the camp, that last year in the Philippines on the Cabanatuaan farm passed more rapidly than I could have ever believed possible. The farm work was a salvation to us. Without work to occupy our time we would soon have gone mad, I am sure. The treatment from the Japanese was severe, and although they knocked us around constantly, there was only one death at their hands while I was at Cabanatuaan. One fellow attempted to escape, was caught, beaten, and bayoneted to death. His body was then put on display. There were dozens of holes in his body, which had been brutally beaten almost beyond recognition.

The other nine prisoners in his group of ten, whose execution had been promised, weren't punished as far as I know. To my knowledge no additional escapes from that camp were attempted.

# 16

# EXODUS FROM THE PHILIPPINES TO JAPAN

BY THE MIDDLE OF JUNE 1944, nearly all of the prisoners in Cabanatuaan who had never contracted dysentery and many who had recovered completely had been shipped to Japan. Whether they needed more men to work in Japan or whether they wanted to get as many men as possible out of the Philippine Islands before the Americans retook the place, we didn't know. While the rumors had us winning the war, the reports hadn't changed much in the more than two years we had been interned. During late June the Japanese called for another detail of five hundred men.

As was the usual practice, the American officers asked for volunteers before they began drafting men. My Texas friend and I talked the matter over carefully because the work on the farm was becoming more demanding and the food rations were becoming smaller. We were reluctant to leave for fear the Americans were really as close as rumors said they were. However, we had only rumors to go on, and it was the common belief that food and treatment would be much better in Japan.

After weighing all of the information available, we decided maybe it would be in our best interest if we did volunteer to go. As it turned out, it wouldn't have made any difference; most of the five hundred men had to be drafted anyway.

Thus we, along with the others, submitted to the medical test for the purposes of determining whether or not we were free from dysentery. Both of our tests apparently were negative, so that cinched the deal.

By the 28th of June the five hundred men had been chosen, and we were on our way. The departure wasn't a happy occasion, because we were separating from friends, and because no one knew for sure what to expect. The Japanese guards had told us on more than one occasion that all POWs would be killed if the Americans tried to free us. There was no question but what they were capable of that act; past experiences with them had clearly verified that. It could be that all of us would find ourselves in situations much worse than those we were presently experiencing. At least at Cabanatuaan we had become used to the routine and to those who guarded and supervised our labors.

The Japanese marched us back down to the town of Cabanatuaan. There, after we had spent a couple of hours sitting in the sun, they jammed us into boxcars and took us to Manila once again. Crammed together as we were in the hot cars, the trip was a miserable one.

Late in the afternoon we were unloaded in the Manila train yards and marched over a familiar route through the city toward Bilibid Prison. I hadn't been in Manila for over a year, and yet everything looked just the same. Even under these miserable circumstances, I felt good being back in this city I had learned to love.

Before I realized it, we were at the prison gates, and they were being opened. The buildings, the prison walls, the guards inside all looked just the same. Only the Americans within the prison had changed. These men were like living dead people. We looked bad enough, but alongside of these Bilibid prisoners, we appeared fat and sassy. These men were being starved to death. Most of the Navy personnel, we learned, had been shipped out, and those left were slowly dying from starvation.

The following day a detail of 510 men from the island of Mindanao joined us. This made a total of 1,010 men in our detail bound for Japan. Among the group were fellows from my former squadron. During the next few days, we were busy swapping tales and talking about other squadron members. In general, the prisoners from Mindanao were in better physical condition than we were, but they had also suffered harsh treatment at the hands of the Japanese. Many of them, like us, had worked on a farm. They had been brought from Mindanao to Manila in an old, slow-moving inter-island vessel.

On July 1 we were assembled and readied to go. Then something happened making it impossible for us to leave. So we spent two more nights in Bilibid Prison.

Because the men were so restless and uneasy, the American officers accompanying us put pressure on the Japanese to secure smoking tobacco from the Filipinos. The Japanese finally obliged by securing a big pile of leaf tobacco. It was divided among everyone, and the smokers tried to crumble it so that it could be smoked. It was the strongest, most foul stuff

I have ever smelled. A little of it went a long way, but it could be smoked and seemed to be a bit better than nothing at all. I gave my share away.

On July 3 we lined up again, and this time we marched out through the gates and into the street. The Japanese paraded us down through the main part of the city of Manila. They never missed an opportunity to put us on display. Many of the Filipinos laughed and jeered, but we didn't mind. By this time we were toughened to this sort of reaction. There were those other Filipinos who secretly gave us the "V for victory" sign.

The walk to the pier was long, and before we could board the ship, we had to stand around on the docks for several hours. Their army was no more efficient than ours. There were many ships in the bay, but the one we were finally directed toward was by far the worst-looking one of the lot. It was a captured freighter, an ancient coal burner, which, we were told, had once belonged to the Canadians.

Once aboard we were put into the two forward holds—505 men in each one. Around the edges of the hold the Japanese had built large bays. I was among the group assigned to an upper one. The holds of the ship were small, and even with the bays, there wasn't enough room for everyone to sit down at one time. It was dark and foul-smelling in the hold and, to make matters worse, the Japanese covered the top immediately with huge pieces of canvas.

Hot, hungry, and mashed together in the hold of that stinking ship as we were, we were in no frame of mind to be tolerant of each other. Tempers were on edge. It was nearly midnight before we were given a canteen cup full of water and another canteen cup of cooked rice.

There was little sleep for anyone that night, and along toward morning we heard the engines begin turning over and could feel the vibration of the ship in motion. Later in the morning we learned from the mess crew that the ship had merely pulled out into the bay and anchored.

The canvas covering remained tightly stretched over the black hold, and before long the heat and humidity in the hold began to slowly drive us mad. Our bodies were covered with sweat, and our skin soon broke out in a burning rash. We shouted for the Japanese to give us some air, but they only laughed in our faces and threatened not to feed us or give us water to drink.

There were no sanitation facilities in the hold at all until the Japanese finally tossed down several five-gallon cans. I guess it was a good thing we weren't getting much to eat or drink because it was almost impossible to reach a can.

During the second night the engines started up again, and this time they kept going. In the morning a few men at a time were allowed on deck for a smoke. The first to go out reported that the ship was just off Corregidor but heading back for Manila. That day the Japanese left the hold uncovered and allowed a small smoking group on the deck all the time. My turn to go didn't come until late afternoon. I went out for a breath of fresh air rather than for a smoke of the foul tobacco rolled in thick paper.

Each night during the next two weeks the ship attempted to slip out of the bay only to turn back and anchor again. The conditions in that dirty foul hold were almost unbearable. Our bodies were wet with sweat all the time, and the bedbugs and fleas and body lice competed with each other for our blood.

A big fellow in the group, who according to those who knew him was a former cook and bully and a coward on Bataan, had thus far survived internment. Now, unable to control his emotions, he went completely berserk in the hold of the ship. He became so violent and dangerous that he had to be held down. In their attempt to restrain him, the fellows choked him to death. That death could not be concealed because so many had observed the incident. The Japanese, not fully aware of what actually happened, furnished a chunk of iron to tie to his legs, and he was dropped overboard. Little did we realize then that the good old Yanks we had waited for so long were the very ones bottling up the bay while we were going crazy in the terrible heat.

To add to our discomfort, the Japanese harassed us constantly. Concentrated as we were, we were captive audiences for their continual verbal abuses. As much as they disgusted and angered us, they didn't stimulate within us feeling and expressions of hostility nearly so readily as did an American general in our group.

Many instructions to us were delivered by the Japanese through the general, the ranking American officer aboard, who always began with, "Men, the Imperial Japanese forces have directed me to . . ." That introduction was bad enough, but combined with his squeaky voice, it was almost too much to bear.

During one period of repeated announcements, the general began with his "Men, the Imperial Jap—" only to be interrupted by a prisoner who shouted, "Drop dead, general, your imperial majesty!"

"Drop dead too, you loudmouth son-of-a-bitch," was the general's reply.

Men booed and taunted the general terribly and shouted all kinds of insults, including accusing him of being a squeaky flunky of the Japanese.

At that moment I was sure there was little hope for us. We had deteriorated to the level of the lowest, even to that of the Japanese themselves whom we so despised. That was about as low as one could get. After more than two years of torture, suffering, and the loss of thousands of our friends, some of us had stooped to this. For me this despicable incident was a horrible experience, perhaps more so than anything I had encountered to date.

After two weeks of pure hell, our ancient craft in a pitch-black night finally slipped out of the bay and into the China Seas in a rising storm. By the following morning the storm was raging, and the upper decks were awash much of the time. Then the Japanese informed us that we would be allowed on deck at will.

Despite the wind and water, the men jammed the deck to be in the fresh air. From this time on, the voyage became slightly more bearable. At least we were free part of the time from the suffocating heat of the hold and the torment of the vermin.

Our ration of food for the trip continued to be a cup of cooked rice and one cup of water per day. The amount of water was about sufficient, but the small amount of rice served only to torment us. At mealtime one could observe men eating their rice one kernel at a time to make it last longer. We all yearned for more food. We could survive on rice alone, we had found out, if the servings were large enough. When a man died, his neighbors just let him lie for as long as possible so they could draw his ration of food. The dead bodies remained until the stench required that they be discarded. Tied to a piece of iron, even bloated bodies would sink rapidly.

The storm lasted for the eight days it took the ship to get to Formosa. Most of us were sick from the constant battering of the waves, the boredom of the journey, and our terrible cramped living space. When we approached the area where we were to dock, we were all ordered below decks again, and the holds were once again covered with the canvas. By morning, however, we were once more permitted to emerge from the black holes.

From the ship we could see part of the business section of what appeared to be a fairly large city. We imagined our coal burner had stopped for the purpose of refueling. By midmorning we were notified that we would be permitted to get down on the dock and bathe in fresh water.

Only small groups were allowed ashore at one time, so the bathing process lasted for a couple of days. The residents of the city, who were inquisitive to see what a bunch of scrawny, hairy American prisoners of war looked like, got an eyeful because we stripped right in the street and scrubbed and soaked in the fresh water. We later learned they were used to seeing naked people bathing; they did their own bathing in public bathhouses.

Here in this Formosan port we again sat for two weeks in heat almost as unbearable as that in the Philippines had been. We fortunately couldn't be forced to remain in the holds, however, because the lower holds of our ship were being loaded with coarse salt. Thus we were able to move around the crowded deck.

By early August the ship was finally loaded, and we were herded below while the ship steamed out of the port. From then, all the way to Japan, we had authorization to go on deck whenever we wanted to. From Formosa we traveled only during the daylight hours and would anchor close to land at night. It seemed that a chain of islands extended all the way from Formosa to Japan.

At one other out-of-the-way spot, trouble developed in the engines, and we were forced to anchor for longer than two weeks while repairs were made. Our efforts to persuade the Japanese to permit us to go ashore, or at least to get into the water, were not fruitful. They wouldn't even consider our request.

On the final leg of our journey to Japan, we traveled in convoy with a destroyer escort. American submarines harassed us constantly. What a pleasure it was to hear the destroyers frantically firing depth charges. In our own minds we were convinced that the Americans in the submarines knew for a fact that we were aboard the freighter and would never torpedo our ship. Later we were to learn just how foolish these beliefs were.

The crew members of our ship were all Chinese, and we constantly tried to get up-to-date news from them. As it turned out, they, too, were prisoners. They were, however, permitted much more freedom aboard than were we. They were also given privileges denied to us, and they always appeared to be well fed and amply supplied with cigarettes. As far as we were concerned, that put them on equal status with the Emperor.

As our ship sailed farther north, we began to suffer from the cold. The daytime temperature was pleasant enough, but nights were cold, and the air became damp. After four years in the Philippines our blood was thin, and the food we were getting didn't generate much heat or energy.

Finally, on the evening of the third of September, we were again herded below deck, and the hold was covered. The Japanese informed us that we were approaching port and the end of our journey.

After sixty-two days aboard the "hell ship," sixty-two days of filth, suffocation, body sores, swollen feet and legs from beriberi, bedbugs, lice, fleas, and starvation, we had finally reached our destination. It was inconceivable for us to believe conditions anywhere could be worse than what we had just experienced. Shortly, we were to find out.

Japan. Our final camp, Fukuoka Camp #17, was located at Omuta on the southern island of Kyushu, approximately forty kilometers east of Nagasaki.

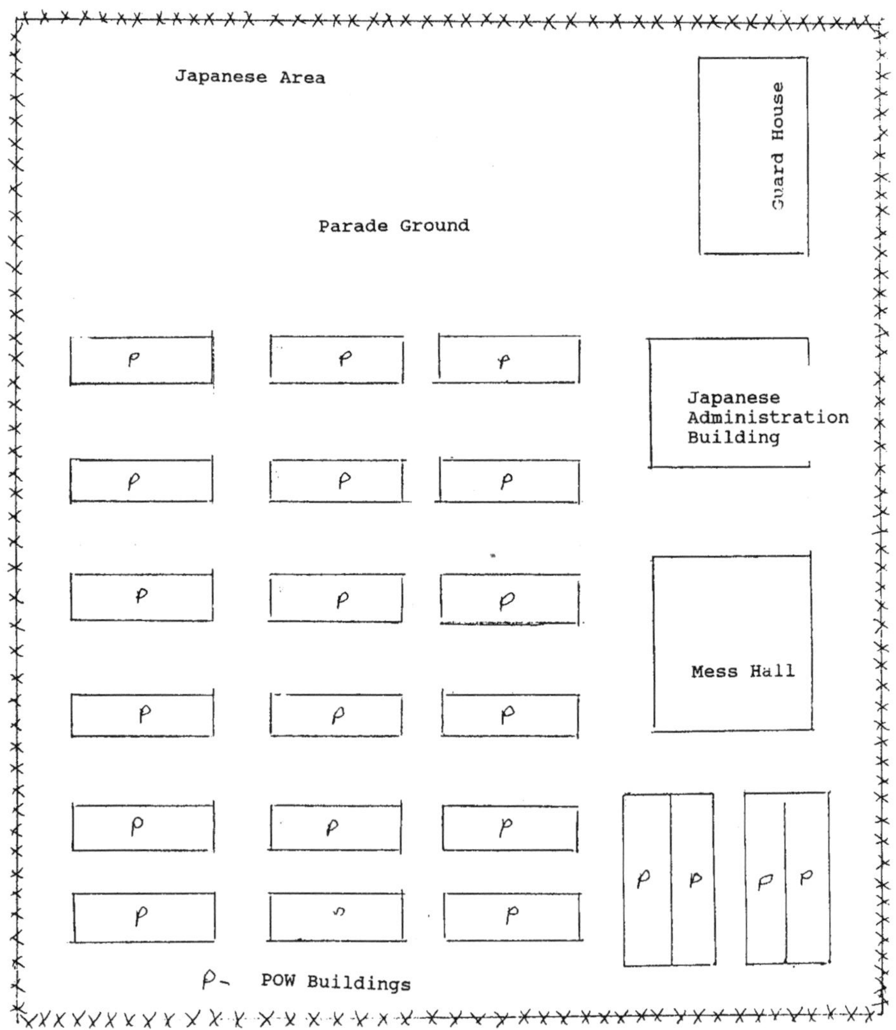


Fukuoka Camp #17, Omuta, Japan

Camp 17. Courtesy Roger Mansell.

Camp 17. Courtesy Roger Mansell.

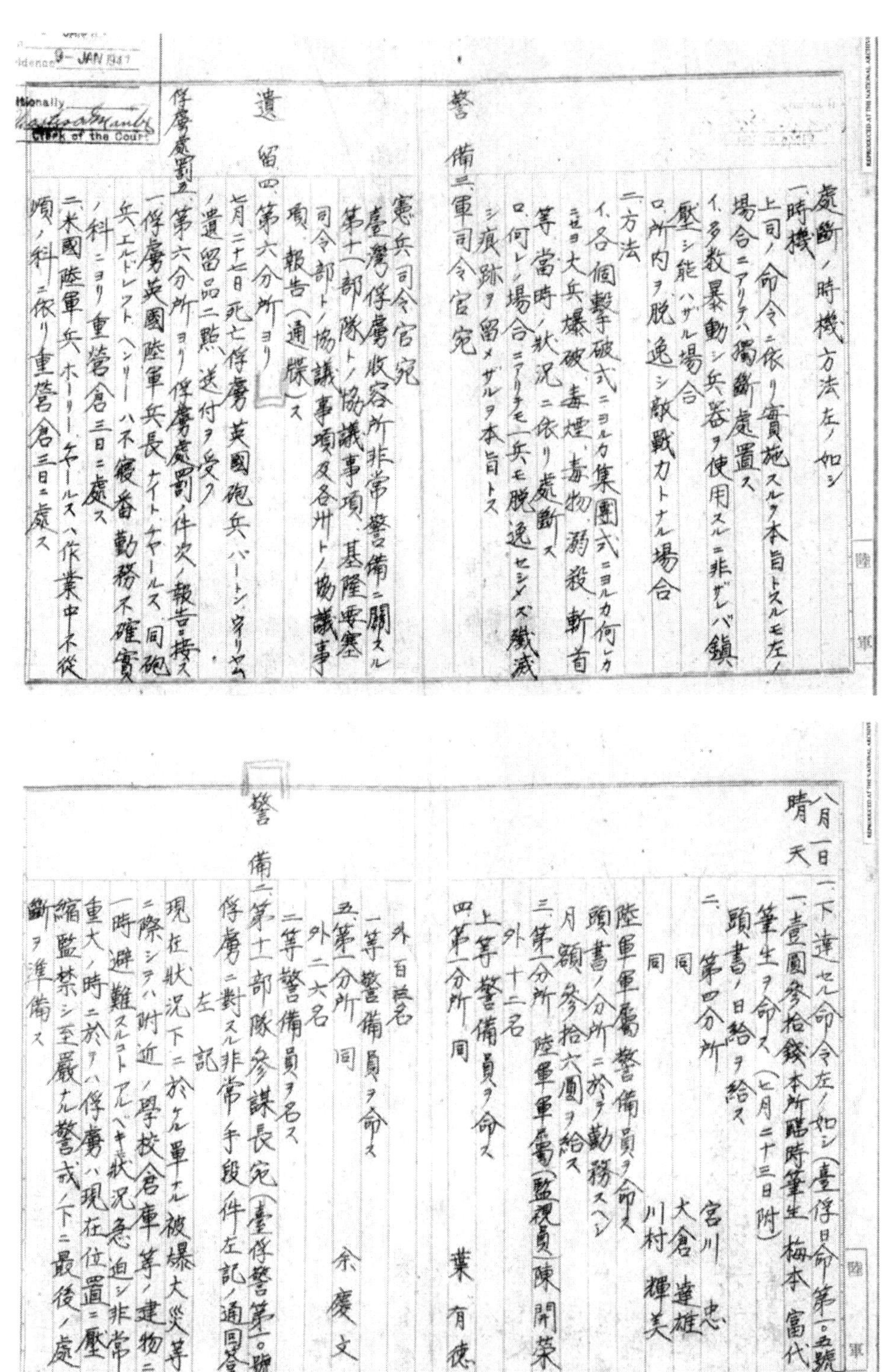

處斷ノ時機方法左ノ如シ

一、時機

上司ノ命令ニ依リ實施スルヲ本旨トスルモ左ノ場合ニアリテハ獨斷處置ス

イ、多数暴動シ兵器ヲ使用スルニ非ザレバ鎮壓シ能ハザル場合

ロ、所内ヲ脱逸シ敵戰力トナル場合

二、方法

イ、各個撃破式ニヨルカ集團式ニヨルカ何レカニセヨ大兵爆破、毒煙、毒物、溺殺、斬首等當時ノ状況ニ依リ處斷ス

ロ、何レノ場合ニアリテモ一兵モ脱逸セシメズ殲滅シ痕跡ヲ留メザルヲ本旨トス

警備三、軍司令官宛

憲兵司令官宛

臺灣俘虜收容所非常警備ニ關スル第十一部隊トノ協議事項、基隆要塞司令部トノ協議事項及各州トノ協議事項、報告(通牒)ス

遺留四、第六分所ヨリ

七月二十七日死亡俘虜英國砲兵バートン・ウヰリヤムノ遺留品二點送付ヲ受ク

俘虜處罰五、第六分所ヨリ俘虜處罰ノ件次ノ報告ニ接ス

一、俘虜英國陸軍兵長ナイトチャールス同砲兵エルドレットヘンリーハ不寝番勤務不確實ノ科ニヨリ重營倉三日ニ處ス

二、米國陸軍兵ホーリーチャールスハ作業中不從順ノ科ニ依リ重營倉三日ニ處ス

八月一日 晴天

一、下達セル命令左ノ如シ(臺俘日命第一〇五號)

一、壹圓參拾錢 本所臨時筆生 梅本富代

筆生ヲ命ス(七月二十三日附)

二、第四分所

頭書ノ日給ヲ給ス

同 宮川忠

同 大倉達雄

川村輝美

陸軍軍屬警備員ヲ命ス

頭書ノ分所ニ於テ勤務スヘシ

月額參拾六圓ヲ給ス

三、第一分所 陸軍軍屬(監視員)陳開榮

外十二名

上等警備員ヲ命ス

四、第一分所 同 葉有德

外百參名

一等警備員ヲ命ス

五、第一分所 同 余慶文

外二六名

二等警備員ヲ命ス

警備二、第十一部隊參謀長宛(臺俘警第一〇號)

俘虜ニ對スル非常手段ノ件左記ノ通回答ス

左記

現在状況下ニ於ケル單ナル被爆大災等ニ際シテハ附近ノ學校、倉庫等ノ建物ニ一時避難スルコトアルヘキ状況急迫シ非常重大ノ時ニ於テハ俘虜ハ現在位置ニ壓縮監禁シ至嚴ナル警戒ノ下ニ最後ノ處斷ヲ準備ス

Kill them all, 1944. Courtesy Roger Mansell.

The following translation was found in File 2015, designated as Document No. 2710, certified as Exhibit "O" in Doc. No. 2687. The date indicated, "1 August xxxx" appears to have the year lined out with a pen. The year appears to be 1944 in the original typing. The number "2015" is penciled in the upper right corner. No other marks were noted on the sheet.

---

Document No. 2701 Page 1
(Certified as Exhibit "O" in Do. No. 2687)

From the Journal of the Taiwan POW Camp H.Q. in Taihoku, entry
1 August 19xx

---

1. (Entries about money, promotions of Formosans at Branch camps, including promotion of Yo Yu-teku to 1st C1 Keibiin - 5 entries)

2 The following answer about the extreme measures for POW's was sent To the Chief of Staff of the 11th Unit (Formosa POW Security No. 10)

3. "Under the present situation if there were a mere explosion or fire a shelter for the time being could be had in nearby buildings such as the school, a warehouse, or the like. However, at such time as the situation became urgent and it be extremely important, the POW's will be concentrated and confined in their present location and under heavy guard the preparation for the final disposition will be made.

The time and method of the disposition are as follows:

(1) The Time.

Although the basic aim is to act under superior orders, Individual disposition may be made in the following circumstances:

(a) When an uprising of large numbers cannot be suppressed without the use of firearms.

(b) When escapees from the camp may turn into a hostile fighting force.

(2) The Methods.

(a) Whether they are destroyed individually or in groups, or however it is done, with mass bombing, poisonous smoke, poisons, drowning, decapitation, or what, dispose of them as the situation dictates.

(b) In any case it is the aim not to allow the escape of a single one, to amilhilate [sic] them all, and not to leave any traces.

(3) To: The Commanding General
The Commanding General of Military Police

Reported matters conferred on with the 11th Unit, the Kiirun Fortified Area H.Q., and each prefecture concerning the extreme security in Taiwan POW Camps."

---

English translation of Document 2710, "Kill them all," 1944.

WORKING THE MINES

The Japanese practice drift mining for coal. Tunnels are supported or timbered as the coal is removed. Prisoners transported to Japan to work in the mines receive their first new clothing in two and a half years. By Benjamin Steele.

Japanese camp commander punishes Gene Jacobsen (holding shovel) and Al Roholt in Camp #17. By Benjamin Steele.

Working Topside

Topside work at a Japanese coal mine is strenuous. A cut is made into a mountainside to make roadbeds for tracks. Prisoners load large rocks onto flatcars and then roll the cars to a fill and dump them. By Benjamin Steele.

## 17

# CAMP NO. 17, OMUTA, JAPAN

OUR SHIP, WE LEARNED the following morning, had docked at Port Moji on the northern end of the island of Kyushu. Before we were permitted to disembark, we were again lined up and examined for signs of dysentery. The Japanese, satisfied we were fit to honor their noble land, allowed us to go ashore. What a sight we must have been! Our hair and whiskers were again long and matted from sweat and dirt. Our filth-covered bodies were disgusting to us and must have been completely revolting to the Japanese, who prided themselves in keeping as clean as possible. What clothing we had smelled bad and was full of lice. No wonder the Japanese sprayed disinfectant over us as we marched down the gangplank.

Once on the dock we were immediately divided into groups of approximately one hundred men. The group to which I was assigned was marched to a large shed and locked inside. What happened to the other groups of men we had no idea. Not until after the end of the war did we learn of the many different POW camps spread throughout Japan.

It was inside the shed that we had the pleasure of meeting for the first time our Japanese interpreter. He was a young fellow, probably in his late twenties. Having been reared in Riverside, California, and having graduated from the University of California, he spoke perfect English. To hear him talking within a group of men, one would never suspect that he wasn't one of the prisoners. That fact created serious problems for us because, even though he had spent most of his life in our country, his loyalties were definitely with the Japanese, and we laid no claim to the sneaky rat. We soon learned he would pull every dirty trick on record and invent others to get the Americans into trouble whenever he could. He was truly a dangerous human being and was responsible for the severe punishment of many prisoners of war.

During the day in the shed we were given a large chunk of brown sourdough bread. This was the first bread I had eaten since long before the fall of Bataan, and although it was of poor quality, it tasted better than any bread that I had ever eaten. Our spirits zoomed. If bread like this was provided where we were going, maybe there was other American chow.

The bread was all the food we were given that day, and even though I ate mine slowly, I had the worst case of indigestion I had ever experienced.

In the evening, shortly after dark, we were marched from the shed through a poor section of the city to the railroad station. Japanese civilians lined the streets, and from their actions we got the impression that they weren't too fond of us or of Americans in general. They spit on us, threw rocks and other items at us, and hurled insults. We couldn't understand what they were saying, but it appeared that they were slightly unhappy about something. Our guards had a full job of keeping them back. Although we couldn't really sympathize with them, we knew about how they felt and only hoped their actions were an indication the war was going badly for them.

At the station, much to our surprise, we were, dirt and all, put into passenger cars. If we hadn't been crammed in so tightly, the ride wouldn't have been half bad. Our pal the interpreter, whose name was Yamamuchi, warned us to keep the blinds pulled. After our very recent experience with the Japanese public, we understood the message clearly.

Our train trip lasted only until two or three in the morning. As we unloaded, we read the name *Omuta* on the station sign. From the station we were marched for hours through the dark streets of what appeared to be a very large city. Not until after daylight did we come to the outskirts of this city and into the industrialized area. The road went past a large coal mine, and out near the bay we could see what appeared to be the high walls of a camp. It wasn't long until we were marched through an opening in those walls and out into an open field.

The morning was bleak, gray, and misty, but the prison camp, which was to be our new home, looked even bleaker. Over by the barracks we could see Japanese guards moving about, but very few prisoners did we see.

Again the Japanese inspected us, our clothing, and our possessions. They took any pencils or paper the fellows had, as well as anything of value at all. After all the times we had already been herded together and shaken down, the Japanese didn't get much stuff, I can assure you.

The Japanese brought several fifty-gallon drums over to the area and ordered us to fill them with water and get the water boiling. As soon as the water was scalding hot, all pieces of our clothing were piled in. Were we ever glad to see those body lice get what was coming to them!

While the clothing was boiling, we took turns clipping each other's hair and whiskers with hand clippers that the Japanese loaned us. They then notified us that it was our responsibility to see that our hair was kept closely clipped all the time. Following the haircuts, we were allowed to go to the small bathhouse and bathe ourselves. We were even given small pieces of soap. After going through the cleansing process, we went over to the barracks area and received our assignments, fifty men to a building. The buildings were long and narrow, each containing three large rooms and a small front room.

Five men, including the barracks leader, were assigned to the small front room and fifteen men were assigned to each of the three large rooms. The buildings seemed to be fairly well constructed and were fairly clean. Inside and stretching the full length down one side of each building was a cement walkway. Along the wall was a bench.

Our instructions were to remove our shoes and step from the walk up to the bench and into our rooms. That didn't present too much of a problem initially because many of us didn't have shoes when we arrived in Japan. At the back end of each building, but within the building, were wooden toilets.

Each man received a comforter. Hard, small straw pillows were strewn about on the floor, which was covered with woven straw mats. The floor also served as our bed.

The following day we were given another physical examination. Why they examined us, I'll never know; they never did anything to help us. Each prisoner then received a number. While holding our numbers up in front of us, we were photographed. We were much skinnier than most criminals I had seen, but nevertheless, with shaved heads and bony faces, we looked like real criminals, for sure.

My number was 1151, "sen-hyaku go-ju ich." From that time on, the Japanese called us by our numbers. The name by which I was called was "go-ju ich."

That same day we each received several pieces of new clothing. The issue consisted of a forest-green-color coat and trousers made of flimsy sackcloth material for wear back and forth to the mine. Also furnished was a g-string and a white, short-sleeved shirt, and a cap to wear in the mine. To stack on the shelves in our rooms for eyewash were a suit of heavy green Japanese NCO clothing and an overcoat. Provided in addition were a pair of split-toed rubber-soled shoes somewhat like American sneakers without laces.

Our numbers were stenciled on each piece of clothing so we and the clothing could be easily identified.

Just outside each room was a board on which we hung our wooden number tags. When we were in the room, our tags had to indicate our presence there. Before going to chow or to roll call or to the toilet or to work, we had to place our tags in the proper place indicting where we had gone. If a guard came by the room, which one would do regularly, and he found a POW's tag hanging in the wrong place, he would put it in his pocket. When he found the culprit, he would punish him, sometimes severely. On a fairly regular basis a guard would pick up tags even when they were properly placed, just to make life more miserable for us. The slapping and kicking were no big deal for us, but when we were deprived of a meal as punishment, we suffered severely.

Each evening at a specified time we would fall out on the parade ground for "tenko" (roll call). Everyone had to count off in Japanese. To miss a number meant the receipt of a hard slap across the face or sometimes even a beating, depending upon the mood of the guards at that particular time. This treatment motivated us to learn to count to at least fifty, the number of men in our building.

All during our internment as prisoners of war, the Japanese guards demonstrated their enjoyment in seeing us suffer. Rarely was there any compassion demonstrated in any way. I couldn't understand then and still am unable to comprehend why those people exhibited such hostility and brutality. One might expect an incident from time to time, but viciousness was a regular part of their behavior toward us.

Sometimes, especially during the winter months, we would stand in the bitter cold and snow for hours before the Japanese guards would come to count us. They seemed to delight in making life as miserable for us as they possibly could. As a result there was much undeserved suffering among the prisoners when a great deal of it could easily have been avoided. Frostbitten feet were common, as were colds. Deaths during the cold period were often the result of pneumonia.

It wasn't long until we had met and had held long discussions with many of the five hundred Americans already in the camp. They informed us gloomily that we had been sent to a terrible place. These men had been in the camp for over a year, working in the coal mine. They told us the work was hard, the guards in the camp and the Japanese supervisors in the mine were brutal, and the Japanese camp commander was a tyrant. The food was a little better prepared than they had back in the Philippines, but the rations were small and consisted almost entirely of rice and thin soup. Rarely was there any meat, and if meat was served, it was in tiny pieces in the soup.

It didn't take us long to verify that the American officer in charge of the mess hall was worse than any of the Japanese. He was a despot of the worst kind, and at the slightest provocation he would deprive a man of his food. I saw men severely punished by him for entering the mess hall with their caps on. Worse than that, he would turn men over to the Japanese guards to be punished. He was a bad one, and we prayed that he would be dealt with before the thing was over. Even the Japanese were wary of him. They called him "skoshi dono" (little god).

After three days we, the new one hundred men, were taken to the parade ground, and recruit drill, Japanese style, commenced. Their drills were very similar to ours, and we soon learned the commands given in their language. We even became quite proficient at goose stepping.

The training completed, we were taken down to the coal mine and schooled in underground mining operations. We learned how to timber a ceiling, how to operate a jackhammer, how to use dynamite for bringing down a long wall of coal as well as for breaking huge rocks, and we were also taught the Japanese lingo used in the mine. The importance of knowing the names of all of the tools, timbers, wedges, etc., was rigorously stressed.

On the 19th of September, 1944, my 23rd birthday, we entered the mine for the first time and worked almost daily from then on. Each morning we would arise from our straw mats long before daylight and go to the mess hall to get a bowl of rice to put into a little wooden bento box to take to the mine. We were also served a second bowl of rice and a bowl of soup for our breakfast.

After we had finished our soup and put both servings of rice into the bento box, we would march to the guardhouse to be counted and searched. A supervisor from the mine would then take charge and march us to the mine area, which was about two miles away. There were always Japanese soldiers to guard us and to make sure our behavior was appropriate.

By daylight or shortly after, we would arrive at the mine and immediately draw our lamps. Next, all would assemble in a large hall to be assigned to specific work details. There also the Japanese would pray to the mine god, and of course they insisted we join with them in the ceremony, which consisted of a lot of chanting and bowing.

The Japanese mine official, one with two stripes across his lamp indicating he was a big shot, would then call out a Japanese worker's name. The worker would present himself before the supervisor and bow low. The official would call the numbers of four or five of us prisoners, each of whom would respond loudly and sharply, "Hai!" and bow. The size of the detail would depend upon the nature of the assigned work for the day.

By seven or seven-thirty we would catch the train and ride down into the mine, which extended out under the bay. The ride was a long, cold one, and we were always happy when it was finished.

After getting off the train, we would go to the underground storeroom and get our tools. Our Japanese overseer would then lead us to our job.

Once on the job we would take off all of our clothing except the g-string and our caps and shirt. The shirts were made of material of poor quality and soon wore out. Many of us worked barefoot and saved the split-toed shoes for walking back and forth to the mine in the snow.

We would then eat our rice and go to work. When the supervisor stopped at noon to eat his lunch, we either slept or tried to kill the lice in our clothing. Lice killing was an activity that required considerable patience and skill. Lice could be found hiding in the seams, primarily, but occasionally could be found more out in the open. At noon we always wished that there was food to eat because we were always hungry, but we found we could work better during the entire day if we ate what we had before the work began in the morning.

About five in the evening we would turn our tools in and make a run to catch the train out of the mine. Topside again we first had to be searched, and then we would turn in our lamps and batteries. Following that, we would go to the bathhouse and attempt to wash off the dirt and grease of the day in water already muddied by several hundred men who had arrived there ahead of us.

After the bath we would be marched back to camp. Once in the camp the guards would always search us and count us again before allowing us to go to our sleeping quarters to get our mess kits.

Over at the mess hall we were given another bowl of rice and soup.

After chow was roll call, and by that time it was usually dark and all generally went immediately to bed. There was absolutely nothing else to do, and everyone was too tired to do anything anyway. This was our schedule day after day with very little change and nothing to break the monotony.

For the first two or three months there were only six hundred prisoners of war, all Americans, in camp. With the exception of those who worked in camp and those too sick to work, all were assigned to the coal mine. Apparently we had been hired out by the government to the mine owner, a Baron Von Mitsui or someone with a similar name. A number of different shifts of men were sent to the mine daily. I happened to be assigned to a permanent day shift. Others went at different times during the day or night.

In the mine there were three levels. The first level seemed to be worked mostly by the Japanese and the Koreans. The second level was by far the best as far as working conditions were concerned. This level was dry and the temperature was good, not too hot or too cold. The third level was way down and was wet and miserable. Water was running along the floor of the tunnels and dripping from the ceiling everywhere. This was the level where our shift was first sent to work. It was like a terrible nightmare to have to work down there.

The entire mine had already been worked out and was extremely dangerous. Before the war it had been condemned, and it was easy to see why. On many occasions we were sent into caved-in tunnels to dig out equipment, and a lot of the timbers we used were ones salvaged from caved-in sections of the mine.

Shortly before Christmas of 1944 new men began to arrive in camp. Those who came in during the following six months were of all nationalities. There were Englishmen, Canadians, Australians, and Scots taken prisoner in Malaysia and Singapore. Javanese and European Dutch were captured in the Dutch East Indies. Finally, there were more Americans from the Philippines. All of the men had tales to tell of the horrors and death under the rule of the Japanese conquerors. Some had weathered attacks from American submarines on the way to Japan and had seen ships loaded with POWs sunk with all passengers lost. American planes had also taken their toll from among the transports sailing from the southern islands to Japan. None of those carrying Allied troops had been properly identified by the Japanese as POW ships.

Most of these new men were assigned to work in the mine after going through the proper training to qualify them for the work. A large number of British soldiers were later assigned to work in a zinc smelter.

Of course, with all the new men arriving, more buildings had to be built to accommodate them. Crews of Japanese carpenters were working in camp all the time. We were quite sure the construction wasn't going on for our benefit alone. The Japanese were building for future activities.

Included in the building projects was a huge mess hall. The place was large enough to seat many men and provided better cooking facilities. It still didn't provide more food, though. In this mess hall was always a supply of hot tea boiling in a huge wooden vat. Most of us drank the strong stuff all the time. We were confident that the constant boiling made the liquid pure and that was more than could be said of the tap water in the camp or that running in the mine.

While we worked in the mine we were paid fifteen sentos per day. The mine owner was supposed to furnish cigarettes for us to buy. Supposedly, we were to be able to buy ten cigarettes every other day. The cost for the smokes was thirty-five sentos. At fifteen sentos per day, we didn't earn enough money to even buy cigarettes. In reality we did have enough money because the cigarette rations were few and far between. In order to manage, two men would team up and smoke together. Holders had been whittled out of pieces of bamboo so that all of a cigarette could be smoked.

The first thing after chow in the morning two men would smoke half a cigarette. The other half would be smoked before going into the mine. Out of the mine in the evening one-half of another cigarette would be smoked, and after supper the other half would be used. Before the men went to bed, their custom was to splurge and smoke a whole cigarette together.

Many times there was no tobacco at all, so some of the men would smoke leaves or anything else that looked at all like tobacco. It would have been much simpler to quit smoking and get out of all of the misery. I didn't know many who did quit, though. How the smokers talked of those good old sweet-smelling American cigarettes.

Because of the lack of proper diet, boils were common. One fellow in our room had more than fifty boils on his body at one time. He was in terrible pain constantly. The Japanese still insisted that he work in the mine, even though he was covered with open sores. Some of the larger boils, carbuncles, had three or four large cores in them. Until the cores were removed, the open sores would not heal.

At one time three boils formed on the back of my right leg. The leg had become swollen and was very painful, but the boils would not come to a head. It became extremely difficult for me to walk.

Finally, I went over to the Australian doctor in camp and asked to have the boils lanced. While the pain from the cutting was excruciating, the doc's work almost remedied my problem. Infection from two of the boils shot out when the boils were punctured, and much of the pain in the leg subsided. The other boil continued to give me problems for a long time. Those three were the only boils I had, and they finally healed, leaving scars. It was in this camp that many of us experienced having a tooth or teeth removed without the benefit of a deadening drug. A major in the dental corps carried with him a pair of forceps, and each time before extracting a tooth he would say, "Join me in praying that the tooth doesn't break."

Meatless meals were the order of the day, and with the exception of a few mangy dogs that the Japanese occasionally brought into camp, we rarely had any meat to eat. One day, however, they brought in part of a whale. It looked terrible and smelled worse. The mess-hall people cooked and served it to us with our ration of rice. Most of the fellows gobbled it down.

Even as hungry as I was for meat, I couldn't stand the smell and gave mine away. I was thankful afterwards that I didn't eat the stuff, for the meat was rotten, and many men were poisoned. None of them died, but many prayed that they could because they were so violently ill. For a couple of days there were no work details, and I had two days of rest while the sick recuperated.

Problems such as this upset the coal production schedule, so the Japanese imposed ways of working us to the extent of our abilities and strength to make up for days lost. At the mine they initiated make-believe contests with other mines in the vicinity or among the various shifts at our mine. The winners would be given a steamed biscuit, two or three cigarettes, a little piece of soap, a small handful of salt, or a drink of rice wine. They didn't have many takers on the wine, but everyone was eager for salt and most for cigarettes. In our poor physical condition, it was difficult for us to work, and without salt it was almost impossible. We often wished we could have carried off the pounds of coarse salt that had been loaded on the ship in Formosa.

Another incentive was the possibility of bathing in clean water. At the mine was one bathhouse for all of the miners, POWs, Japanese, and Koreans, and the first ones out of the hole got the clean water. The water was in a pool about the size of a large room in an American house.

Once in the bathhouse the procedure was for the men to dip water out of the pool and wash themselves before getting in. They didn't do that, though. Imagine what the water looked like after a few hundred coal miners had bathed. It was almost impossible to get clean, especially after having used a greasy jackhammer all day.

As we caught on to their strategy, the Japanese enjoyed little success as they prodded us to exceed our quota of work more rapidly to enable us to get out of the mine early. They never gave up trying, however.

On one particular day our detail was shoveling coal into cars pulled alongside a long wall. Occasionally while the cars were being changed, we could rest for a few minutes. On our detail was a prisoner who was apparently suffering from some form of sleeping sickness. Any time he wasn't in action, he would immediately fall asleep. When the new empties were pulled alongside the coal wall, we again began to fill them.

The sleeper, not hearing us go back to work, continued to sleep, leaning on his shovel. Before one of us could awaken him, the Japanese supervisor came close to him and shouted directly into his face. The sleeper, startled, awakened quickly, and with his fist hit the Japanese supervisor smack on the nose as hard as he could hit. The supervisor went down and sat in the coal, too surprised to move. We hurriedly told the supervisor the fellow was "kichagai no" (sick in the head) and didn't know what he was doing.

The supervisor avoided the fellow all the rest of the day, and in the evening, instead of reporting him to the soldier guards, gave the sleeper two cigarettes and a piece of soap. The Japanese were completely ill at ease around prisoners who had mental problems. They didn't want anything whatsoever to do with them.

As the weeks wore on, the Japanese were able to spare fewer of their civilian workers to mine coal. There was no question they were badly in need of additional workers. Because of this shortage, Americans in charge of each barracks were assigned to help supervise the workers in the mine. Why these particular people were chosen, we didn't know.

The sergeant who was our noble leader was a punk from one of the southern states. He had been a guerrilla in the Philippines for a short period of time, and after being captured he had worked for a spell with a

Japanese outfit on the northern part of Luzon. From them he learned some of their language and really made that knowledge pay off for him. He was deceitful and a liar of the first order who was looking out for his own welfare at the expense of others.

Because of his ability to speak a little Nipponese, he was in fairly good standing with the Japanese and used that to his advantage. The American captain assigned to our group was his pal, and the two of them ruled our group of fifty men with the rigid regulations they devised and implemented.

Assigned one day to the task of breaking and moving rock in the mine, we were placed under the sergeant's supervision. The Japanese overseer had left our detail to check on other work groups. Immediately upon the departure of the supervisor the obnoxious sergeant began to issue orders. One member of our crew, not willing to put up with his nonsense, told him to go to hell. The sergeant made a lunge for the fellow and was knocked down for his trouble. He picked up a rock and came back again. We grabbed him and held him away from his challenger. I believe his opponent would have bashed his head in if the Japanese supervisor hadn't returned earlier than anticipated. We did have time to warn him to keep his mouth shut, and that he was smart enough to do. He reported the incident to his buddy, the captain, though, who threatened to expose the entire group of us to the Japanese. Not all of the Americans were saints by any means.

For a period of about six weeks I worked on a detail under the supervision of a civilian by the name of Sonbu San (Mr. Sonbu). There were five of us on the detail in the beginning, and we worked in an abandoned section of the mine trying to salvage conveyor machinery. The ceiling was bad, and there were no supporting timbers at all. At first we were all frightened to be in the place and kept one eye on the ceiling all of the time.

After a few days in the abandoned area of the mine, I got over being frightened. The other fellows seemed to get worse instead of better, and finally they had to be taken off the detail. I know that I was no braver than they, and I hadn't given up caring by any means. From time to time there were serious accidents, and workers were badly injured or killed. I continued to be sensitive to the possible danger but had lost my fear even though huge chunks of stone continued to fall from the cavernous area in which we worked.

The recovery of the machinery must have been terribly important to the mine owners because they continued with the salvage effort. Each day Sonbu San and I would return to our work place and doggedly dig away the fallen debris. During the time the two of us worked together, we didn't become close friends, but he seemed to have a certain amount of respect for me, and I appreciated the fact that he had plenty of savvy concerning working in the coal mine. He appreciated my company and my help, especially after I was no longer forced to accompany him on his daily dangerous mission. Because of his knowledge, I knew that he would always be careful and use good judgment.

Rarely were we questioned concerning our work, and never were we visited by a roving Japanese supervisor. Consequently, there were times when neither of us worked very hard, and on numerous occasions we slept for two or three hours before leaving the mine in the early evening.

When we were finally pulled off that work assignment, Sonbu San was transferred to a different job, and I rarely saw him after that. When I did, he always hollered something to me and waved.

After that lengthy experience I was assigned to work with a Japanese whom we called "the kicker." With just a hatchet and a little handsaw for tools, he was a genius at timbering a mine tunnel. There were six of us on that first detail with him—four fellows to handle timbers and two of us to help put them up.

The first day we cut a set of three timbers and had them in place against the ceiling. The Japanese had climbed up to wedge them against the ceiling. He was standing on a log held on a slant by several of the other workers. I had my hands full of wedges and was handing them to him as he called for them.

As he worked, he jabbered constantly in Nipponese, and it was difficult for me to understand what he was saying. Wanting a certain wedge and not being able to make me understand, he became violently angry and kicked me hard in the face. The blow hurt, and before I realized what I was doing, I dropped the wedges and grabbed his foot, leaving him standing on the other foot on the slanted timber. Then I twisted his leg. The pressure on his hip and knee was intense, and the pain generated must have been fierce.

He raised his hatchet to strike me, and I applied more pressure, as much as I possibly could.

Still holding the foot, I looked him right in the eye and said, "Don't you hit me, you little devil, or I'll tear this leg right out of you! And don't you ever hit or kick me again!"

With hatchet poised, he looked at me for a long few seconds and then slowly relaxed his arm. I cautiously released the pressure on his leg, still staring fiercely at him. Then, we went quietly back to work.

I was sure that he would turn me over to the guards that evening when we got out of the mine, but he didn't. In all, I must have worked with this fellow every day for about three months. And except for the first day, we got along just fine. He occasionally beat the other workers, but never did he touch me. Each morning I would tell the new men that they were to allow me to work right close to him and they were to stay out of his reach. He had a terrible temper and had great difficulty controlling it, and seldom did he seem to want to control it.

# 18

# STILL ALIVE IN '45

ONE FEBRUARY MORNING, along about ten o'clock, a Japanese runner came through the mine with the word that all prisoners of war were to be taken out of the mine. Our hearts pounded! Could this be the day we had been awaiting so long?

The Japanese overseers had no information and neither did the other workers whom we met at the train as we left for the surface. The atmosphere was one of excited tension as the train slowly made its way to the top of the tunnel.

Once out of the mine we were turned over to the Japanese guards from camp. We soon realized this wasn't the day nor was it going to be a picnic. Someone from one of the other shifts was missing when the miners were counted prior to going back to camp.

After a search of several hours, the man was finally found in one of the abandoned tunnels, but it was too late for us to go back down into the mine again that day. Because the fellow was obviously ill, mentally and physically, he was not beaten by the Japanese. He had to be helped back to camp, and on the way he reported that he had decided there was no use trying to go on, and so he had gone off by himself to die. He had just given up, and he did die in camp several days later.

The feeling of desperation was being shared by more men daily, and the constant brutality of the Japanese guards and the civilians in the mine didn't help matters any. The Japanese were professionals when it came to dealing out punishment, masters in the art of torture. And they seemed to get much enjoyment out of their efforts.

Most of the punishment was administered by the guards in the guardhouse at the entrance of the camp. Their practice was to bind a man's hands behind his back and then go to work on him. Their methods of torture varied. Some they would just beat, but others would be given repeated charges of electricity. Some would have to stand for hours at attention holding an item out in front of them. One Marine was thrown into a cell for stealing food. Reported by the American mess officer, he lived for over twenty days without food. All the while he cursed the Japanese and spit in their faces. When he finally died, his body, hardly more than a skeleton, was put on public display. Hate alone must have kept him alive for that long period of time.

On another occasion four fellows each stole a carrot from off a truck and were caught. It was during the winter, and the ground was covered with snow. These four men—an American, two Englishmen, and an Aussie—were completely stripped of their clothing and were forced to stand naked on a table in the unheated mess hall, each holding the carrot he had taken out in front of himself.

The sight of those poor guys made everyone else sick. Later, they were taken outside in front of the guardhouse to stand in the snow. Two of the men, both Englishmen, died from exposure. One of the others had to have both legs amputated. The fourth kept his legs but was crippled for life.

Our honorable American mess officer, the Navy lieutenant, also saw to it that many Americans and others were punished by the Japanese for simple infractions of his unreasonable rules. How we hated that man—even more than we hated the Japanese guards!

The prisoners of war were not the only ones to get punished. The Japanese workers, suffering from shortages of all types, were constantly tempted to improve their lot. One day in the mine one Japanese worker stole another's lunch. The thief was caught and nearly beaten to death by the other Japanese workers. Again it verified to us that the Japanese just delighted in beating someone. They didn't seem to be particular concerning which nationality.

During the winter with the cold and the snow, the morale of all of us hit rock bottom. Often we were forced to stand in the snow in front of the guardhouse for hours waiting to be counted. A number of men died from pneumonia, and their bodies were cremated. The buildings weren't heated, and even though we went to bed with all of our clothing on and huddled together, some nights we almost froze. On those cold days it was a relief to get into the mine and out of the snow and the cold. We knew the Japanese civilians weren't much better off, though, because they used to steal coal by filling their tiny lunch boxes. The boxes were so small that they held only a handful of coal, so to take a chance of getting caught for only that much coal proved to us that they were in bad circumstances. Once caught, they were beaten severely.

As the days passed, it seemed to us that pressure was being put on the Japanese supervisors, and they in turn were putting greater pressure on us. The work became so difficult along toward spring that some of the fellows would have their arms broken to get out of going to the mine. They would lay their arm across two logs and have a buddy hit it with a club. At first it paid off, and they were permitted to stay out of the mine. Later, so many were coming out of the mine with broken arms that the Japanese wised up and made them go to work, even though they were severely handicapped.

One day I saw a fellow stand on the railroad track and let a loaded coal car run over his feet and cut off his toes. In spite of the pain and the loss of his toes, he figured he saved his life because he got out of going back into the coal mine.

Another fellow persuaded a colleague to break his leg for him. When the fellow swung the heavy piece of timber, he hit his friend on the ankle, crushing the bones in his foot and ankle. Our Australian doctor informed him that he would be crippled for life, but he didn't care. He was permanently retired from the mine.

The way the work assignments were arranged, we were supposed to get every tenth day off. The Japanese paid no attention to Sundays; all days were alike to them. On the tenth day only a skeleton crew was supposed to go to the mine. That crew would have to build rock structures to help hold up the ceiling along a "long wall." The Japanese always worked this detail like mad because they wanted part of a day off, too.

On this particular "tenth" day I was working with Al Roholt. He was the fellow from Wisconsin who had challenged the barracks sergeant. We had been drilling and blasting rock for use in filling the cribs being constructed. Being on the day shift, we spent a great deal of time drilling and blasting rock, and the work was hard. The jackhammers were old and heavy and constantly battered us as we drilled holes in preparation for the blasting that was to follow.

He and I were then ordered to go into abandoned sections of the mine and carry out any timbers we could salvage. With those timbers the workers would build a crib to be filled with rock.

We had made several trips for timbers and had gone back into an abandoned tunnel for another usable log. The one we found and dug out was big and water-soaked. I am sure that it weighed almost as much as the weight of the two of us combined.

After carrying the "Kabok" (huge log) a short distance, we threw it off our shoulders to take a break. No sooner had we sat down than a Japanese came around the corner of the tunnel. He was a "two-striper big-shot." He shouted, asking in Nipponese why we weren't busy. We told him that the log was heavy and that we were taking a short rest.

He was a young, handsome fellow and he was also angry.

Looking at us for a moment, he abruptly called us to attention with his shrill "Kiotski!"

Then he hit me.

He didn't hit as a man would with his fist, but swung as a woman might. Standing at attention as I was, he knocked me down. I didn't mind that so much, but he also broke a piece of one of my back teeth.

He hit Al as I was getting up. I spit the piece of tooth out into my hand and turning to Al said, "I think I'll kill the son-of-a-bitch! He has nothing to do with us!"

I wondered why I should take any more. There is an end to everyone's endurance, and I had about reached mine. The guy had no business even talking to us. We weren't on his detail; we were doing our work and deserved a rest.

I knew I could have easily choked him to death. Then it would have been simple to bury him in that deserted area.

Whether he could understand English or whether he simply sensed my frame of mind, I don't know, but he took off down the tunnel like a rabbit. It was undoubtedly most fortunate for me he did leave.

Sometime during the early spring of 1945, the Japanese moved most of the Allied officers out of our camp. Yet much to our sorrow, the mess officer was not among them. Early in the morning of their departure, we assembled on the parade ground, and the Japanese permitted the ranking American officer to speak to us.

"Men, I told you at Christmastime last year I hoped 1945 would be our year. I am telling you now this is the year we have been waiting for so long!"

We cheered with joy at those words and didn't care if the guards knocked us around for the noise and our behavior. If the officer was ever punished for his pronouncement, we never knew, for he and his colleagues moved out almost immediately.

Not long after that day, and after I had been working in water in the mine for two or three days in a row, I started early one morning to get terribly stiff in my joints. By late afternoon I could scarcely walk and had to be helped out of the mine and back to camp. I could tell that a fever was developing, and by chow time I was too miserable to eat.

My roommates helped me into the room and covered me with their comforters. I slept, and when I awoke in the night, I couldn't move a finger without crying out in pain. The pain throughout my entire body was so intense that I could hardly stand it.

Two of the fellows persuaded the building guard to come to look at me. He had them go to the Japanese area and get a stretcher. They soon returned, and with the help of the other guys in the room, they were able to put me on the stretcher. I was then carried to the building reserved for men too ill to work. There I was placed on a bed, off the floor.

The Australian doctor who examined me informed me I was having an attack of rheumatic fever. He said, "I have absolutely no medicine to give to you, so the only thing I can do that may be helpful is to keep you in this building until you are able to go to work once again."

For about forty-eight hours I ran a high fever with pain so terrible I couldn't bear to move any part of my body. On the third day the fever broke, and I began to sweat. The water just poured from my body. With the sweating I began to feel a great relief from the intense pain. Before the day was over, I could bend my knees a little and move my fingers. After a couple more days, even though I was very weak, I could walk slowly around the room by staying close to the wall for support.

During each of the first two days when the fever was at full strength, I had been given a chunk of bread to eat. I was unable to eat the bread, so it was placed by my head where I could guard it from thieves. During the night rats jumped onto my bed and ate the bread right by my head. Although they walked over my face and I knew what they were doing by my head, I could do nothing to stop them. I was grateful they didn't start gnawing on my face.

Within a week, although I was still sick and very weak, I was put on what was called limited duty. That meant that I was to work on details inside the camp.

The first day at work a small group of us was assigned to the job of covering a cement air-raid shelter with dirt. We had marched over to the Japanese area and were left under the supervision of an American sergeant.

My friend, Al, had been ill too, so he was assigned to the same work detail.

I had a short-handled shovel and he, a pick. He would pick a little dirt loose, and then I would shovel a little. The sergeant told all of us to take it easy, and he would warn us if any Japanese came near.

Al and I were resting when, all of a sudden, we heard a loud "Kiotski!" (attention) shouted.

We turned around, and there stood the Japanese camp commander. A short fellow whose two-fisted sword trailed along on the ground, he had come up on us between the buildings, and no one had seen him.

Looking at Al and me, he shouted, "Nan no?" (What are you doing?)

We explained to him as best we could we were all sick men and were working slowly because we were so weak. He then motioned for Al and me to come over to him.

"I guess he wants us to work over there," I said. With that I picked up my shovel and started over toward him.

As soon as I got close to the man, I could see that he was very angry. His little pig-like eyes were just shooting fire.

In rage he grabbed the shovel from me and attempted to hit me in the face with the edge of the blade. I ducked from it enough for the edge to miss me, but the flat of the blade struck me full in the face. As weak as I was, it knocked me to the ground. As I was getting to my feet, he knocked Al down. He then turned on me once again.

How many times he struck me with the shovel I don't know. But I was sure he had broken my back. He must have tired himself, for he finally quit and told us to go with him.

We were frightened terribly, for we had seen some of the punishment dealt out at the guardhouse.

Once at the guardhouse he jabbered some cock-and-bull story about the two of us refusing to work. Any fool bothering to look at us carefully could have seen that we were in no condition to work. We should have still been in bed.

Between the commander and the guards, they concocted the idea that we should be punished by being forced to kneel on two rough bamboo poles—one pole at our knees and the other one under our shins. A Japanese then stood on our feet to make sure that all of our weight was on the bamboo poles. With that the commander started to leave the guardhouse. As an afterthought he returned and gave me the shovel to hold over my head.

Within a matter of minutes the pain in my legs from the bamboo poles and in my arms from holding the shovel was almost unbearable.

I could hardly believe that this was really happening to us. If I attempted to lower the shovel, I would get a kick from one of the guards for my trouble. To make matters worse, Al could put his hands down occasionally to shift his weight. As he moved, the rough bamboo poles cut deeper into my legs. He didn't realize what he was doing, and when I told him, he quit moving.

After an hour or so, my arms and shoulders were so numb they didn't hurt as much. Neither did my legs, because the circulation had been cut off. My body seemed almost completely paralyzed. My mind was still clear and for the first time, I questioned whether or not I would be alive to see the Yanks and tanks arrive. I wanted to cry but tears wouldn't come.

The clock in the guardhouse, I remember, had said 2:15 p.m. when we were brought in by the camp commander. At 5:30 the shifts from the mine began to come in, and we became the objects of interest.

The hatred for the Japanese and the desire for revenge could easily be read in the men's eyes, but there was nothing they could do to help us. Many of them had been in about the same predicament and could empathize with us. They knew what we were experiencing. Just before six in the evening, the Japanese commander left camp, and with him left our hopes of ever getting free.

At six the guards changed, and we had to get a few parting kicks. The new guards were about to take over on the fun when they were abruptly halted by their sergeant. He cut out all of the monkey business in a hurry, and after posting the new guard, he came over to talk to us.

After we had explained the situation to him, he just shook his head in disgust. I know he really felt sorry for us.

"As much as I would like to," he said, "I am afraid to let you go."

He did tell me to give the shovel to Al, though, who turned to me and said, "If I have to take the shovel, I'll never make it."

He was in worse physical condition than I, and I had no doubt of the truthfulness of his statement. He had courage plus and was never one to look for an easy out. By that time I was so numb it didn't matter, anyway, so I told the sergeant that I had better keep the shovel because the camp commander had given it to me.

He looked at me for a moment, and then he took the shovel and stood it against the wall near me.

Later in the evening the sergeant put a piece of American gum in his mouth and chewed it a second. He then took it out of his mouth, strolled over and slyly put it into my mouth. This was some more of the stuff sent over by the Red Cross the Japanese were using.

He then repeated the performance for Al. There was no doubt but what he feared one of the guards would see and report him. They didn't trust each other at all. Later he stood in front of us and offered us drags from his cigarette, which we refused. He was doing his best to help us as much as he dared.

At nearly midnight we were still on our knees and had by that time almost completely given up on hope of survival. All of a sudden the skies seemed to open up and let out all the wrath stored up there. The guards became excited and began yelling and running around like they were out of their minds. Not until the bombs had begun to hit did we realize what was happening. Here were those good old Yanks we had waited for so long, and as far as I was concerned, they could never have chosen a more opportune time.

The guards ordered us to go into a cell, but we were too stiff to move. Having their hands too full with this new problem to waste time with us, they dragged us into a cell, left us lying on the cement floor, and slammed the door shut and locked it. The last thing I remember before slipping into unconsciousness was seeing the red flames from the nearby burning barracks leaping into the night. I kinda grinned to myself and shouted, "Burn the whole damn place to the ground!" and passed into unconsciousness.

When I awakened, it was still night. I could hear Al breathing heavily, so I knew he was still alive. With that I must have passed out again. When I finally awakened the second time, the sun was streaming in through the windows from the west. I attempted to rise up but was still so stiff and sore that I could hardly move. I spied my friend sitting against the wall watching me. He grinned and said, "Hi!"

With some help and encouragement from him, I was finally able to get to a sitting position near him against the wall. I had been beaten badly and was terribly sore over all parts of my body. My legs were stiff and bloody from the cuts made by the rough bamboo poles, and the pain in my back was excruciating.

After discussing the situation, we finally made our way to the window to observe the damage. We could see the bombers had destroyed many of the buildings in camp. Crews of men were busy cleaning up the mess.

Although we knew everyone would be crowded into the already overcrowded undamaged buildings, we were happy with what we were observing. We couldn't help but wonder about the mine. Had it been hit also? Even though the guards might take it out on us, we still had the satisfaction of knowing the Japanese were finally getting what had been owed to them for a long, long time.

Although it was terribly painful for us to move about, we finally were able to sit down on the floor once more to discuss our predicament. The ragged tears on my shins caused by the bamboo cutting into my legs were horrible, and my shoulders, back, and hips hurt each time I moved, even a little. But we were alive and excited about the bombing of the camp.

We figured if the Allies were bombing us, they were probably hitting the rest of Japan also. The thoughts of such a possibility delighted us even though we were presently in a great deal of trouble. Of course we had no idea how long we were going to be kept in the guardhouse. We were afraid that we might be the first to feel the camp commander's wrath over the new calamity. Now that we knew the Americans were really getting close, wouldn't it be terrible not to be able to see the thing through? We couldn't help but shudder at the thoughts of possible outcomes as a result of our incarceration. Many other men had been destroyed for no more excuse than they would have for getting rid of us. One thing we knew for sure: we were hungry and thirsty.

That day and night finally dragged by, and two more days and nights passed. On the fifth day after the encounter with the Japanese commander, the interpreter came into the guardhouse, and we called to him. He didn't know we had been confined to the guardhouse. We told him the circumstances of our imprisonment within a prison, and after some indecision, he finally sarcastically agreed to see what he could do for us.

That afternoon he returned with an affidavit for each of us to sign. The affidavit read, "I, the undersigned, under the peril of death, agree never again to attempt to overthrow the Imperial Japanese Government."

We signed the document, and he opened the cell door.

"Now that you have signed the paper, if you ever get into trouble again, it means that you will be put to death."

With that pleasant farewell parting, we returned to the building where we belonged.

Back in our room we found instead of fifteen men in each room, there were now thirty. We learned that no one had been killed during the bombings but that the Japanese area of the camp had been burned out almost completely. It seems that the incendiary bombs had really done the job they were supposed to do. The men who had been to the mine since the bombing said most of the city had been burned as well as many of the mine buildings. Included among the latter was the building housing the mine god. In fact, it was the first to go. At the mine we did no more praying for protection after that. At least we didn't pray to the mine god. I guess the Japanese figured if the god couldn't take care of himself, he couldn't take care of them in the mine.

The day after we were freed from our prison cell, we were both sent back to the mine. In spite of our injuries and pain, we were happy to be away from camp, even if it meant going back to the coal mine.

Our belief had always been that when the end of the conflict got close, our treatment from the Japanese would get either much better or much worse. Again we were wrong. It was almost as though they chose to completely ignore what was taking place. We had no way of knowing what information they were receiving from their superiors, but any fool could have read the handwriting on the wall by this time. The end just had to be getting near.

Earlier the Japanese had constructed concrete air-raid shelters for themselves, and we dug dirt cellars for our occupancy. As soon as the Americans began bombing the area, the Japanese required that we daily bundle the clothing they had given us and place the bundles in the dirt cellars before leaving for the mine. In the evening when we returned from the mine, we would go to the cellars and get the clothing bundles. We were responsible for those clothes and were warned that we would be punished if they were destroyed.

When the air-raid warning sounded at night, we would grab our bundles of clothing and run for the cellars. These holes were damp all over, and many places were wet from water that had leaked through the roof.

On occasion we would be forced to spend almost the entire night in those holes. There was little opportunity to get much sleep while down there because of the dampness and the crowding. The following morning, on those occasions, we were forced to go to the mine as usual whether we had been able to get any sleep or not. Along toward the middle of the summer, we got to the point where we just ignored the air-raid alarms, and the Japanese didn't seem to care.

By late July most of the city and surrounding area had been destroyed.

The Japanese were still bound and determined to keep the mine operating at any cost. I am sure the airplane crews must have known we were working in the mine because, after that first raid, neither the camp nor the mine area was bombed again. Surely the Americans would have completely destroyed the mine had they not known we were working there.

The Japanese and Korean civilians who came to work in the mine were faring no better than were we. One morning one of the supervisors came to work without shoes. I was assigned to work with him that day. Once we were in the mine, he sobbingly told us he had lost his home and family in an air raid the night before. Everything he owned had been destroyed. Yet he demonstrated no special hatred toward us that day—only tremendous sorrow over his own great loss.

He said that, in spite of his tragedy, the mine officials had still required him to report for work.

As I have said many times before, those Japanese went all out and played no favorites. We really felt sorry for this poor guy. All that we could do, though, was offer our sympathy, and that couldn't do him much good.

Finally, with the big push from the Allies, conditions got so bad in our area there were practically no Japanese left to work with us in the mine. The mine authorities, still undaunted, assigned a larger number of the more experienced men to supervise the work of the individual crews. I was assigned as supervisor of a detail consisting of four Englishmen and a Scotsman.

Our job daily was to timber tunnels. Having worked with one of the best timber men in the mine for a long period of time, I understood well the nature of the work. Occasionally one of the big bosses, a three-striper, would come around and check the quality of our work. It was an absolute must the work be of high quality because many of our prisoner colleagues depended upon us to assure their safety as they worked in the tunnels we timbered.

On our day off during the first part of August 1945, we were lying on the floor of our room, wishing as we always did when we had time, when the air-raid alarm sounded. Before we had time to move, the planes were overhead. We looked up, and flying over us at a very low level were six big American bombers. We were horror stricken because we knew Japanese antiaircraft batteries were protecting the area.

The guns began firing. Sure enough, they scored a direct hit on one bomber. The big plane seemed to explode in the air, but two men were able to bail out and get their chutes open.

Pieces of the burning bomber went in all directions. We watched the other five bombers fly on while the two chutes floated lazily to the ground. We wished that we could rescue and protect the men from the brutality of angry Japanese.

The two parachutists had no more than hit the ground when a flight of American fighter planes peeled off over the area. They dived down over the camp with guns blazing, and we dived for the ground. None of us had time to get to the shelter area.

The fighter planes came over so low that we could see the pilots in their cockpits. Although it looked as if they were gunning for us, we knew that their targets were actually the gun emplacements. However, because the antiaircraft guns were so close to our camp, the American pilots couldn't help but scatter a few bullets into our area too. We were hoping for some sign from them that they knew we were in the camp, but they went about their business, ignoring us completely.

When they finally left, excitement ran high. Everyone except the Japanese was in the height of his glory. Those were land-based fighters, we were sure, so we knew the Yanks must have airfields nearby. That could mean only one thing: the Allies were winning, and we would undoubtedly soon be free.

By now we had lost most of our fear of the Japanese taking their spite out on us. We figured if they had been going to kill us, they would have done that before now. Also, if they had to negotiate for surrender, we would be prize possessions for them to bargain with. Right then we felt that the tables had been turned, completely. Once again this was evidence that we still didn't understand the Japanese fully, nor did we have any really valid information concerning the present state of affairs between the Allies and the Japanese.

## 19

# SENSO YAMU!

ON THE MORNING OF August 15, 1945, we went to work in the mine as usual. As we stood in a large hall in front of the Koshiki No (head supervisor), he told us that our continuing work detail was assigned the job of timbering a tunnel ceiling.

With our assignment we hurried to the tunnel, hoping to catch an early train into the mine. Our strategy was to get to the pile of marutas (logs) before the Japanese workers to secure an ample supply of logs, eliminating the need to enter abandoned mine sections to salvage timbers. We found what we were seeking and promptly carried the logs to the job site.

By noon we had all the timbers cut as well as an ample supply of wedges. We were just beginning to put the timbers into place when a young Japanese fellow came running up and announced we were to stop working and report with tools to the underground mine office and toolshed.

"Nan no? Nan no?" we asked, wondering what the problem was.

"Wakaru nai!" (I don't know) he responded.

Speculations were immediate, and my pulse began to beat a little faster as I permitted myself to hope. Having gone through almost the same experience once before, I hardly dared think that this might be the long-awaited day.

When we met the other work details at the toolshed, excitement had reached its peak. We had known for some time the Americans were close to Japan. After three and a half years, the end could be near.

The supervisor in charge of our mine area had the few Japanese workers lined up and was jabbering at them. He was excited, and they were excited! Although we had learned some of their language by this time, he was talking so fast no one could understand him clearly. We did hear the words "Senso yamu" (war is over) repeated, however.

Finally, the supervisor led us to catch the train to the surface. Twenty minutes or so later, we reached the loading platform just as the noon shift was arriving. No sooner had they gotten off the train, than they were ordered to go topside again. When we excitedly gathered around them and plied them with questions, they reported nothing unusual in camp. Our surging hopes sank. They told us they hadn't even seen any American planes during the morning. Surely these men would have heard if the war really had ended.

The train out of the mine finally started, and we slowly rattled upward. In spite of the information from those on the noon shift, we were still guardedly optimistic. When we arrived at the top of the tunnel, much to our pleasure the guards allowed us to leave the mine without the usual shakedown. As we checked in lamps and batteries, the mentally retarded fellow who was to receive them ran around shouting, "Senso yamu! Senso yamu!"

As much as we wanted to, we couldn't bring ourselves to believe him. They could have told him anything.

Once the lamps were stored, the guards told us not to go to the bath but allowed us to stand around the assembly ground, nor did they force us into the usual marching formation. They even broke loose a few cigarettes. No one was permitted out of the immediate area, however. Even though we had to put our clothes on over dirty bodies, no one complained. We knew we could bathe back in camp.

As we stood around talking, we agreed something most unusual was going on, but we couldn't figure out just what. We really wanted to believe hostilities had ended but just couldn't bring ourselves to that conclusion for fear we might be wrong. The disappointment would have been severe. Cautious hope seemed better for now.

Finally, one of the fellows happened to notice that the Japanese airplane spotter was no longer in the lookout tower, and he excitedly shared the information with us. The suspense continued to mount.

After nearly an hour of waiting and talking, we were ordered to fall in for our usual, but early, hike back to camp. This time, however, we walked casually instead of marching over the road we had traveled so many times.

As we walked, men began making predictions only to have others puncture their bubbles. We were now bursting with hope but had learned long ago not to be overly optimistic. During the past three and one-half years we had experienced so many disappointments, some not easy to handle.

Finally, the Scotsman from Banforshire, Scotland (at least that's where he said he was from), came out with, "If when we get back to camp, the Jap camp commander gives us that Red Cross chow he has been holding out, you'll know for sure that the war is over!"

Reaching camp in high spirits, we lined up in front of the guardhouse as usual, only to learn that the guards didn't choose to count us. We were even dismissed without being searched. That just couldn't be!

Free to leave, we had started toward our barracks when the Japanese camp commander came out on the porch of the headquarters building and through the interpreter said, "Each building send men for Red Cross boxes."

Not only did a shout go up, but also caps, canteens, and lunch boxes. The Scot's prediction was coming true!

What a happy occasion that was as those small Red Cross boxes emerged and were being distributed. It is almost impossible to describe our joy. The entire camp took on a holiday air. Even the guards were happy!

That night no one went to sleep. We sat up enjoying our food and the thoughts of freedom and going home. For the first time in three and one-half years the major subject of conversation changed from food back to pre-war topics. It was almost impossible to believe we were really going to be able to go back to the good old USA!

"Do you think our government will pay us for the time we have spent as prisoners of war?"

"What if people back home think we were cowards for surrendering, like the Japs said they would?"

"If you get money, what are you going to buy with it?"

"Will my gal back home still be waiting?"

"I wonder if our folks know we are still alive?"

"Is a Ford better than a Chevy or a Plymouth?"

"How will it really seem to get back in the USA once again?"

Such questions went on and on, nothing being considered inappropriate or unreasonable.

Although we had not as yet been informed officially that the war was over, the Japanese guards optimistically assured us this was a fact. They seemed as happy as we were that the conflict was finally finished. No one hated anyone that night.

The following day we were keyed up and tired but gloriously happy!

We assembled on the parade ground and received a new outfit of Japanese NCO summer clothing, leather shoes and all. None of us was too excited about putting on Japanese army uniforms, but the new clothing felt good. The pair of shoes I got had thick gum soles. They really felt wonderful on my feet, and I promised myself if I really did get back home, I was going to fit my feet with the nicest, most comfortable shoes I could find. I was also going to have plenty of good hats and work and dress gloves for my hands, which had taken a great deal of battering and bruising working for the Japanese. We were even given one of the Japanese military caps with the star on the front. That day there were no work details, and we thoroughly enjoyed the rest. Besides, we needed time for trading.

I was eager to get chocolate bars, although the first piece I ate caused me to become a bit nauseated and dizzy. That feeling, resulting from the rich food to which I wasn't accustomed, soon passed, and I really had a craving for chocolate candy.

There were those who wanted cigarettes more than anything else so gladly traded their chocolate bars, powdered milk, and jam for smokes. We even shared our stuff with the guards who had made our lives so miserable while we were in that camp. We found out some of those guards could speak a bit of English. They could have helped us on many occasions had they been willing and unafraid to do so.

On the following day, the seventeenth of August, we assembled on the parade ground once again. Dressed in our new clothing, which even included Japanese underwear, we didn't look half bad. We were terribly skinny, but our spirits helped make us feel like supermen.

The Japanese camp commander, sword and all, mounted the platform and, with the help of the interpreter, haltingly and with much emotion read to us the copy of the formal declaration of Japan's defeat and surrender.

As he read the statement, the most wonderful, warm feeling permeated my entire body, and I felt nothing but joy and peace. All the contempt and hatred I had felt for the Japanese soldiers during the past forty-two months completely evaporated. At that moment I forgave the Japanese and experienced the overwhelming joy of forgiveness.

No longer did I have any negative feelings toward political and military leaders here or at home or anywhere else. It is difficult for me to express completely my feelings at that time, but they were nothing short of magnificent. I felt bursting with love!

My conclusion was then and continues to this day that those feelings were blessings, showered upon me by the Lord because He loved me!

The Japanese camp commander also said he knew our treatment hadn't been the best but that food and supplies had been extremely limited, and severe discipline had been necessary to maintain order within a camp of over 1,700 prisoners of war.

He looked so miserable and unhappy I couldn't help but feel sorry for him. Here was the man who had beaten me on the head and across my back with a shovel, who had made me kneel on bamboo poles and hold the shovel over my head. Now, all of the fighting spirit and pride was gone from him. He stood before us a broken man with tears streaming down his face.

Surrender of an entire nation must have been a terribly agonizing and humiliating experience for a country that had taught its people that death at one's own hands is far more acceptable and honorable than surrender. I wondered seriously how all the living Japanese could now justify the dishonor they had brought upon themselves or had settled upon the nation from the actions of its leaders. Having experienced what they must now be feeling, I truly felt sorry for them.

The Japanese CO said he had received orders that the guards were to remain in camp for two more weeks, during which time all former prisoners of war were also to remain in camp. It felt good to now be referred to as "former" prisoners of war.

"This," he said, "is for your own safety. At the end of the two-week period we will turn over to your senior officer all of our arms and all Japanese soldiers will depart from the camp."

During our long months of internment I had thought with a great deal of pleasure that some day I would get satisfaction from seeing the Japanese fall from glory. I had given much serious thought to methods of revenge. Now that victory was actually ours, I no longer desired any type of revenge. Here on the platform before us was the person responsible for causing many men to suffer and die. Yet I couldn't bring myself to hate him any longer; I felt only pity and sorrow for him. All of his arrogance was gone, and he seemed now only small and miserable.

# 20

# WAITING FOR THE YANKS

THAT DAY, AUGUST 17, 1945, will always be a memorable one for me. What a super, super day! While we were still required to remain in camp, we were actually free. What a glorious feeling! I wanted to sing, shout, jump for joy! We could walk anywhere we wanted in the camp without interference or trouble. While I guess that wasn't actually too much of an achievement, to me it was wonderful.

During all of the time we had been in the various prison camps, through air raids and all, our camps were never identified as POW camps. Now that the war was over, the Japanese got around to properly marking our place of residence. They put a large "P O W" on the parade grounds and another on top of the mess hall. This did help the American supply planes to spot us, and we concluded it was for that purpose the signs were put up rather than for helping to assure our safety from our own forces.

The guards remained in camp as the Japanese commander had said they would, and with the bulk Red Cross food that accompanied the small, individual boxes, life became far more bearable. Although time began to drag, we survived the two weeks without problems erupting. As promised, the Japanese turned their guns and other arms, including swords, over to our American CO, a dentist, along with the camp itself. Our CO then ordered us to remain in camp, and for some time everyone obeyed. Then dissent arose as men began to ask why we couldn't just leave camp and go home. We were so eager!

Shortly after the Japanese left the camp to us, we ran out of food. The Red Cross provisions as well as the stored rice were completely depleted. Worse yet, there were no more cigarettes in camp. Everyone had become suddenly too prosperous, forgetting the possibility of lean days ahead.

After lengthy discussions, we decided the mine owner had gotten a lot of work out of us, and consequently he should continue to have responsibility for providing food for us until the Americans arrived.

That decision reached, word went to the mine owner that he had until noon the following day to provide our camp with an ample amount of good food and cigarettes or we would take over the mine and close it down completely. We had guns and ammunition now, and we knew we could do just what we threatened to do. It was our firm belief that these demands were completely reasonable.

We then proceeded to divide ourselves into groups in case action had to be taken, and each group was assigned a specific responsibility once we arrived at the mine site.

The following morning we met on the parade ground and formed into our respective groups in preparation for going to the mine should the owner not be willing to comply with our demands.

The owner must have either decided we meant business or received counsel from government or military officials that he should respond properly to our request, because shortly before noon five heavily loaded trucks rolled into camp. One of the trucks was loaded with nothing but cigarettes. Two of the other four trucks carried huge sacks of rice while the other two were loaded with canned food. It seemed quite likely now we would have plenty to eat for some time, but we had learned we would have to ration ourselves better than we had done earlier. The food was taken to the mess hall, and the cigarettes were immediately distributed to the men.

The mine officials had not only responded to our requests, they also sent workers out to take care of the camp. They even put cooks in the kitchen to prepare the food for us. We wondered how these new cooks would get along with the American mess officer, but we learned that he had shut himself up in his private room in the mess hall building. I hadn't seen him at all since we had been advised of the surrender of Japan. He must have known he was in serious trouble because, without the Japanese guards to back him up, he no longer had any authority over any of us. He should have understood clearly the mood of the men whom he had so thoroughly mistreated. The hatred for him had been so intense among the men that he had been marked by us as a war criminal who deserved punishment more than any single Japanese soldier. He was nothing better than a vicious traitor who had betrayed his country, fellow Americans, and other prisoners from Allied countries.

With nothing to occupy our time, it wasn't long until almost everyone became uneasy and restless. To keep us from becoming too disorderly, we finally received permission to go out of camp to the beach and dig for clams. Not only was this sport for me, a person who dearly loved fishing, but the efforts were most rewarding. Some mornings we each collected a large bag full of clams. When the tide began to come in and the water got deep, we returned to camp and had the clams boiled briefly. Then we shucked them. Mixed with rice, they were especially rich and good. I thoroughly enjoyed the clam-gathering activity.

One evening, to liven things up a little, some of the fellows got the idea we should have a camp show. There was a great deal of talent among the men, and all were eager either to participate or just to watch the activities.

Numbers had been presented by several Americans, some of the English fellows, and several Aussies. We had among the American contingent a big, raw-boned Texan who sang cowboy songs and played the guitar. I have no idea where he was able to get a guitar.

When his turn came for additional numbers, he began by singing the song "The Bastard King of England."

He hadn't gotten very far along with the number when a British NCO stepped up and told him not to sing that song. The number stopped and so did the program for a time. Everyone held his breath for fear there would be a battle—or afraid there wouldn't be one. From time to time relations between the Americans and the "Blue Bloods," as the British soldiers liked to refer to themselves, had become a bit strained. To them, America was a land of mongrels, resulting from the intermarriage of immigrants to the United States over a period of nearly two hundred years. In spite of the surge of emotions, good sense prevailed and everyone settled down. It would have been terrible for anyone to get hurt now after all the suffering under the domination of the Japanese. Tempers cooled and the show went on.

One afternoon early in September we were routed from our barracks by the largest four-engine American bomber we had ever seen. The plane, a B-29 we learned later, circled out over the bay and then came back over camp flying extremely low. We could see the fellows in the plane waving to us.

As the plane flew over the second time, its crew threw out several magazines and a note telling us that they were coming back over the camp to drop food. We all jammed the parade ground cheering and watching the bomber circle and return. As it approached camp again, still at a very low level, we could see the bomb bays open. I couldn't stop the feeling of uneasiness that began to creep over me.

Once one experiences bombs being dropped on him, he doesn't quickly forget the danger, the damage, and the casualties. We agreed with each other that no one in his right mind would drop anything from a low-flying plane into a field packed with men. How wrong we were!

Over the camp once again, fifty-gallon drums, fully filled, parachuted from the plane. That huge monster was much too close to the ground for the chutes to have time to open, and fifty-gallon drums came hurtling down through the air, crashed into the ground and smashed. The jubilance turned to panic as men scattered in all directions seeking safety from the falling gasoline drums. Jammed on the parade ground as we were then, we were extremely lucky not to have been killed. A drum hit one of the barracks and tore a gaping hole through it.

Most of the food and cigarettes in the drums were ruined, but the clothing wasn't damaged. The salvageable food and cigarettes, as well as the clothing, were promptly distributed. The magazines telling of the defeat of Japan were also passed around. From what we read, it was apparent General "Dugout Doug" MacArthur had returned to the Philippines in glory several months before the war ended.

Two days later another of those huge bombers flew over the camp. It circled and approached once more. Again the bomb bays opened. This time the plane was at a proper height.

Twenty chutes loaded with supplies dropped. Two of the chutes gave way, and the cases broke loose and came hurtling toward the camp. We all dived for cover, but a case hit one of the fellows and mangled his leg at the hip. He was immediately attended to by the Australian doctor, but the report was to the effect that he died later from the shock and the loss of blood. Everyone was broken-hearted. We wished we had never seen the American supply planes. The poor guy had sweated out three and a half years of hell at the hands of the Japanese only to be killed by a case of food dropped from a circling plane by our own people.

From then on the planes came every two or three days. After that incident, though, we would always make sure that we got out of the way of the chutes in case any of them broke open. I always ran to the edge of camp and crawled into a coal car turned on its side.

We were of the opinion, once we were able to get all of the food we wanted, we would never again complain. Well fed as we were rapidly becoming, our thoughts and conversation began to dwell on other topics, such as getting out of Japan. To make matters worse, men from other prison camps in Japan drifted in to see us. We asked ourselves, "If others can roam around the country, why shouldn't we be able to do so?"

Finally, the fences came down and became firewood. With nothing to keep us in camp, we armed ourselves with cigarettes, soap, and GI overcoats and started for the country in search of fresh fruit, vegetables, chickens, eggs, and anything that might be interesting.

Al and I went together. We walked down through what was left of the city, and at the railroad station we boarded the first train that came along. This we rode into the country until we felt that we were adequately removed from the heavily populated area. Then, not knowing where to go, we just struck off down a country road that ran through rice paddies.

The countryside was beautiful in early September with green fields stretching over low-lying rolling hills and dotted with trees and an occasional farmhouse. Houses appeared to be a bit flimsy to us when compared to the sturdy ones that were characteristic of the American countryside.

As we moseyed along, dirt roads narrowed into nothing more than paths leading off to the scattered homes and farm buildings.

Until we came to a house with several chickens in the yard, we saw nothing to stimulate our bartering spirits. Then, approaching the home hesitantly and cautiously, we knocked at the door hoping to negotiate a trade. A young, attractive, and extremely shy young lady stood before us. Before we could say anything, she quickly moved her hand back and forth in front of her face while saying, "Nai, Nai" (no, no). It was apparent she was frightened and perhaps of the opinion we were there to do her harm.

"Chichi San" (person in charge), we repeated over and over, until she finally turned back into the house.

Presently an elderly man approached slowly, bowing low. He graciously invited us into the house and motioned for us to be seated on the floor. The interior of the home was beautiful. It was apparent to us that at one time the man had been well off financially.

The old gent could speak a bit of English, and with the small amount of Nipponese we knew, we were able to communicate very well. With tears running down his cheeks, he told us how happy he was that the war was over. Choking back tears, he explained to us that many young men from the area had been killed in the war and that numerous people had suffered terribly from the lack of food, clothing, and fuel to heat their homes during the cold winters.

After we had talked for a while, the young lady reappeared with bowls of cooked vegetables. Foolishly we declined because we truly were not hungry and knew they needed the food far more than we did. Tearfully, he apologized for the poor quality of food, and we were unable to convince him that our refusal was because, finally, we had all that we wanted to eat.

After a most enjoyable visit we parted, but without chickens. We just couldn't bring ourselves to ask him for them. As we left, we expressed our hope he would enjoy the soap, cigarettes, and the overcoat that we left for him.

That experience over, we agreed we couldn't take anything from these people. What they had they needed badly. We did continue our wanderings through the countryside, however, speaking to those whom we met and waving to others not within speaking distance. It made us feel rather good about things in general.

Going back on the train later in the day, we observed several Japanese soldiers get on with a huge box of swords. Where they were going with them, I don't know. When we admired their swords, the fellows insisted we each select one for ourselves. They were friendly, extremely eager to please, and happy to accept the balance of our cigarettes and soap.

Back in camp we shared our experiences with those who had gone in different directions and learned from them the people with whom they talked didn't have much food to exchange for items that we had available for trade. One group of our men had taken a cow from a farmer and had brought it back into camp to be slaughtered for food for themselves. They didn't need that cow for food, and when we told the guys that the cow may have been the farmer's only source of income, their response was, "Tough shit! Let 'em starve!"

I felt bad and somewhat angry over that response because we had known well what it was to be terribly hungry and should now have compassion for those who were less fortunate than we were.

As the days wore on and as our physical condition improved, we became almost desperate to be on the move. There was nothing attractive about the camp, and we were becoming desperately homesick knowing we were eventually going to be able to go home. We just wanted to go!

Although we were warned repeatedly that it might be dangerous for us to leave camp any time and especially after dark, we took the chance and went out one night anyway. One small section of the city had been left standing, and we made our way to that area. Upon our arrival there whom should we meet but one of the former supervisors in the coal mine. Some of the fellows thought they wanted sake and asked him if he had any. He said he didn't, but that he could get some for a price.

By this time it was clear the Japanese were well informed concerning the nature of the supplies parachuted to us by the Americans.

For fifteen packages of American cigarettes he advised us he could get all of the sake all of us could drink. He couldn't arrange for it until the following day, however, so five of the guys made a deal with him and agreed they would meet him the following evening for a big party. For several reasons, I didn't want to be involved in the deal. In the first place, I could see the possibility of a bunch of drunken former prisoners of war getting into trouble, and trouble was one thing I was going to make every effort to avoid. I had made up my mind I would avoid anything that might keep me from getting back home. Second, I had given away or traded all of my cigarettes. Finally, I didn't like sake and just didn't want to get involved in any nonsense. I had other long-established plans that had far higher priority.

After a period of negotiations, we continued our wanderings and finally would up at a little tea house. Later, I learned this was a Japanese house of prostitution, but I didn't know it at the time. The prison camp experience hadn't made me a lot savvier concerning some things in Japanese society.

About a dozen girls, all pretty ones, were serving tea. So, we ordered some. By this time we had plenty of Japanese money among us, having each sold a GI overcoat for what seemed like a heck of a lot of money. Our military must have had a lot of extra overcoats because they parachuted many hundreds into our camp at the warmest time of the year in our area. We could have used them to good advantage during the past winter, but now the only value they had to us was the price one could bring on the Japanese market.

We noticed when we went into the tea house there were several Japanese policemen standing just inside the door. When one of the girls served tea to those of us at our low table, she asked for a cigarette. One of the fellows pulled out a package and held it out to her. She snatched the pack out of his hand.

Before I realized what was happening, one of the policemen had stepped over and slapped the girl hard enough to knock her to the floor. She quickly got to her feet and gave the package of cigarettes to the policeman. He then handed it back to its owner. In English he then said, "I think now if you would like to offer her a cigarette, she would be pleased to accept just one."

A cigarette was offered, and she accepted—one.

On the fourteenth of September a newspaper man from the States appeared in our camp. Where he came from, I never learned. Someone said that he was a reporter for the *New York Times.* He may have been; I don't know.

After talking with several of the men and officers who had been left with us, he collected a few of the fellows who were in the best physical condition and headed for the mine. There, they rounded up all of the Japanese mine supervisors, one-, two-, and three-stripers, and lined them up in a building. Then, with the men he confronted each Japanese supervisor. If the supervisor had treated the prisoners reasonably well under the circumstances, he was sent home. When they identified one who had been mean to the men, they worked him over.

Hearing of the activity later, I was glad that I hadn't been assigned to the detail and felt we had no business taking matters into our own hands. I hated to see any of our men involved in the kinds of behavior so characteristic of the Japanese soldiers and mine supervisors during our internment. That kind of conduct didn't impress anyone and made us no better than the Japanese guards. I wanted us to be better men in all respects.

The following morning, the fifteenth of September, we all assembled on the parade ground with the reporter on the platform in front of us. For several hours he told us about the military campaigns in Europe and the surrender of Germany. Then he elaborated in detail about the battles in the Pacific, the return of General MacArthur to the Philippines, and the release of the American POWs there. Finally he got around to telling us of the bombing of Hiroshima and Nagasaki with the atomic bomb. We could hardly believe all we were hearing, but we found ourselves hanging on every word that he said.

Around noon someone in the huge crowd of men hollered, "When are we going to be able to get out of here?"

All joined in!

"Well," the reporter said, "the army of occupation isn't due to get into this area until about the middle of October."

Everyone groaned.

"However, " he continued, "the American Army has landed on the southern tip of this island. C-46s and C-47s are being used to fly supplies to them from Okinawa. Those planes are going back to Okinawa empty. You know, if I hadn't been home for five years, I would try to get down south and take a chance of getting a plane out."

That counsel was all that was needed to motivate us to action. Fellows began easing themselves out of the crowd.

One of the Japanese fellows who had marched us back and forth to the mine had been assigned to supervise the maintenance work in our camp, so we located him and asked him for help. During the year he hadn't been what one would call friendly to us, but he had never lost his temper with us and had never permitted us to be abused by anyone in his presence. He came across to us as being an honest fellow who did have some feelings of compassion for us.

We asked him to draw a map for us showing us exactly where we would have to go to reach the American occupation forces on the southern part of the island. He did so willingly. Once we were satisfied we could follow his directions successfully, we bade him goodbye and gave him all of the stuff dropped to us that we didn't want to carry.

The old fellow couldn't believe what was happening to him! What a payoff he was getting for treating us in a halfway human way. No question but what he was going to be set for life, given the current prices for those items that were greatly in demand in Japan at the time. He had enough GI overcoats to supply the local population for several winters at least.

Just outside the camp we stopped a fire truck and got the Japanese driver to take us to the railroad station, which was only a short distance from our camp. By the time we reached there, nearly a hundred men had assembled. There was also a sizable crowd of Japanese men and women waiting for a train.

Among ourselves we agreed we would commandeer the first train coming into the station heading the way we needed to go. The newspaper reporter had told us General MacArthur had passed the word that American POWs should feel free to utilize any transportation available to get out of Japan, so we felt confident we were doing what was quite proper.

Thus, we informed the station master concerning our plans, and he responded most agreeably. We got the impression that he was as eager for us to go as we were to get out of Japan.

As we stood waiting and talking, a very dignified-looking, high-ranking Japanese army officer appeared. He was well dressed and carried a long, beautiful two-fisted sword, the kind highly prized by both conqueror and conquered alike.

One of our bunch immediately walked over to the officer and demanded the sword to be taken home as a souvenir. After some hesitation, the officer unbuckled it and handed it over to the jerk.

I held my breath because I knew how proud the Japanese officers were and how important the beautiful swords were to them. I wouldn't have been a bit surprised to see the officer kill the American rather than give up the sword.

To make matters worse, another bright guy demanded the shiny leather boots. That left the officer standing in his stocking feet to be gazed at by his shocked countrymen. I wasn't very proud of either of those Americans right then. To take the boots, especially, was about as low a trick as I have ever seen pulled by either Japanese or Americans during and following our long period of internment. I decided then and there that there wasn't too much difference between some men, no matter to what race they belonged. I still recall vividly the humiliation we had suffered at the hands of the Japanese soldiers as they repeatedly swarmed over us on Bataan and on subsequent numerous occasions.

After several hours of waiting, a train, composed of an engine and a coal car and two passenger cars, finally arrived, and we all promptly piled on as quickly as the incoming passengers got off. Because space was at a premium, some of the fellows were forced to get into the engine cab and others into the coal car. No one seemed to mind that he didn't get first-class accommodations.

Following some delay caused by the indecision of the Japanese crew, we got under way and headed off into the night. What a completely hilarious experience! We hollered and laughed and sang every song that any of us had ever known. Time passed rapidly, and before we realized it, it was midnight and the train came to a stop.

Helpfully and courteously, the Japanese crew advised us that we had come to a junction and it would be necessary for us to change trains. It just so happened that one was standing by waiting for us. We didn't mind the change in trains a bit because the new one had more cars, providing room for everyone to ride in style.

In good spirits we thanked the train crew who had brought us this far and shared with them some of the items we still had left.

On the second train we rode throughout the balance of the night and until nearly noon of the second day. As we traveled across Kyushu, we saw few buildings standing anywhere. The towns along the railroad tracks had been leveled, apparently by American bombers. What devastation!

When we reached the end of the rail line, the Japanese crew advised us that it would be necessary for us to cross the bay by boat if we were to continue our trip to contact the American troops. Those men were very polite and extremely helpful. This bit of news didn't serve to discourage us in any way.

The harbor was close, and from where we were standing, we could see several reasonably large ships docked close together. Selecting the largest one, we headed for it, planning strategy as we walked.

As we approached the ship, we spotted four Japanese civilian sailors squatting on the deck, eating their noon meal. A delegation of several broke out of the main body of the ex-POWs to negotiate passage, and I was a member of that small group.

The sailors listened to our request but were not nearly as cooperative as the train crews had been, and they promptly, flatly refused us the trip even when we told them we had money and could pay them.

Withdrawing from the ship, we joined the others for a conference. It wasn't long until a Navy chief exclaimed, "Kick 'em off, and we'll take the ship. We can operate it as well as they can!"

With that bit of encouraging information, we decided it might be time to demonstrate our seriousness in getting to our destination.

Approaching the sailors the second time, one of the fellows drove his souvenir sword into the deck of the ship and said somewhat fiercely, "Listen, you guys! General MacArthur said we had the authority to use any means of transportation necessary to get out of Japan, and this boat is necessary for us to reach American troops. We are going to get across this bay with you or without you. If you want to take us across and get paid for your troubles, fine. If you don't, we'll put you off the ship and ferry ourselves across."

With that bit of new information, it was the Japanese sailors' turn to hold a conference.

They finally agreed they would ferry us across at a cost of three yen per passenger. Of course we all piled on the boat, eager to get this leg of the journey behind us.

The body of water was much larger than we had imagined. In fact, at one time we couldn't see land in any direction. However, the water was as calm as could be, and we were happy about that because the ship had settled fairly low in the water. At about midway, the engine stopped, and it was only through the efforts of our own men that it began running once more. Otherwise the trip across was quite uneventful, but it took nearly three hours.

It was getting along toward evening when we docked on the other side of the bay. As the trip came to an end, we reminded ourselves to be sure to pay our fare as we disembarked. We stationed one of the Japanese sailors at the exit to collect the money.

Almost everyone, knowing he would probably have no further use for the Japanese money, gave the sailors all he had. The boat operators just couldn't believe what was happening. By the time the last man had disembarked, the Japanese sailor fee collector was standing in a pile of money. The sailors were happy and so were we!

Leaving the beach, we walked through what had once been a fairly large city. Nothing was left but ashes and rubble, and we saw very few people.

After hiking down the road for at least two hours, we came to a military establishment of sorts. Two huge tunnels had been dug into a hill along the side of the road. In front of the tunnels were parked several Japanese army trucks. Seeing no soldiers in the area, we went over to the tunnels and shouted for someone to come out to talk with us. What we really wanted was permission to use the trucks to transport us to our destination.

After a brief wait, a Japanese officer appeared. One of our group, acting as spokesman, asked if we might use the trucks to take us to the Americans. The officer hesitated and then finally said we could use the trucks if we would permit them to be driven by Japanese drivers who would return them later in the night.

We were in complete agreement with that proposal and all of us hopped into the trucks.

The Japanese officer provided the drivers, and more than that, he tossed into each truck several large boxes of Japanese hardtack. We were grateful because we hadn't eaten since noon of the day before. The crackers were shaped like our American soda crackers, but they were not nearly as tasty. They were all right, though, and served to take the edge off our hunger.

On what we hoped was the last leg of this part of our journey, we were hilariously happy. In spite of the pleading of our Japanese drivers, the men wouldn't sit down but instead stood up in the trucks singing and shouting. As heavily loaded as they were, this made the trucks even more top-heavy and in danger of turning over. For the Japanese drivers we were becoming difficult to manage. Consequently, our progress down the road was becoming extremely slow. Finally, we became impatient and put one of our own men under each steering wheel. The Japanese drivers seemed to be relieved that they no longer had to be responsible for keeping the trucks right side up on the road.

As the trucks picked up speed, the fellows began to shout and sing even louder in anticipation of reaching American troops. We were almost hysterical with happiness over the thought of being back with our own people once again.

As we rounded a bend in the road and drove into a small town, we ran smack into an American military roadblock. Here were Jeeps and half-tracks set up in preparation for the worst. It appeared as though the troops had prepared to prevent an attack on their position.

When the soldiers saw who had been making all the noise, they piled out of their vehicles. Did they ever look good to us! And, what huge human beings they were! No wonder Japan had to surrender!

The Yanks in their Jeeps and half-tracks led the way down the road toward their camp, and singing and cheering in the Japanese trucks we followed. Our happiness was overwhelming.

# 21

# RETURN TO THE PHILIPPINES

IT WAS NEARLY MIDNIGHT when we reached our destination, but the American commanding officer got out of bed and welcomed us enthusiastically. How good he made all of us feel!

He impressed us with his sincerity in extending greetings and congratulations and even expressed his pleasure that we had selected his occupation site as our first contact with American forces. On behalf of the government of the United States he expressed appreciation for our war efforts in the Philippines and for our courage and tenacity in surviving the hardships of prison camps. He also assured us that Allied forces in demanding unconditional surrender of Japan had settled the score with that country for its sneak attack on Pearl Harbor and for its treatment of Allied prisoners of war. Later, I was to learn much more about the statement concerning settling the score with Japan.

"Planes are flying into a Japanese air base close by," he said, "and they are returning to Okinawa empty. I promise you we will get you out of here just as rapidly as space becomes available. My hunch is most of you will be flown out sometime tomorrow. To enable us to schedule you, we will need your names and the names of your former organizations. We will want to inform the authorities you are on your way home and are eager to keep moving. I do know a repatriation camp has been established for you somewhere in the Philippines, so I suspect you will be entertained there for a brief period until passage to the United States can be arranged for you.

"Where in the world did you get those Japanese uniforms? I wish we were equipped to provide American military clothing for you, but you will have to wait until you reach some place where a quartermaster organization is well supplied.

"Our men will set up tents for you, and we can give you a folding cot to sleep on, a pillow, and a blanket. I am sorry, but that is the best that we can do for you on short notice. However, I suspect even that might just be a step up from what you have been used to as prisoners of war. We'll get the cooks out of bed, and they will be only too happy to prepare food for you. What would you like for an early breakfast?"

Everyone, as though the answer had been rehearsed, in unison shouted, "Hotcakes!"

While food was being prepared, we showered and received assignments to the cots in tents hurriedly erected for us. For each cot, we also received a mattress and a pillow. This was the first actual bed we had been given to sleep on for a long, long time, and no one was about to make a fuss over not being able to have sheets and pillowcases.

Before long the chow bell sounded, and we made a mad dash for the mess hall. We were served not only stacks of hotcakes but also ham and eggs, juice, coffee, jam, and syrup. Boy, what a meal! And, did we ever appreciate it!

When we finally did leave the mess hall and hit the sack, I know we must all have gone to sleep with big grins on our faces. At least I know I did. I was so happy!

I slept right on through the regular breakfast, and it was ten or later before I finally crawled out of the sack. Some of the other fellows had already left the tent, and some were still sleeping.

After a warm shower with plenty of soap, I felt just super. "What a great old world this is," I kept saying to myself.

At the mess hall I was welcomed heartily and had my choice of breakfast or lunch. It all looked so good that I took some of both.

Another fellow and I then checked in to the administrative office to see what our chances of getting a flight were.

"How soon can you be ready to go?" the sergeant asked.

"We are ready to go right now!" I responded.

Everything we had to our names was on our backs, so within a few minutes we piled into a truck for the airfield.

This American infantry outfit, part of the army of occupation, was quartered in wooden barracks similar to temporary, two-story barracks our army had built in the States before the war. On the way over we asked if these barracks had been built especially for the American soldiers and learned that Japanese suicide pilots had been stationed and trained here.

Approaching the field, we could see the airstrip was littered with Japanese planes of all types and makes. The bombed hangars reminded me of the ones we had left at Clark Field in the Philippines after the Japanese had their holiday. A long runway had been cleared of wreckage, and all of the craters had been filled to enable the American planes to land and take off.

We boarded a battered C-46 and sat along the sides of the plane facing each other. The plane looked as if it had seen better days. When we weren't given parachutes, I really began to worry, but the crew chief assured us that there was nothing to worry about.

"These planes," he said, "never crash. They are the Army mules of the Air Force and are just as dependable as a mule on a farm down in Mississippi."

While flying between Japan and Okinawa, the pilots and crew of the plane told us more about the war in the Pacific and of the liberation of the Philippines. I was pleased that the prisoners still at Cabanatuaan had been freed by Army Rangers even before the island of Luzon had been secured but was saddened to learn the beautiful city of Manila had been almost destroyed. We learned that instead of declaring Manila an open city as our forces did at the beginning of the war, the Japanese fought from within the city and then shelled it as they retreated to the north. Some sections of the city had to be taken block by block, house by house, by the American forces. Especially difficult to take was the old Walled City area.

The time passed so quickly that we were circling for a landing at Okinawa before we realized that we were anywhere near the base. We couldn't see much from the air that looked exciting, only airstrips, more planes, and buildings. It looked almost as though the whole island was one huge airfield.

The plane made a smooth landing and quickly rolled to a stop at one edge of the field. From the plane we went by truck directly across the airstrip to a Red Cross wagon parked on the far edge, some distance from where the plane had landed. Here we unloaded and were directed toward the Red Cross wagon and refreshments we had been told would be happily served to us.

Standing beside the lunch wagon were four of the prettiest American ladies I had ever seen. At that very moment I realized what it had all been about. These beautiful creatures represented right then much of what was terribly dear to us. They were so pretty that we were almost afraid to go near them.

One of our problems, one that had not occurred to us until that very moment, was the fact we had been living away from society for so long our language had become quite gruesome. I never used profanity when I was growing up and didn't adopt the practice to any serious extent as a POW. But I felt extremely ill at ease in the presence of these lovely ladies. It was several months before I felt secure enough to become involved in an intelligent conversation with a woman and enjoy it.

At the wagon the girls were serving donuts and coffee. One of the fellows and I each selected a donut and stepped back. On the other side of the wagon I spied bottles of Coke and candy bars. Saying, "Let's get a Coke!" I grabbed my buddy.

One of the girls heard me and brought two bottles over to us. She could see we were bashful, I am sure, and seemed to delight in our shyness. I just couldn't get over how pretty and how nice they were.

After finishing the refreshments, we reluctantly left the girls and went next to the supply depot, where we were stripped of our Japanese clothing by a sergeant, who clearly expressed his disgust for our being willing to wear the clothing issued to us by the Japanese. "You are no smarter than the stupid Japs are," he growled.

We tolerated him in good humor, realizing that he had no way of knowing how grateful we had been to get new Japanese clothing. Had we reported to him in the Japanese clothing we had been wearing in the mine for a year, he would have had a legitimate complaint.

He issued to each of us a complete set of American military clothing and a barracks bag. Then we got a tent assignment, went to dinner, and again stuffed ourselves with good American food. As we went through the chow line, I piled my plate as high as I could and ate all I took. Some of the regulars who entered the mess hall to eat complained all through the meal about the quality of food. They thought it was horrible; we thought it was just wonderful. It was difficult for us not to level with them, but we concluded we had better keep our mouths shut.

After eating, we went over to the Red Cross hut to see if we could get another glimpse of the girls. While we were there gawking, we received toilet articles and writing paper. There were also boxes of candy bars, so I stuffed my pockets. I wasn't quite ready to believe there could be a continuing supply. My strategy and that of the other former POWs continued to be: Get all that you can while you can!

The following morning after a marvelous breakfast, we were loaded into B-24s that shortly lifted off for the Philippines. Six of the huge bombers were in the flight and took off one after another.

We had been airborne only a few minutes when our plane developed engine trouble, making it necessary for us to return to Okinawa. Once on the ground again it didn't take the mechanics long to locate the problem, and within an hour we were back in the air. While on the ground we did learn from the crew members that they were truly sorry the war had ended because they were having such a good time bombing Japan, unmolested by enemy planes.

Back in the bomber once again, we didn't have much to do to kill time during the flight. Planks for seats had been set up inside the bomb bays, and we sat or stretched out on those. There was no way to see out of the plane, and because of the noise from the engines, talking was difficult.

The feeling the plane was losing altitude must have awakened me. I could sense that something was happening and felt uneasy. We had been required to put on parachute harnesses as we entered the plane, and I promptly reached for one of the parachutes that we had been directed to snap on to our harness in case of an emergency. Studying the parachute and the harness I could find no way of snapping the two together. On the front of my harness were large metal rings, and on the chute were large metal rings. I couldn't believe what I was seeing.

Looking through the pile of parachutes carefully, I was able to find a parachute with snaps and noted that some of the fellows had snaps on the front of their harnesses. I was very happy we weren't experiencing an emergency and thought to myself, "Now, this is the Army I remember."

From one of the crew we learned we were circling Clark Field. I couldn't believe that in a few hours we had flown from Japan to Okinawa and from Okinawa to Clark Field in the Philippines. What a difference from the sixty-three days it took our POW ship to sail from Manila to Port Moji in Japan.

The pilot opened the bomb bays to enable us to look down, and we were amazed by what we saw. This just couldn't be the field the Japanese had hit nearly four years before. The base spread out over many acres and was dotted with hundreds of buildings and airplanes. Runways seemed to crisscross it in at least a dozen places.

Our plane finally landed, and we were immediately taken by truck to a nearby mess hall at the edge of the field. Everyone seemed to be afraid we might be hungry again.

As we walked toward the mess hall, the first person I saw was a Filipino who had been one of our squadron bunk boys before the war. I shouted at him, and when he spotted me, he came over on the run. Tears were streaking down his cheeks as he threw his arms around me and welcomed me back to Clark Field. He seemed overjoyed to see one of his old friends once again.

We were able to talk for only a short time. Among other things, he told me he had lost his wife in Manila during the Japanese retreat. He asked me about many of the fellows from our squadron and shared information about several others. Some of the Filipinos did love the Americans and would remain loyal friends forever, we knew.

Our visit was promptly terminated as we were rushed from the mess hall back to the truck again. Apparently the planes that had left Okinawa before us had landed at Nichols Field in Manila, where we were supposed to have landed. We learned that our plane had again developed engine trouble, and for that reason had landed at Clark Field instead.

Our truck took us from Clark Field to the railroad station, and there we boarded a train. The train was an old-fashioned one, but it was clean and apparently in good running order. American soldiers were operating it, and in no time we were rattling toward Manila. The closer we got to our destination, the more excited I became. I was enjoying every bit of our trip and knew life in the future was going to be just super for all of us. I felt as though we had launched the celebration of a lifelong holiday.

By the time we actually reached the city it was so dark outside that we were unable to recognize anything we could see. The train didn't stop as we had anticipated it would but continued on south of the city to a repatriation camp set up for returning American POWs. We learned the British had established a camp nearby for the repatriation of their men.

From the train we went to the military headquarters building and were checked in. Then we went to the supply depot, where we were given a complete new issue of everything given to a brand-new recruit. In addition we received blankets and some other odds and ends. By the time the supply people had finished issuing clothing and the other stuff, our overseas bags were packed full. We could really think of no purpose for steel helmets right then, but we got them anyway. When I reached for the bag of goodies to throw it on my shoulder, a soldier stopped me.

"I'll take the bag for you," he said.

I told him that I could carry it without trouble, but he asked, "Do you want to get me in bad with the people? I was assigned to carry your bag, and that's what I gotta do."

I felt foolish but didn't argue, and together we moved away from the supply building toward the sleeping area.

We were quartered six to a tent and moved in to find our beds all made up for us. Seemed like we were in a make-believe land! "How could things change so much so fast and we scroungy ex-POWs be on the receiving end of all of these good things and services?"

Once settled in, we headed for the nearest mess hall. There we learned that the mess halls would be open twenty-four hours a day to serve us. We had the privilege of requesting the cooks to prepare whatever we wanted. They weren't pressed too hard because, at the moment, we were still extremely interested in quantity. And we knew that whatever we were served would be a thousand times better than we had been used to for so many months.

That night as I lay in my bed, I just couldn't believe we were really back among our own people once again. Everyone was so good to us! All our worries about being perceived as cowards had been entirely unnecessary. We really should have known better, but our captors had constantly harped on that subject. For three and one-half years we had lived with serious feelings of guilt for having surrendered, and now we were being treated like heroes. I felt so good about everything I just didn't want to go to sleep. Everyone was so wonderful and this was only the Philippines, not home.

"If this is an example of what we can expect, our lives are really going to be something, at least for a few weeks!"

The following morning we were all sent to the medics for thorough physical examinations. They were conducted in a huge room by doctors who were sitting along the walls and end of a long building. There must have been at least twenty doctors involved in the activities. Each doctor was assisted by a nurse, all of whom were beautiful, and each doctor checked us for only one thing.

On our way around the horseshoe-like grouping, we were given at least half a dozen shots, I believe, and by the time we reached the end of the line, we felt like we had been through another war. By this time we had been out of the coal mine for over a month and our weight was increasing fairly rapidly. We still looked somewhat scrawny and grubby, but we were on the mend.

Standing by the last doctor was an older nurse, and by her were stacked several cases of whiskey. Each fellow, as he finished with the examination, was given a large water glass about half full of the amber stuff. The fellow ahead of me politely refused the drink and said to the nurse, "Give it to the doc." With that, the nurse turned around and tossed the drink down neatly.

When my turn came, I gave her mine, too. I watched her closely, thinking she might go down with booze, but it didn't seem to faze her one bit. "Maybe the nurses change off and take turns being the last in line," I thought to myself. "Perhaps one of their fringe benefits."

It was to these doctors I first formally reported my experience with malaria and the fifteen five-grain quinine pills. Several doctors gathered around to hear my story, but none believed me, I am sure. I tried to convince them that they should do research on that type of massive treatment, but they just shook their heads and, I imagine, thought I had something loose in mine.

After the examination we next went to an interrogation tent. There we were given an opportunity to write anything we wanted to about our experiences and to bring charges against any person of any nationality who we felt should be punished. As I settled down to report my experiences with the mess officer in our camp in Japan, the officer in charge announced, "None of you former prisoners coming from Camp Number 17 in Fukuoka need to bring charges against your mess officer. We have already gathered enough information from those who arrived here ahead of you to convict and hang him a dozen times."

This announcement provided some relief, and after having a few things to report about our Japanese camp commander and providing the other specific information requested, I went back to our tent. Right then, I really didn't want to say anything negative about anyone. What was past was past. What I wanted to do was devote all of my thoughts and energies to the future. The past was bleak. Not as bleak as it had been a few weeks or months earlier, but still bleak. The future was all sunshine!

That same morning we learned we were restricted to camp for a minimum of three days until we were completely processed. While I was hoping to get into Manila promptly, I wasn't too disappointed, because there were a great many interesting things going on in camp. Eating ranked at the top of those attractive things taking place.

Down at the recreation center and PX, we learned that everything was on the house. That is, food items and drinks—pop and beer—and smokes were on the house. I honestly cannot understand why I didn't explode. It wasn't that I ate a great deal only at mealtime, I ate a great deal continuously. The only two reasons for not eating more than I did were that I didn't have any more room, and that I really needed to pause for sleep from time to time.

When I wasn't eating or sleeping, I scouted the camp to see how many of our squadron members I could find. One of the first acquaintances that I bumped into was a fellow from Corregidor whom I had met at Cabanatuaan prison camp. He was an old soldier compared to a great many of the rest of us, and he looked good. I recalled his telling me that before the war he was a beer drinker and had a waist measurement of forty-six inches.

"One of the good things coming out of this war," I remember his saying, "is that my stomach has shrunk from forty-six inches to a mere thirty-two. Never again will I let myself get that huge."

When I met him, guess what he was doing—drinking beer, and lots of it. I almost reminded him of what he had told me but figured, "What the heck. He's probably old enough or has enough time in to retire. Why disturb his much-deserved vacation?"

Much to my joy whom should I run into next but my old pal Sad Sack. He was the guy who had gone with me to find a bivouac for our squadron when we first moved on to Bataan at the outbreak of the war.

Sad hadn't changed a bit. He still had that Corpus Christi, Texas, drawl and was just as full of the devil as he could be and couldn't wait to begin making up for lost time. Together we talked for hours, and then we set about rounding up other members of our squadron.

As close as we could figure from the information generated, thirty-eight of our former colleagues out of the pre-war group were still alive. Those figures were not accurate, we knew, because those present had lost track of many of those with whom they had been the closest before the war and during internment. We later learned that sixty-four actually made it through the ordeal. One hundred and thirty-six officers and men were killed in the war or died while prisoners, we later learned.

Two of the three days passed, and during this time I received a radiogram from home. Later, I learned my Scottish friend with whom I had worked in the mine had slipped out of Camp No. 17 and had found his way to the Allied troops. When he reached a place where he could, he cabled my parents and told them I was still living and would be returning home soon. Not having secured his address before his departure, I never did have the opportunity to express appreciation to him.

From the radiogram I learned I had three brothers in the war. Two of them were in Europe and one was on Guam. My older brother, who was in the Air Corps, had fought up through North Africa, through Italy, and into Germany. He was a master sergeant and a line chief.

The brother just younger than I was a lieutenant in the Signal Corps and with his company made the landing on Normandy. The fourth brother, Whitey, was in the Seabees and had fought the war in the Pacific. This news pleased me greatly, especially the information they were all well. I could just imagine what my parents had gone through having four sons in the military all at the same time.

While in the repatriation camp, I learned that all POWs had received a one-rank promotion. Prior to the war I had earned three promotions in less than a year and during the three and one-half years of internment, I advanced one more step. In addition, we all received a partial payment in the amount of two hundred dollars.

On the final day of our quarantine, I received word to report to headquarters, and there I learned that I should be ready to sail for the United States at 8:00 a.m. the following morning.

"What should I do?" I asked myself. I wanted to go home in the worst way, but knowing I would probably never get back to the Philippines again, I desperately wanted to see Manila one more time.

From headquarters I learned that if I didn't take this ship, my name would be placed at the bottom of the list, and I would have to wait my turn once again.

Returning to our sleeping quarters, I asked the fellows what they thought I should do. All of them agreed I must be nuts not to jump at the chance to go home. As undecided as I was, their eagerness and encouragement did the trick. The following morning I caught the truck that was to take us to the docks in Manila.

As the truck approached the city, I could see that the once beautiful Filipinos Boulevard was no more. The sea wall had been leveled to enable landing craft to move freely from ship to shore. It appeared the entire area between the road and the sea was one huge storage area.

The city itself was in ruins. Once beautiful buildings were now only piles of rubble. It appeared to me it would take years of hard labor and much money to restore Manila to its former status as a jewel in the Orient. It saddened me greatly to see what the retreating Japanese troops had done to what was once one of the most beautiful spots in the entire world. What treachery! Right then I was only too happy to get away from the depressing scene as rapidly as possible.

## 22

# HOME AT LAST

AT THE DOCKS WE IMMEDIATELY boarded the ship and were assigned to a deck near to the bottom under the waterline. The heat was almost suffocating and promptly revived memories of my earlier experience in the hold of an old Canadian freighter on the way to Japan from Manila. I began to have second thoughts about going home by ship. There had been talk that it might be possible to catch a bomber returning to the States.

Luck must have still been with me, for even though I was one of the last soldiers to board the ship, I found an empty bunk while others were still searching. It was above two other bunks, but it was vacant, so I threw my bag up and climbed up right after it, sweating profusely.

Lying on my back looking up into the ceiling that was fairly close to my face, I noticed a small vent directly above me. I reached up and twisted it a bit and immediately was engulfed in cold, not cool, air. How wonderful it felt!

That problem solved beautifully, I lay there puzzled about myself. I was really having trouble understanding my feelings. Here I was, free and on my way home, exactly what I had prayed and longed for over such a long time, yet I was experiencing uneasiness and doubt. It seemed there were things in the Philippines I ought to tend to before leaving. Even though we had given that country everything, even the lives of all but a small group, I felt it wasn't quite right for me to abandon the place without checking to see that everything was left in good shape. It was as though the struggle really wasn't over yet, and here I was, bugging out. I knew that I didn't want to spend the rest of my life in the Philippines; I just felt that there was some unfinished business that needed my attention.

Although the heat throughout most of our deck was almost suffocating, the mood of the men was festive, and in spite of myself, I was beginning to join in. Besides, there was an announcement that the ship's store was open, and I needed to see what was available.

While the ship was crowded with American and British soldiers and some of the conditions were not great, there was practically no complaining. We all crowded the decks to get a final look at Corregidor and Bataan as the ship slowly moved away from the docks at Manila and out into Manila Bay. The devastation around Manila wasn't really visible from the ship, although the harbor was littered with hulks of vessels of all types. And as we sailed past Corregidor, we could see little of the damage inflicted by the Japanese as they wrested the stronghold from the battered American forces. There was also the struggle to retake it from the Japanese.

The days between the Philippines and Hawaii were filled with talk, eating, card playing, and dreaming of the good things yet to come. Because of the large number of men aboard, the food lines were long and the meal times irregular. We had only salt water to bathe in, but we could bathe any time we wished, and that in itself was a great improvement over conditions of the past few years.

We were happy when we reached Pearl Harbor and were anxious to go ashore and see the sights, but the ship docked only to refuel and to take on additional provisions. Those in charge were much too wise, I am sure, to allow a couple thousand men to get into mischief ashore. It could have taken days to round them up again. Actually, we didn't mind too much because we knew that the sooner we left Hawaii, the sooner we would reach home.

After twenty-three days aboard the Coast Guard ship *Dykstra,* the big day finally arrived. Word was passed we would sail under the Golden Gate Bridge about three that afternoon. Sometime during the day a blimp with "Welcome Home, POWs" painted on her side flew over the ship. We all cheered and shouted and were in a hilarious mood.

I remember the day was clear, and the sun was shining just beautifully. Someone shouted, "There she is!"

Sure enough, in the distance we could just barely make out the outlines of the bridge, but she was unmistakable. To us the "Golden Gate" was just as much a symbol of freedom as the Statue of Liberty had ever been to anyone.

As we sailed closer to her, we saw two small ships coming out to meet us. They drew along the sides of our much larger vessel and were crowded with beautiful girls, all waving and throwing kisses. Wouldn't you know the people in Frisco would think of everything!

We were boisterous and cheered loudly as we passed under the beautiful structure, awed by the large banner hanging from her welcoming us home and congratulating us for a job well done. There were a lot of rough, hard men aboard that ship, but there were few dry eyes in the crowd that day. No one was ashamed to cry, either. This was the gateway to everything we held dear. Here was the beginning of all our dreams and plans for the future. We had been tried severely and had survived the worst the Japanese had to offer. Now, we were the conquerors, and they were the defeated! All the hell we had gone through was being compensated for in these few minutes.

Almost too soon our ship docked and the gangplank was lowered. The dock was jammed with people looking for a familiar face. Every once in a while someone would see his gal or his folks and would let out a yell. I knew none of my family would be there at the docks but didn't mind at all. Home was only a short distance, and what was a day or two now?

Our turn to leave the ship finally came, and we jogged down the gangplank. No sooner had we hit the dock than some lady grabbed my pal, Max, and kissed him and swung him around. She grabbed me next and repeated the performance.

I could see from the look on Max's face he didn't know her, and I was sure that I didn't know her, either. From her we learned that during the time we had been gone, his sister had married, and this lady was his sister's mother-in-law.

From the docks we were taken by truck to Letterman Hospital in San Francisco. There we were assigned to wards and had to give up all of our clothing. In exchange we each received a suit of corduroy pajamas and a robe, though, and were told we could walk around the hospital area wearing those. The thing I was most interested in right then was an opportunity to telephone home.

We learned we could make telephone calls, but we had to wait for our turn. We realized everyone was eager to contact loved ones and understood the necessity for cooperation.

My turn finally came about eleven o'clock that night. When I heard my dad's voice, I was overcome with happiness. About all I could get from my mom were sobs of joy. I assured them that I would telephone again when the congestion had ended. With the information that everyone at home was well, I went back to my ward and happily to bed.

During the third day of my stay at Letterman Hospital, I learned I was to have visitors. A cousin of mine who lived in Berkeley was coming to take me to his home. He and his lovely wife had made arrangements for me to be a guest in their home overnight.

What a great time I had with these beautiful people and their small son! From them I learned about the activities of my family and many things that had happened during the war years. We hardly had time to sleep that night.

The following day my buddy, Max, telephoned from the hospital to tell me we were being transferred to Fort Lewis, Washington, to be stationed at Madigan Hospital. The Red Cross train was leaving at 5:00 p.m., so I made it back to base in plenty of time. Before long we were aboard the hospital train and on our way once again.

Once aboard the train, we were all put to bed. Again we had to give up our clothing. We realized those in charge didn't want to chance losing any of us at one of the train stops, and we were not at all upset with the restrictions imposed upon us. At least, I wasn't upset because I was tired and badly needed the rest the travel provided.

Never before or since have I seen such service as we were given on that train. We were treated so well and so graciously that I honestly felt guilty. We even had our meals served to us in bed.

Early in the morning of the third day we arrived in Tacoma, Washington. My buddy's mother and dad and sister were there to meet him. I was almost overcome with emotion at that reunion. His parents were such warm, gracious people, and as soon as they learned that Max and I were from the same squadron, they just adopted me as one of their sons.

From Tacoma we went to Madigan Hospital at Fort Lewis, where we were assigned to wards. We were required to be in the wards during the morning for consultation with the doctors, but we could obtain a daily pass beginning at one in the afternoon.

It was at Madigan that I had long talks with doctors concerning my treatment for malaria. Even though they listened to my story intently, it was difficult for them to believe a single heavy dose of quinine had completely cured me of malaria. I began to wonder more than ever if I hadn't had help from the Lord then, as well as on many other occasions during our internment by the Japanese.

Max's mother and sister returned to their home in Montana after a few days, but his dad remained there in Tacoma with his new automobile to make sure we had transportation. In the short time I was with him, I learned to love this rugged Montana wheat farmer who generously offered to establish me as a farmer on land adjacent to the many hundreds of acres that he owned and farmed.

During the last ten days of October while we were at Madigan Hospital our lives were just one good time after another. We did our best to catch up on all the movies we had missed and made sure we never passed up a meal, supplemented with generous snacks in between.

Then Max decided it was time for him to go home to get reacquainted with other members of his family and with former friends. He was able to arrange for a ten-day leave, and in the company of his father, he left me to suffer alone at Madigan Hospital.

During his absence I remained fairly close to the ward, wrote lots of letters, and visited with the other fellows and the nurses in the hospital. We received notice there might be an opportunity for us to return to Japan to testify against Japanese war criminals. No one I knew had any desire to return, and I surely didn't want to go back to the Far East just then. At that point I had had about all of Japan that I ever wanted.

One afternoon early in November I was aroused from a snooze by the nurse who told me that I had a telephone call from Seattle. I replied I didn't know anyone in Seattle and for her not to torment me with nonsense like phone calls from Seattle.

"Listen," she said. "There is a call for you from Seattle, and I promised faithfully that I would have you return the call."

I responded, "I told you that I don't know anyone in Seattle!"

"I told you I promised the caller you would return the call and you are definitely going to do just that!"

"Was it a man or a woman who telephoned?" I inquired stubbornly.

"It was a woman!"

"I definitely do not know any women in Seattle!"

The nurse dialed the Seattle number and passed the telephone to me.

"Hello," was the woman's response.

"Who is this?" I asked.

"Guess!" she responded.

"I haven't the faintest idea who you might be, and I am a poor guesser. Who the heck are you anyway?"

"I'm Barbara," she said gleefully.

"Barbara? Barbara who?" I asked.

"Barbara Perkins!"

When she said this, I almost fainted. This was the girl with whom I had been so much in love when we were in high school.

My next question was, "Barbara Perkins! You mean that you aren't married yet?"

She responded with a laugh saying, "No, of course I am not married!"

"What the heck are you doing in Seattle?" I asked.

"I am a WAVE in the Navy stationed here."

She then asked me how I was feeling, and I assured her that I was fine. I still couldn't believe what I was hearing.

"When can I come to see you?" she asked.

"Any time," I told her, "or I could go to Seattle to see you."

"Oh, no! You had better stay in the hospital and I'll come and see you. How about this evening?"

I told her tonight would be just fine and gave her specific directions so she wouldn't get lost on the hospital grounds.

A pass secured, I began to get all spruced up.

During the afternoon I couldn't help but wonder if she had changed much, and why she hadn't gotten married. She had been a good-looking gal and surely must have had opportunities. "Well, she will soon be here and I will probably get all of the answers," I said to myself.

At 7:30 p.m. she walked into the ward. I watched her intently as she walked right past me and down through the line of beds. All the stories of starved POWs must have reached her, and I knew she was looking for a rack of skin and bones. Although when the war ended I had weighed only a hundred and nine pounds, the war had been over for two and one-half months, and during that time I had put on sixty pounds.

She was decked out in her Navy blues and was about the prettiest little lady I had ever seen, even prettier than I had remembered her being. Believe me, the other fellows in the ward sat up taking notice and expressing their appreciation with whistles and appropriate comments.

I waited until she had gone the full length of the ward and returned before I approached her with, "Are you looking for someone in particular?"

From the expression on her face it was easy to tell that she couldn't believe what she was seeing.

"Where is this skinny little guy I am looking for?" she must have been asking herself.

Although I would have liked to take her into my arms and just hold her, I didn't. We shook hands instead.

For only a few minutes we sat and visited, and then I asked her if she would like to go into Tacoma for a movie and dinner. We could talk afterwards, if we still weren't talked out.

Her response was enthusiastically positive, so off we went. Very few people owned automobiles right after the war, so all were quite used to riding the bus. The constant glances from the other occupants on the bus assured me I was the envy of every other GI who was watching.

After the movie and dinner I told her I would go back to Seattle with her on the bus, if she wished. The distance wasn't far, and once in Seattle, we took a taxi to her apartment. She was sharing off-base quarters with three other WAVES who were working in downtown Navy offices.

Telling me that she had several albums filled with pictures of the "good old days," she invited me into the apartment to see them. Of course I was eager to continue our talk and the association, so I went into the front room with her. Her associates were all asleep, so we confined our talk to low whispers.

We had looked at many photographs and had fun laughing at some of the memories they brought back when a large picture fell from the album to the floor. I picked it up and looked at it. It was a picture of a handsome Air Force lieutenant. His face wasn't familiar to me, as were those of most in the other pictures, so I asked her who he was.

She said, "I had just as well tell you about him, I guess."

With that she showed me a newspaper clipping announcing her engagement to the lieutenant. She said he was still overseas, and they were to be married when he returned.

Although I felt terribly disappointed, I congratulated her and was honestly happy for her. She had met the fellow at college.

There was much more to talk about, and before we realized it, the night had nearly passed. I learned she had graduated from college and had taught school for one year before joining the Navy.

She finally asked me, "How long will you be at Fort Lewis?"

I told her I didn't know for sure but probably would be there for some time, perhaps until Christmas.

"Well," she said, "we can have lots of good times while you are here."

"No," I responded thoughtfully and deliberately. "I loved you once and never did get completely over that. I could easily fall in love again. You are promised and not to me. The next time I fall in love it's going to be for keeps and not just for good times."

Before I realized what was happening, she was in my arms. In that instant I was completely overcome with joy. I couldn't believe this wonderful thing was happening to me! What a marvelous, exciting, and exhilarating feeling! Twice in a matter of three months I had been gloriously blessed with amazingly beautiful feelings. For the second time since the end of the war God had poured His blessing out upon me. I knew without a doubt that He truly loved me!

Navy WAVE Barbara Perkins

During the next half hour or so, before I left Seattle floating on air, we had set the wedding date for a few days later. I was so gloriously happy!

On the bus ride back to Madigan I simply couldn't believe what was happening to me. Just a few weeks ago I was a prisoner in a foreign land, being guarded by men who demonstrated nothing but hatred and contempt for me, and now I was a free man and back in the country I loved so dearly and about to be married to the most wonderful, most beautiful girl in the world! For the second time during this postwar period I felt close to God. It was almost as though He had put His loving arms around me and blessed me first with freedom and now with this exciting, wholesome girl who was to be my wife.

Back at Madigan Hospital I promptly telephoned my dad informing him I was to be married in a few days. His response to that bit of news was "Oh, son, I would really like to talk with you before you get married!"

"I would like to talk to you," I responded.

"Please don't do anything until I get there!" he requested.

I assured him that I wouldn't.

Staff Sergeant Gene Jacobsen, 1945

He must have hung up the phone and jumped into the car, because he was at the hospital early the next morning, looking tired and a bit shaken. With him was Lewis, the fellow from home who had so generously befriended me when I was so ill with dysentery in Cabanatuaan Prison Camp in the Philippines. He was such a super fellow!

It was great to see Dad, and we immediately secured a room at a motel near the base to enable him to get much-needed rest. During the afternoon and evening we talked, and the next morning I took him to Seattle to meet my bride-to-be.

I still chuckle as I recall that experience. He waited in the automobile, and I went into the house to get Barbara. When we came out, he stepped out of the car. Seeing Barbara, he got sort of a dazed look on his face.

"Why didn't you tell me it was Barbara Perkins whom you were going to marry?" he pleaded.

"You didn't ask me who my bride was to be," I responded.

He was overjoyed and greatly relieved, for he had known Barbara and her family for years. The three of us then spent a few hours together before Dad left for home after assuring us he would deliver our good news to all family members and friends at home.

Barbara made arrangements for us to be married at the large home where she was living and also contacted the Mormon bishop of the ward where she had been attending. It was my responsibility to secure the marriage license, which I learned wasn't a simple process.

Not being familiar with Air Force rules and regulations pertaining to marriage by enlisted men, I secured a copy of the appropriate military document and learned it would be necessary for me to secure permission from my commanding officer before proceeding with the ceremony.

I then proceeded to get an appointment to talk with the CO of Madigan Hospital. When I approached his secretary, she asked, "What is the nature of your business with the colonel, Sergeant?"

"I want to receive his permission to be married."

"You want to *what?*" she exclaimed.

"I want to receive his permission to be married," I repeated.

"Just have a seat, Sergeant, and I will see if the colonel can see you."

She entered the colonel's office, and I could hear the conversation between her and her superior. It went something like this.

"Colonel, Staff Sergeant Jacobsen is in the outer office, and he wishes to speak with you. He wants your permission to get married."

There was a period of silence, and then I heard the colonel ask, "He wants to what?"

"He wants to receive permission to be married."

"I don't believe it. This, I have to hear for myself."

The secretary stepped back into the outer office and, turning to me, said, "The colonel will see you right now, Sergeant."

I stepped past her and into the colonel's office and was immediately invited to be seated. The colonel then asked me to tell him about the woman I wished to marry.

This I was pleased to do and went into some detail about our earlier lives together and about our recent reunion. He listened intently and then, rising to his feet, he put out his hand and said, "I am aware of the regulation which states an enlisted man should secure the approval of his CO before entering into marriage, but in all of the years I have been a commanding officer, you are the first man who has extended to me that courtesy.

"By all means, marry the girl, and I wish you both well. It sounds to me as though you are getting a wonderful wife and you deserve her. May God bless you!"

That very evening Max and his dad returned from Montana and were excited to hear the news of my wedding plans. Barbara and I had agreed I should ask Max to be my best man and his dad to give the bride away. Barbara's mom would be at our wedding, but her father would not be able to attend. Both Max and his dad responded enthusiastically when I asked them to participate with us.

The following day they took me to the government offices where I was to secure the marriage license. With that in hand, I was ready for the big event.

On November 10, 1945, Barbara and I were happily married and our lives together began.

# EPILOGUE

TWO WEEKS FOLLOWING OUR MARRIAGE, November 23, 1945, Barbara received an honorable discharge from the Navy, and through the graciousness of the good people at Fort Lewis, we were authorized a room in the base guest house. Both of us were eager to return to Montpelier, Idaho, to spend Christmas with our families, and on December 20, I was given a ninety-day leave of absence with instructions to return to Fort Lewis for discharge on March 10 of the following year.

What a wonderful Christmas we celebrated that year! My older brother, a former master sergeant in the Army Air Corps, had been discharged earlier. He had been a line chief and had participated in the North African and Italian campaigns. Our brother just younger than I also returned home just before Christmas. He had not received his discharge yet but was anticipating it shortly. He had served as a lieutenant with the Signal Corps in the European campaign and had had harrowing experiences, which he shared with us. Whitey, our youngest brother, was still with the Seabees on Guam and wasn't to be discharged for several more months.

Our dad was well and just as rugged as ever. The war had made an impact upon him, and he had mellowed from the man I had known when I was a kid. Mom was the one who had suffered more than any or all of us. Having four sons in the war at the same time was a terrible burden for her to bear. And, although friends and neighbors informed us that she was constantly cheerful and optimistic, the war years had taken their toll. She was extremely thin and lived just more than another year, dying at the age of forty-eight.

During the first eight months following my discharge, I was able to spend many hours with her. The love we had shared with each other continued, and I was with her continuously during the final two weeks of her life. During one of those days she asked me, "How long do you think you can put up with me?"

My response to her as I held her in my arms was, "Let's see. You put up with me for the first nineteen years of my life and prayed daily for my welfare during the next five years, so I am committed to caring for you during the same number of years."

Barbara and I were saddened that she was unable to see our first child, a son, who was born just a few days before her passing.

Hardly a day passes that Barbara and I don't think and talk about our parents and anticipate with great joy our future life with them in the hereafter.

At the encouragement of Barbara and her mom, I carefully recorded war and prison-camp experiences in hopes this story could be written sometime in the future. This activity kept me well occupied until my discharge.

Early in March we drove with Barbara's parents to Fort Lewis, Washington, where I received my separation papers.

During the summer Barbara and I took time off to visit Max and his parents in Montana. By this time he had married a lovely girl from North Dakota, and they had settled in their home just across the road from the home of his parents.

After a few days with those good people, we drove to the small Montana community where Lloyd Irvine had spent his earlier life. Lloyd was the fellow on the Tayabas work detail who asked me to promise I would find his parents, if I survived prison camp and returned to the United States. You will recall that he died sitting against a tree and I buried him in the jungle of Southern Luzon.

We arrived in the town about eight o'clock in the morning and drove down the one main street that, except for two fellows talking to each other, appeared vacant.

As we drove past them, I turned to Barbara and said, "One of those fellows is Lloyd's dad."

"How do you know that?" she asked.

"Because Lloyd looked just like him; the likeness is unbelievable!"

At the end of the street we turned the car around. As we approached the two men, they parted and one crossed the street just in front of us.

I stopped the car, and, stepping out, I approached the man whom I had identified.

"Mr. Irvine!" I called.

"Yes," he responded, "But how did you know? I don't recognize you."

Gene Jacobsen (l) and Ben Steele (r) in 1995 in the area where they were confined in Bilibid Prison, Gene for seven months, Ben for nearly a year.

"You had a son, Lloyd, in the service in the Philippines, didn't you? You just have to be his dad because in appearance, he could have been your double."

Yes, I am his father," he responded with a puzzled look on his face.

"Lloyd and I were in the same squadron in the Philippines. We were taken prisoner together by the Japanese, and I was with him when he died."

The man broke into tears, and I just stood there while he wept.

When he was able to compose himself, we walked over to the car, where I introduced him to Barbara. Then, the three of us drove to his home, where we spent most of the morning with him and his wife.

I gave Lloyd's father the message I had been entrusted with and told him all that I knew about Lloyd and about our lives in the 20th Pursuit Squadron and in prison camp. While I described in detail the area where I buried Lloyd, I said nothing about his physical condition at the time of his death.

Lloyd's father was still president of the LDS District in which he lived. He and his wife remained good friends of ours and visited us twice each year as they passed through Logan, Utah, on their way to General Conference of the Church of Jesus Christ of Latter-day Saints in Salt Lake City. We greatly enjoyed their association and friendship.

During June 1962 I was able to take my family to the Philippine Islands, where we visited many places of interest. Our travel schedule was such that we were able to spend nearly half a day at the American Military cemetery on the site of the former Fort McKinley. Finding the graves of former squadron colleagues was an intensely emotional experience for me, and I began to feel anger over the loss of so many great young men. It was there that I started to write a poem to record and convey the feelings I was experiencing as I meditated on the deaths of so many former colleagues.

It wasn't until after my second visit to the same cemetery in 1996 that I was able to complete the poem that would express my feelings about our frustrations and sorrows as soldiers on Bataan and then as prisoners of war of the Japanese.

### Voices From the American Military Cemetery at Fort Bonafacio, Manila, in the Philippine Islands

On marble pillars carved in stone
The names of former corpsmen known.
Young they were, valiant and brave,
Assigned too early to an unknown grave
In a station still unknown.

Standing alone in that hallowed place,
Each name read recalls a face,
A catching laugh, a smile, a glow
Of months with them so long ago,
Far from their present resting place.

They are dead, how blessed am I
Standing beneath a tropic sky,
Free from prison pains and care,
Breathing deep of freedom's air,
One of the few who didn't die.

As I stood in quiet, I could hear
Their voices speaking loud and clear:
"You're well, we're not, and we won't be
Until you strive to set us free
From the heavy burdens that we bear.

It isn't death that pains us so,
Although we hadn't planned to go
So young, without our mission through,
The one we were supposed to do
And failed, we all now know.

"Why was the country we loved so dear
Willing to sacrifice us here,
Abandoned, long before we fell,
To suffer each his own private hell
When victory could have been so near?

"What happened to the planes and tanks
Promised to the starving Yanks?
Eager to serve our country well,
Instead we experienced a living hell
Far from home in the form of thanks."

As I stood and read the names inscribed
Of the brave men who fought and died
I felt my anger rise and stir
Through tears that caused the scene to blur
Recalled other names—those who lied.

Our four-star general topped the list
Of faces visible through the mist
Joined by our exalted President,
Who never shared his real intent
Or concern for those who would be missed.

Generals there were and quite a few
Who seemed to know not what to do
And the British Prime Minister, the President's friend,
Who wooed and swayed him to the end
Until his war at home was through.

And so, these restless dead still yearn
For the folks at home to finally learn
The truth about the "Rock" and Bataan
Although the years have come and gone
Their complete respect from us to earn.

A group of cowards we were not
As some have said and others thought.
The task assigned was far too great,
For desperate men a pending fate,
A futile war nobly fought.

Who will take up the cause for these men here?
Courageous and faithful, men without fear,
Who plead with us to set them free
To join the ranks of you and me
And those at home who hold them dear.

When men are called to serve in war,
Whether near at home or in places far,
Is it too much for them to ask
Support that's needed for the task
The nation's honor not to mar?

For them no freedom, no honors, no fame.
At home life went on just the same.
Few knew just why we lost the cause.
The nation hardly seemed to pause,
So still they suffer in their shame.

# AUTHOR'S CHRONOLOGY

| | |
|---|---|
| September 19, 1921 | Born in Bloomington, Idaho. Reared in Montpelier, Idaho. |
| June 1939 | Graduated from Montpelier High School. |
| September 17, 1940 | Enlisted in the U.S. Army Air Corps; assigned to the 18th Pursuit Squadron, Hamilton Field, California. Squadron was to be assigned to Alaska in January of the following year. |
| October 1940 | Volunteered for a transfer into the 20th Pursuit Squadron, shortly bound for the Philippine Islands. |
| October 1940 | Boarded the luxury liner SS *Washington,* which had been chartered to sail to China to bring home wives and children of American civilians living in Shanghai. |
| November 23, 1940 | When the ship docked in Manila, proceeded with squadron members to Nichols Field in the Barrio of Baclaren. |
| November 20, 1940 | Assigned as clerk in the squadron supply. |
| December 27, 1940 | Promoted to private first class with specialist rating, which increased monthly salary from $21 to $36 per month. |
| March 29, 1941 | Appointed as acting supply sergeant with rank of corporal. |

| | |
|---|---|
| July 1, 1941 | Promoted to the rank of sergeant with monthly salary increased to sixty dollars when the squadron was transferred to Clark Field with P-35s and P-40s. |
| November 1941 | Thirty-five B-17 bombers arrived from the States along with officers and enlisted men. Half of the bombers were assigned to the Island of Mindanao. Several National Guard tank and field artillery companies also arrived at Clark Field. |
| December 8, 1941 | Japanese bombers and Zero fighter planes attacked Clark Field, destroying American planes on the ground. |
| December 24, 1941 | Squadron ordered to abandon Clark Field and move to the Peninsula of Bataan. |
| January 1942 | Transferred to the Philippine Army along with squadron members. Was issued World War I British Enfield rifle and ammunition and assigned to infantry duty at the Battle of the Points. |
| April 9, 1942 | Bataan was surrendered to the Japanese by General Edward P. King. |
| April 12, 1942 | Death March began at Mariveles, southern tip of Bataan. |
| April 20, 1942 | Arrived at Camp O'Donnell. |
| June 2, 1942 | Assigned to the Tayabas Road-Building Detail. |
| August 15, 1942 | Taken from Tayabas Detail to Bilibid Prison in Manila. Severe illness from beriberi, hepatitis, pellagra, and starvation. |
| March 17, 1943 | Transferred to Cabanatuaan Prison Camp to work on a 300-acre farm. |

| | |
|---|---|
| July 2, 1944 | Selected to be sent to Japan to work in the coal mines. |
| July 4, 1944 | Loaded aboard old Canadian freighter for trip to Japan. |
| September 4, 1944 | Disembarked at Port Moji on the island of Kyushu—starved, ill, and terribly dirty. |
| September 5, 1944 | Sent to Camp No. 17, at Omuta, in the Province of Fukuoka. |
| September 19, 1944 | Birthday and first day in the coal mine. |
| August 15, 1945 | Ordered out of the mine at noon and sent back to camp. |
| August 17, 1945 | Informed by weeping camp commander that the war had ended and the Allies had been victorious. Experienced the joy of forgiveness. |
| September 12, 1945 | Commandeered Japanese train for trip to meet U.S. Army of Occupation. |
| September 14, 1945 | Reached Army of Occupation camp and flew to Okinawa the following day. |
| September 15, 1945 | Flew to Clark field in the Philippines and traveled by train to POW repatriation camp south of Manila. |
| September 20, 1945 | Boarded American Coast Guard troop ship for travel to America. |
| October 16, 1945 | Landed at San Francisco and proceeded to Letterman Hospital. |
| October 18, 1945 | Transferred by Red Cross train to Madigan Hospital at Fort Lewis, Washington. |

| | |
|---|---|
| November 10, 1945 | Married Barbara Perkins, U.S. Navy WAVE and my high-school sweetheart. |
| December 21, 1945 | Given 90-day furlough to go home to Montpelier, Idaho, with my wife. During furlough recorded my three-and-one-half-year experiences as a prisoner of the Japanese. |
| March 6, 1946 | Received honorable discharge from the Army Air Corps. |
| March 19, 1947 | Son, Michael, was born in Montpelier, Idaho. |
| February 29, 1949 | Daughter, JoAnn, was born in Logan, Utah. |
| June 10, 1949 | Graduated with honors from Utah State University. |
| September 6, 1951 | Became principal of the Lincoln Elementary School in Montpelier, Idaho. |
| June 1954 | Barbara and I received Master's degrees at Utah State University. |
| June 1954 | Entered the doctoral program at the University of California, Berkeley. |
| August 1956 | Accepted an assignment at the University of California, Davis, California. |
| January 31, 1957 | Our younger daughter, Sue, was born in Woodland, California. |
| June 1957 | Graduated with doctorate from the University of California, Berkeley. |
| August 1957 | Accepted professorship at Utah State University, Logan, Utah. |

| | |
|---|---|
| July 1960 | Became Associate Director of the University Extension Services and Director of Summer School at Utah State University. |
| July 1962 | On leave from Utah State, accepted a one-year assignment with the University of Utah to establish a Faculty of Education at the Haile Selassie University in Ethiopia. |
| July 1964 | Accepted the position of Assistant Dean of the Graduate School of Education and professor of Educational Administration at the University of Utah, Salt Lake City, Utah. |
| July 1965 | Accepted the request of the Haile Selassie University President and the Ethiopian Minister of Education to serve for two years as Chief of Party of the University of Utah team there. |
| September 1972 | While on a year's sabbatical leave from the University of Utah, was sent by the LDS Church to provide in-service training for school administrators in Western Samoa, Tonga, and New Zealand. |
| August 1975 | Received unpaid leave of absence from the University of Utah to serve for two years as Superintendent of Saudi Arabian International Schools for children of expatriate oil-field workers in the Eastern Province of Saudi Arabia. |
| January 1, 1982 | Requested and was given early retirement from the University of Utah to serve as consultant with the Singapore Ministry of Education. |
| June 1982 | Officially retired at June commencement as a Professor Emeritus of Educational Administration at the University of Utah. |

| | |
|---|---|
| November 1985 | With Barbara, accepted a call to serve as LDS missionaries in Zimbabwe, South Africa. |
| 1987, 1997 | Engaged in volunteer work with the Utah School Boards Association. |
| March 1997 | Moved to St. George, Utah, where Barbara and I plan to live out the balance of our lives in beautiful and warm Dixie. |
| 1978–2000 | Publication of *To Japan with Encouragement and Hope.* |
| 2004 | Publication of *We Refused to Die.* |

# ROSTER OF THE 20TH PURSUIT SQUADRON, APRIL 9, 1942

This roster was prepared by James E. Brown, a member of our squadron, on September 30, 1979. He compiled it from the handwritten record of April 9, 1942, and from information from surviving officers and men of the squadron.

When he completed and distributed the document, which included both officers and enlisted men, he indicated that there might be errors and requested input from any of us who had information that he didn't have at the time. He advised us that the roster was not an official one.

### Officers Who Lost Their Lives During the War or in Prison Camp or About Whom No Information Was Available

| | |
|---|---|
| Alder, Glen | Killed in action at Clark Field on 12/8/41. |
| Anderson, M. J. | Killed in action over Manila Bay. He was strafed by Japanese pilots after bailing out of a disabled airplane on 1/19/42. |
| Ansley, F. A. | Unknown. |
| Browne, F. B. | Jumped from sinking Japanese troop ship on 12/27/44. He either drowned or was shot by Japanese troops. |
| Carter | Unknown. |
| Crellen, E. B. | Lost in action over Subic Bay on 3/2/42. |
| Drake, J. | Killed in action at Clark Field on 12/8/42. |
| Duncan, R. P. | Reported as dead. No details. |
| Fulks, W. J. | Died on Japanese troop ship going to Japan on 1/28/45. Ship sunk by Allied forces. |
| Gies, C. P. | Unknown. |

| | |
|---|---|
| Halverson, M. B. | Unknown. |
| Houseman, E. E. | Unknown. |
| Hughes, H. S. | Unknown. |
| Iverson, G. W. | Unknown. |
| Louk, Max | Killed in action at Clark Field on 12/8/41. |
| Louker, J. A. | Killed in action at Clark Field on 12/8/41. |
| McCowan, M. S. | Killed in action at Clark Field on 12/8/41. |
| McLauglin | Reported as dead. No details. |
| Mulcahy | Killed in action at Clark Field on 12/8/41. |
| Mullen, J. E. | Died on Japanese troop ship going to Japan on 1/28/45. Ship sunk by Allied forces. |
| Patrick, T. W. | Killed on a Japanese ship on 1/9/45 by American bombs. |
| Ramsey, P. E. | Killed on a Japanese ship by American forces in 1944. |
| Ranke, H. C. | Died in POW camp. No details. |
| Roberts, R. E. | Died in POW camp. Details unknown. |
| Rousseau, H. S. | Unknown. |
| Shavlin, E. B. | Unknown. |
| Siler, F. L. | Unknown. |
| Sneed, Charles | Killed on 1/9/45 on a Japanese ship by American bombs. |
| Tremblay, E. W. | Unknown. |

## Officers Who Returned to the United States after the War

| | |
|---|---|
| Akins, W. T. | Killed in the line of duty in an airplane accident. |
| Armstrong, F. | Wounded and evacuated to the United States. Killed in the line of duty in an airplane accident. |
| Blass, D. L. | Killed in the line of duty in an airplane accident. |
| Cummings, W. J. | Returned and lives in Texas. |
| Fossey, James T. | Retired to Oklahoma. Passed away in 1999. |
| Gilmore, Edwin B. | Retired as a Lieutenant Colonel. |
| Keator, R. D. | Evacuated and settled in Louisiana. |
| Lunde, Oswald | Evacuated and retired as a Colonel. |
| Matthews, T. R. | Retired in California as a Colonel. |

| | |
|---|---|
| Moore, Joseph H. | Flew KKP-40 south on orders to search for food just prior to the fall of Bataan. Following a distinguished career in the Air Force, retired as a Lieutenant General to San Antonio, Texas. |
| Stinson, Lloyd | Retired as a Colonel. Resides in Florida. |
| Wake, Custer E. | Killed in an airplane accident in the line of duty. |
| White, V. K. | Evacuated. Residence unknown. |
| Woodside, M. H. | Address unknown. |

## Enlisted Men Who Lost Their Lives During the War or about Whom We Have No Record

### MASTER SERGEANTS

| | |
|---|---|
| Heeler, William H. | Died 11/12/42 from dysentery in Cabanatuaan Prison Camp. |

### TECHNICAL SERGEANTS

| | |
|---|---|
| Keans, Arthur J. | Died 4/19/42 from malaria in San Fernando. |
| Walters, Harold C. | Died 7/23/42 in Cabanatuaan from dysentery. |

### STAFF SERGEANTS

| | |
|---|---|
| Bogden, Felix | Died 8/7/42. Location Unknown. |
| Claussen, Manly | Died 6/14/42 in Cabanatuaan Prison Camp from dysentery. |
| Elkins, Lawrence W. | No record since Japanese detail. |
| Fenslow, Edward | Died 6/16/42 at Cabanatuaan Prison Camp from dysentery. |
| Gaultney, Willian | Died 10/7/42 at Cabanatuaan Prison Camp from dysentery. |
| Gleim, Alex | Died 5/21/42 in O'Donnell from dysentery. |
| Hainer, William A. | Killed in action at Clark Field on 12/8/41. |
| Kapalko, Andrew | Killed in action at Clark Field on 12/8/41. |
| Kearney, Ralph J. | Died 7/15/42 in O'Donnell from malaria. |
| Koppen, Howard A. | Died 6/5/42 in Cabanatuaan Prison Camp from dysentery. |
| Nyberg, Carl A. | Died 5/21/42 in O'Donnell from dysentery. |
| Suedkamp, George J. | Died 5/9/42 in O'Donnell from dysentery and malaria. |

| | |
|---|---|
| Turner, Ross C. | Died 8/5/42 in Cabanatuaan from beriberi and dysentery. |

SERGEANTS

| | |
|---|---|
| Bartkus, F.W. | Died 6/3/42 in O'Donnell. No details. |
| Ernest, Donald J. | Died 6/6/42 in O'Donnell from malaria. |
| Fritz, Wendell J. | Killed 4/3/43 in port area. No details. |
| Hainline, T. E. | Died 5/29/42 in O'Donnell from malaria. |
| Hudson, Jack D. | Died in Cabanatuaan. No details. |
| Inlow, Wilmer L. | Killed in action 12/10/41. |
| Johnson, T. A. | Died 6/8/42 in Cabanatuaan from dysentery. |
| Luckey, Ronald T. | Died 7/22/42 in Cabanatuaan from dysentery. |
| Watt, Richard C. | Died 1/12/42 in Cabanatuaan from dysentery. |

CORPORALS

| | |
|---|---|
| Batson, Lewis M. | Died 8/23/42 in Cabanatuaan from dysentery. |
| Hoke, Robert J. | Died on the Death March. |
| Orton, Julias A. | Died 5/31/42 from malaria. |
| Pool, Jack D. | Died on Death March from malaria. |
| Storkel, Eric C. | Died 6/6/42 in O'Donnell from malaria. |
| Thompson, Norman | Died 7/15/42 from dysentery. |
| Whitkavage, George | No record since Japanese work detail. |

PRIVATES FIRST CLASS

| | |
|---|---|
| Barter, Albert E. | No record since Japanese work detail. |
| Brown, Curtis C. | Died 6/3/42 in Bilibid Prison from dysentery. |
| Calder, William H. | No record since Japanese work detail. |
| Casey, Addison | Died 5/28/42 in O'Donnell. No details. |
| Causey, Whitney | No record since Japanese work detail. |
| Darneal, Harold R. | Died 6/7/42. No details. |
| Domenick, Joseph | No record since Japanese work detail. |
| Elliot, Robert W. | Died on Japanese work detail in Tayabas Province. |
| Fulton, Delbert M. | Died 6/4/42 in Cabanatuaan from malaria and dysentery. |
| Griffith, Robert G. | Died 6/6/42 in O'Donnell from dysentery. |
| Irvine, Lloyd W. | Died 6/12/42 on Japanese detail in Tayabas. |
| Massey, Jack E. | No report since Japanese work detail. |

| | |
|---|---|
| Miller, Roland E. | Died in Camp No. 17, in Fukuoka, Japan, from pneumonia. |
| Murname, Daniel J. | Died on 6/18/42 in O'Donnell from dysentery. |
| Peterson, Maylon B. | Died 8/18/42 in O'Donnell. No details. |
| Rosen, Eric Z. | Died 12/14/42 on Japanese ship en route to Japan. |
| Tade, Ray E. | Died 10/17/42 in Cabanatuaan. No details. |
| Webb, Ira D. | Died 5/18/42 on Tayabas work detail. |
| Winn, Will R. | No report since Japanese detail. |

PRIVATES

| | |
|---|---|
| Appel, Dick M. | Died 4/22/42 in O'Donnell. No details. |
| Brayford, F. W. Jr. | Died in prison camp from dysentery and malaria. |
| Boots, Eldon R. | Died 5/26/42 from dysentery on Capan work detail. |
| Bumbar, Cornelius | Killed in action at Clark Field on 12/8/41. |
| Clark, Vincent | Died 5/26/42 in O'Donnell from dysentery and malaria. |
| Clem, Grover R. | Died 6/15/42 in O'Donnell. No details. |
| Cooper, Wilmer W. | Died 6/13/42 in Cabanatuaan. No details. |
| Corkery, Robert O. | Killed in action at Mariveles on 3/8/42. |
| Darnell, H. R. | Died 6/7/42. No details. |
| Dorsey, Marion A. | Died 7/12/43 in Cabanatuaan from malaria and dysentery. |
| Erickson, Vernon A. | Died 4/14/42 on Death March from malaria and starvation. |
| Folz, John A. | Died in prison camp. No details. |
| Foote, Roe V. | Died 6/4/42 in Cabanatuaan. No details. |
| George, Duane P. | No record since Japanese work detail. |
| Gregory, Charles R. | No record since Japanese work detail. |
| Gollishian, E. P. | Died 5/2/42. No details. |
| Hall, George W. | Died 12/1/42 in Cabanatuaan from dysentery. |
| Hartman, Willian | Died 6/13/42 in Cabanatuaan from dysentery and malaria. |
| Harvey, Roy P. Jr. | Died 5/11/42 in O'Donnell from malaria and dysentery. |
| Hildensperger, J. | Died 8/27/42 in O'Donnell from dysentery. |
| Holcomb, Marvin C. | Died 4/26/42 in O'Donnell. No details. |

| | |
|---|---|
| Holmes, Clark A. | Died in O'Donnell from malaria. |
| Hueston, Joe I. | Died 8/10/42 in Cabanatuaan from dysentery. |
| Hufsmith, Richard | Died 6/22/42 in Cabanatuaan from dysentery. |
| Johnson, Harold V. | Died 6/14/42 in Cabanatuaan from dysentery. |
| Krause, Paul A. | Died 6/22/42 in Bilibid Prison. No details. |
| Losey, Ronald W. | Died 6/4/42 in O'Donnell from dysentery. |
| McAllister, L. J. | Died 6/11/42 in Cabanatuaan from malaria and dysentery. |
| Murphy, Patrick | No record since Japanese work detail. |
| Nelson, Warren L. | Died 9/11/42 in Cabanatuaan from malaria. |
| Olinger, Walter T. | Died 6/9/42 in O'Donnell. No details. |
| Prosser, Stanley | Died 8/15/42 in Cabanatuaan from dysentery and malaria. |
| Rizzo, Guido | Died 6/28/42 in O'Donnell. No details. |
| Rolls, Fred W. | Died 9/29/42 in Cabanatuaan from malaria. |
| Seiff, Harry M. | Died 10/14/42 in Cabanatuaan. No details. |
| Shaw, Douglas M. | Died 10/6/42 on prison ship to Japan. |
| Simmons, Charles E. | Dead buddy report. No details. |
| Snow, Robert L. | Died 5/11/42 in Cabanatuaan from beriberi and dysentery. |
| Stratton, Roy R. | Died 6/4/42 in O'Donnell. No details. |
| Sweet, Allen J. | No record since Japanese work detail. |
| Turner, Clifford M. | Died 7/28/42 in Cabanatuaan from dysentery. |
| Warila, Edwin J. | Died 4/30/42 in Baguio. No details. |
| Watson, Alton A. | No record since Japanese work detail. |
| Weiner, Henry A. | Died 8/8/42 in Cabanatuaan from dysentery. |
| Wendland, Robert A. | Died 6/16/42. No details. |
| Williams, Burr D. | Died 5/7/42 in O'Donnell from malaria. |
| Wissing, Edwin W. | Killed in action on 12/8/42. |
| Wyatt, Vernon E. | Killed in action on 12/8/42. |

## Enlisted Men Who Returned to the United States Following the War

### TECHNICAL SERGEANTS

| | |
|---|---|
| Jordan, Murry G. | Died 6/1/74 in Colorado City, Texas. |

### STAFF SERGEANTS

| | |
|---|---|
| Barnhardt, Floyd | Was in Maywood, Illinois, in 1966. No further details. |
| Cote, William L. | Died in the United States during 1975 or 1976. |
| Doss, Leonard | Died in Fort Worth, Texas, during 1993. |
| Gerleman, Russell | Died in Arizona. |
| Huff, James | Living in Napoleon, Ohio. |
| Huth, Lloyd H. | Died in Medford, Oregon, during 2000. |
| King, Arnold | Died in Florence, Arizona. |
| Mitchell, William | Living in Rockport, Texas. |
| Osecky, Benny | Living in Annandale, Virginia. |
| Sperr, Roy L. | Died in Sacramento, California, in 1993. |
| Standfrod, K. D. | Died in San Jose, California. |
| Wissman, Claude F. | Wounded in action, evacuated to Australia. |

### SERGEANTS

| | |
|---|---|
| Albrecht, Edwin L. | Wounded, evacuated to Australia. |
| Idlett, George D. | Living in Herndon, Virginia. |
| Jacobsen, Gene S. | Living in St. George, Utah. |
| Jensen, Gorden T. | Died in 1978. |
| Sayan, Russell D. | Died in Tucson, Arizona |

### CORPORALS

| | |
|---|---|
| Jones, William L. | Died in Van Buren, Arkansas. |
| Joseph, Irving V. | Died in San Francisco. |
| Joy, William J. | Living in Honolulu, Hawaii. |
| Loy, Ernest | Living in Maple Falls, Washington. |

### PRIVATES FIRST CLASS

| | |
|---|---|
| Agnes, Francis W. | Living in Everett, Washington. |
| Bowers, Elmer | Reported dead in United States following the war. |
| Heintzelman, Edward | Died in Loveland, Colorado. |

| | |
|---|---|
| Johnson, V. O. | Living in Sandy, Utah. |
| McDonald, Grant A. | Living in Bountiful, Utah. |
| Miller, Jesse L. | Died in Colorado. |
| Stevenson, Jack | Died in Daly City, California, in 1967. |
| Zenda, John F. | Died in New York. |

PRIVATES

| | |
|---|---|
| Bailey, Stuart | Living in San Ysidro, California. |
| Bennick, Eugene | Wounded, evacuated to Australia. |
| Bristow, John A. | Living in Sacramento, California. |
| Brown, James E. | Died in Niceville, Florida, in 2004. |
| Barna, Joseph L. | Died in West Mifflin, Pennsylvania. |
| Caldwell, Frank | Died in Billings, Montana, during the 1950s. |
| Carrier, David R. | Died in Oklahoma during the early 1990s. |
| Coleman, Gilbert | Died in Lemon Grove, California. |
| Cowley, William | Died in 1992 in Orlando, Florida. |
| Fackender, Ken W. | Died in Fort Walton Beach, Florida, in 2001. |
| Helton, James W. | Died in Phoenix, Arizona. |
| Johnston, George A. | No information. |
| Maberry, Max P. | Died in Montana during the 1960s. |
| Newbold, Don M. | Living in Preston, Idaho. |
| Patterson, David O. | No information. |
| Poole, Harold V. | Living in Salt Lake City, Utah. |
| Quast, Nelson H. | Died in Entiat, Washington. |
| Robinson, Darryl D. | Died in Baker, Louisiana, in 1987. |
| Smith, Frederick N. | Living in Downey, California. |

# About the Artist, Benjamin Charles Steele

Ben, the "Bataan Artist," as he has come to be known, was born on a ranch near Roundup, Montana, on November 17, 1917. He grew up a cowboy and continues to express great love for his early life on the Montana range and for the beautiful trout streams of Montana. During September 1940, he enlisted in the United States Army Air Corps at Fort Missoula and was promptly assigned to March Field, California, for basic training.

Following a six-month assignment with the 7th Material Squadron, 19th Bombardment Group, as aircraft dispatcher, he was in September of 1941 assigned to duty at Clark Field in the Philippine Islands. It was there on December 8 that he survived the first attack by the Japanese when on that day their planes bombed and strafed Clark Field and the surrounding area.

In January 1942, he was assigned to infantry duty on the front lines of battle on the Peninsula of Bataan. There, in the company of Filipino soldiers and Americans representing almost every military discipline, he helped hold back the hordes of Japanese soldiers for a period of three months.

On April 7, 1942, the Allied forces suffered defeat by hunger, disease, the lack of medication, and by the lack of military equipment and ammunition—all far more destructive than the Japanese military forces. Thus, the peninsula was surrendered to the Japanese by General Edward P. King on April 9. Shortly after the surrender the "Death March" from Bataan commenced.

Ben was interned at Camp O'Donnell for nearly two months. Then, on June 2, 1942, he was assigned to the Tayabas Road Detail in the province of Tayabas in southern Luzon. It was in Bilibid Prison following the Tayabas detail, survived by roughly fifty of the men originally assigned, that he began to draw scenes of the interaction of the POWs and the Japanese soldiers.

In January of 1944 he was sent to Cabanatuaan Prison Camp, where he remained until July first of that year. Two days later, along with a thousand and nine other POWs, he boarded an old Canadian freighter seized by the Japanese. Sixty-three days later the *Mati Mati Maru,* so named by the POWs because it was so slow, docked in Port Moji on the Island of Kyushu, Japan. From there Ben was sent to work in the Omine Machi Coal Mine on the island of Honshu, Japan. He remained there until repatriated by American forces following the surrender of Japan to the Allies.

In October of 1994, Ben and I with our wives, Shirley and Barbara, attended the National Convention of Ex-Prisoners of War held in Albuquerque, New Mexico. During the convention week we spent one day visiting the art city of New Mexico, Santa Fe. While the ladies went sightseeing and shopping, Ben and I found comfortable chairs in the town square and began to share POW experiences with each other. It was during this daylong session I learned that Ben and I had followed approximately the same itinerary during the time we were prisoners. We were on the Death March together; we were in O'Donnell together; we were both on the Tayabas road-building detail and were among the few who survived that three-month ordeal; we were together in Bilibid Prison, in Cabanatuaan Prison Camp, and were on the same ship going to Japan. It was in Port Moji that I was sent to work in a coal mine in the province of Fukuoka, and he was sent to work in a coal mine on Honshu.

But the most interesting part of that long visit was learning that while recuperating in Bilibid Prison, he and I had bunked almost side by side. Only one fellow separated us. I was telling him about a fellow near me on the floor in Bilibid who suffered terribly from beriberi, badly swollen from his feet all the way to his chest. It was when I described and named the fellow next to me who suffered from asthma that he told me the asthmatic was right next to him and that he, Ben, was the one so terribly swollen from wet beriberi.

I suddenly realized why I had been attracted to him and why he had become such a dear friend. Together, almost side by side, we had suffered the three and one-half years of torture at the hands of the Japanese.

After the war Ben enrolled in the Cleveland Institute of Art and then entered Kent State University, the institution from which he graduated with the B.S.E. degree. He then began summer school at Denver University and was later awarded the Master of Arts degree from that institution. After a one-year assignment as a high-school art teacher, he was employed

Ben Steele, Montana cowboy and Bataan artist

by the Department of Army as Post Crafts Director at Fort Riley, Kansas. An appointment as Staff Crafts Director, Military District of Washington, Washington, D.C., followed, as did an appointment to the same position at the Third United States Army, Fort MacPherson, Georgia.

In September 1959, he began teaching in the Art Department at Eastern Montana State College, Billings, Montana. Six years later he was appointed Director of the Art Department at that institution and remained in that position until his retirement in June of 1982.

Among his numerous works of art is a collection of eighty drawings and three paintings of prisoner-of-war experiences and scenes. That collection he has given to Eastern Montana State University for its permanent collection. Prior to the time of that gift, the collection was exhibited in numerous locations throughout the United States, including the Harry S. Truman Library.

Ben generously authorized me to select from his book, *Benjamin Charles Steele, Prisoner of War,* those drawings that I wished to include in my book. I am grateful to him for his generosity, for his friendship, his gentleness, his humility, and his love.

Gene Jacobsen